FOUNDATION

THOMAS R. NEUBURGER

FOUNDATION
BUILDING SENTENCE SKILLS

SECOND EDITION

HOUGHTON MIFFLIN COMPANY / BOSTON

DALLAS   GENEVA, ILLINOIS   LAWRENCEVILLE, NEW JERSEY   PALO ALTO

Cover photograph by Jerry Howard

Printed in the U.S.A.

Library of Congress Catalog Card Number: 85-80938

ISBN: 0-395-35803-5

ABCDEFGHIJ-A-898765

Contents

Chapter 21 Punctuation review ₃₀₀

Chapter 22 Spelling skills ₃₁₂

Preface

Many college students have trouble recognizing and correcting fundamental sentence errors in their own writing. In addition, the courses intended to help these students are often not as successful as either the students themselves or their instructors would wish.

FOUNDATION was designed to solve this problem by bringing together the two most effective teaching methods in a single text. Having taught for many years in the City Colleges of Chicago, I found that developmental writing students need a firm understanding of basic sentence structure and word usage as well as plenty of practice in applying this knowledge systematically to their own work. Most texts in this field seem to emphasize one method at the expense of the other. As a result, only a small number of students are adequately served. With FOUNDATION, students can learn to correct their sentence errors consistently and confidently, a crucial step in any writer's development.

FOUNDATION teaches sentence correcting as a set of skills that can be mastered by practice and the understanding of how sentence elements function. Beginning with a detailed study of the recognition of important sentence parts, the text shows students how to make correct judgments about sentence structure and word usage. In each chapter, students learn to locate and correct a great variety of errors by working in easy stages; exercises of appropriate difficulty apply the information learned at each stage to the student's own work, and a writing assignment provides a final opportunity for practice.

A couple of important changes have been made in this Second Edition of FOUNDATION. First, a newly added section, "Paragraphs," covers paragraph and essay structure and the writing process, providing an introduction to the higher-level aspects of college writing. Paragraph editing and sentence combining skills also receive special emphasis in many chapters.

Second, FOUNDATION has been newly organized. All of the skills related to a grammatical or syntactical structure are now grouped together. For example, Chapter 16, "Subordination," not only shows students how to find dependent clauses, it shows how dependent clauses are punctuated, explains the use of *who* and *whom* in adjective clauses, and offers editing tips and combining practice in the proper use of subordinated ideas.

I wish to express my appreciation to all who helped in the preparation of this book. Special thanks go to my colleagues Professors James Russell and Sterling Washington of Malcolm X College for their assistance in building the program from which FOUNDATION grew. I am also grateful to the following reviewers:

Mary P. Boyles of Pembroke State University
Sigrun Coffman of Truckee Meadows Community College
Robert Dees of Orange Coast College
Nancy DeSombre of Wilbur Wright College
Karen L. Greenberg of Hunter College
Sandra Sellers Hanson of LaGuardia Community College
Roslyn J. Harper of Trident Technical College
Timothy A. Miank of Lansing Community College
Robert Naseef of Peirce Junior College
Ann M. Salak of Cleveland State University
Jan Zlotnik Schmidt of the State University of New York at New Paltz
Peggy Stiffler of Chaffey College
Elsie A. Williams of the University of the District of Columbia

Finally, I thank Virginia, Jack, Chris, and David for their patience and love.

T.R.N.

FOUNDATION

Section I

Clauses and sentences

The basic unit of paragraph and essay writing is the sentence. One of the goals of this book is to help you write correct and well-constructed sentences. To do that, we need to look closely at sentences and the clauses they are made of.

1. Recognizing clauses and sentences

A **sentence** is a group of words that has at least one subject and one verb and can stand alone. A **clause** is a part of a sentence that contains a subject and a verb but may or may not stand alone.

Verbs describe an action or tell that something exists or show that something is related to something else—for example, *works, played, was, have.* When you find the verb, ask "who?" or "what?" (for example, "who works?") and you will find the subject.

Below are some examples of clauses. In them the verbs are circled, and the subjects are underlined twice.

We found his latest novel in the bookstore.

The revolution began in 1849.

His early songs sound like Bruce Springsteen's.

When the rain had stopped.

Because her answers are usually correct.

For which he was saving his money.

Independent and dependent clauses

Notice that the first three examples above differ from the last three. The first three can stand alone as complete sentences, but the last three are incomplete.

A clause that can stand alone as a complete sentence is called an **independent clause** or a **main clause.**

Independent (or main) clauses

Juan's little sisters have chicken pox.

This student was both the brightest and the laziest in her class.

Later today we will go for a walk.

A clause that cannot stand alone as a complete sentence is called a **dependent clause.** A dependent clause always contains a word or words that connect it to another part of a sentence. We will call such connecting words **tip-off words.**

Dependent clauses

although the car broke down

since she is allergic to cigarette smoke

which I never saw before

The tip-off words in these examples are *although, since,* and *which.* The tip-off words in the examples on page 2 are *when, because,* and *for which.*

In the sentences below, the tip-off words *until* and *how* tell you that the clauses they begin depend on another part of the sentence.

Until the TV is turned off, I cannot concentrate on my studies.

He did not know *how* he could manage to pay his bills.

Tip-off words, then, are linking words that connect a dependent clause (a clause that cannot stand alone) to another part of the sentence.

The following exercise will help you practice finding the two kinds of clauses. Do it, then check your answers by looking in the back of the book. The answers to all of the odd-numbered exercises in this book are in the Answer Key, starting on page 331.

Exercise 1   Independent and dependent clauses

Each of the following items is a clause.

1. If the clause is an independent or main clause, write **independent** on the line.
2. If the clause is a dependent clause, write **dependent** on the line and draw a **box** around the tip-off word or phrase.

Examples

independent   The banking assistant gave her the forms.

dependent   [That] she was studying for an important test.

_____ 1. Because these events occur frequently.

_____ 2. As we already told you.

_____ 3. My mother remembers this dance from her youth.

_____ 4. Tomorrow one of the deans will be in touch with you.

_____ 5. If she finds her wallet soon.

_____ 6. Whom you were hoping to replace.

_____ 7. Perhaps you can buy some rolls for breakfast.

_____ 8. Although Jerry studied last night.

_____ 9. Of course, the price is too high.

_____ 10. Which my sister recommended.

_____ 11. My brother disliked the movie.

_____ 12. When the college considered your application.

_____ 13. Kirsten's improvement in writing is remarkable.

_____ 14. Recently, the firm promoted Mr. Jonas to royalties manager.

_____ 15. Before the next installment appears in the local paper.

Sentence fragments

To be complete, a **sentence** must contain at least one independent clause.

Sentences

This week the price of coffee finally dropped.

Instead of studying, I watched my favorite TV show.

A group of words that does not contain at least one independent clause but ends with a period, like a sentence, is a **sentence fragment**. Sentence fragments can be dependent clauses or they can be groups of words that do not contain a subject and a verb.

Sentence fragments

A book of mine.

Running in the direction of the main library.

Because they needed funds.

To make your message as clear and precise as possible, you should avoid sentence fragments in any college or business writing you do.

Exercise 2   Sentences and fragments

Tell which of the following are sentences and which are fragments by writing **sentence** or **fragment** on the line.

Examples

sentence   In 277 B.C., the emperor was assassinated.

fragment   For an important test.

_____ **1.** An old forgotten book.

_____ **2.** Over twenty thousand clay soldiers were buried with China's first ruler.

_____ **3.** She bought the perfume on an impulse.

_____ **4.** As good as he ever felt.

_____ **5.** An answer that was correct.

_____ **6.** For the third time this semester.

_____ **7.** She received a perfect math score for the third time this semester.

_____ **8.** Whom you were hoping to replace.

_____ **9.** A good computer system.

_____ **10.** If Jerry had studied last night.

Types of sentences

You know that to be complete a sentence needs only one independent clause. Of course, many sentences contain more than one independent clause. There are actually four kinds of sentences.

Simple sentences contain only one independent clause.

Simple sentences

Independent clause
He jogs.

Independent clause
The hospital is building a new wing.

Compound sentences contain two or more independent clauses. These independent clauses are joined by

1. a conjunction like *and,*
2. a comma + a conjunction like *and,* or
3. a semicolon (;).

Conjunctions used to join independent clauses are called **coordinating conjunctions** because they join equal sentence elements. The main ones are

and
or
but
nor

Usually, a comma is placed before a conjunction joining two independent clauses. But if the independent clauses are short, the comma can be omitted.

Compound sentences

Ind. cl.   Ind. cl.
He jogs but she walks.

Independent clause   Independent
The hospital is building a new wing, and its construction has

clause
already started.

Independent clause   Independent clause
The hospital is building a new wing; its construction has already

started.

Complex sentences contain both dependent and independent clauses.

Complex sentences

<u>Ind. cl.</u> <u>Dependent clause</u>
She walks even when it rains.

<u>Dependent clause</u> <u>Independent clause</u>
Because it needs a better heart clinic, the hospital is building a new

<u>wing.</u>

Notice the tip-off words *even when* and *because* introducing the dependent clauses.

You will find more information about compound and complex sentences in Chapter 15, "Coordination," and Chapter 16, "Subordination."

Combinations of compound and complex sentences are also possible—**compound-complex sentences.** These sentences contain two or more independent clauses and one or more dependent clauses.

Compound-complex sentence

<u>Dependent clause</u> <u>Independent clause</u>
When the sun came up, Larry was hammering the bookcase, and

<u>Independent clause</u>
the dog was howling.

Exercise 3

Independent and dependent clauses in sentences

Each of the following sentences contains two clauses. Write **compound** next to those that contain two independent clauses. Write **complex** next to those that contain one independent clause and one dependent clause.

Remember that a dependent clause always begins with a **tip-off word** (like *if, who,* or *because*) that connects it to the rest of the sentence.

Examples

<u>compound</u> The bookstore has ordered the text; it will arrive in two weeks.

<u>Complex</u> If we pay the bill before January 31, we will get a 10 percent discount.

_____ **1.** The message came yesterday, but no one told Karl about it until today.

_____ **2.** The waitress poured hot coffee for the man who had just walked into the cafe.

_____ **3.** He left a tip that made her smile.

_____ **4.** The tip that he left made her smile.

_____ **5.** He left a large tip, and that made her smile.

_____ **6.** Brad Pelis entered the silent house; Angela was waiting for him.

_____ **7.** He told her that he would leave for Europe on Wednesday.

_____ **8.** You could review by rereading Chapter 12, or you could study the workbook exercises.

_____ **9.** If you want to review the workbook exercises, you should start on page 27.

_____ **10.** You should start on page 27 if you want to review the workbook exercises.

Review exercise 1

Define the following words:

1. clause _____

_____

2. independent clause _____

_____

3. dependent clause _____

_____

4. simple sentence _____

_____

5. compound sentence _____

_____

6. complex sentence _____

_____

7. sentence fragment _____

_____

Review exercise 2

The following short paragraph contains ten clauses grouped in six sentences. Mark each **independent clause** and each **dependent clause** by placing a line above it and labeling it **IC** or **DC**.

Example

<u>   IC   </u>   <u>   IC   </u>
The college was founded in 1848, but it did not receive national
<u>   </u>
attention until the 1920s.

Melanie went back to the window, which she pried open with a screwdriver. As she climbed into the room, something flew right by her face. An open birdcage hung near the window. Melanie peered around her, but she could see little in the semidarkness. She groped for a light switch. Finally, she found it; a loud laugh came from behind the door.

Chapter 1 writing assignment

1. Using complete sentences, list three or four qualities that you think make an ideal parent.
2. Write a short paragraph (about half a page) in which you discuss one of these qualities. Use all three kinds of sentences in your paragraph: simple, compound, and complex.
3. Go over what you have written, making sure that there are no sentence fragments. Carefully add corrections where necessary.

2. Finding the main parts of a sentence

The main parts of a clause, or of a simple sentence, are the verb and the subject. Many clauses also have a third main element: the object or complement. These parts contain the main idea of the clause—its core idea or backbone. All the other words and phrases connected to it merely serve, or modify, this core idea—that is, they limit or refine it in some fashion. For instance, in a sentence like "I drink coffee for breakfast," *I drink coffee* is the core idea, and *for breakfast* restricts or refines it.

The verb

Every clause has a word or phrase (a phrase is simply a group of words) that either shows some kind of action or indicates existence, condition, or relationship.

Verbs that show action (the first group) are called **action verbs,** and they include such words as *to give, to come, to talk,* and *to swim.* Verbs that show existence or condition are called **linking verbs.** Forms of *to be, to become,* and *to seem* are among the most common linking verbs.

Action verbs

To find the action verb of a sentence, ask yourself, "What's happening in the sentence?" Consider this example:

Simon **speaks** Spanish very well.

When you ask "What's happening in the sentence?" the answer is that someone speaks something. Since *speaks* is an action and the other words of the sentence are not, the verb of the sentence is *speaks*, and it is a one-word action verb.

Often, the verb of the sentence consists of more than one word, as in these examples below:

> The answers **were announced** yesterday.
>
> After supper, Claire **will be working** on her paper.

In these sentences, the answers to the question "What's happening?" are the phrases *were announced* and *will be working*. We call such groups of words *verb phrases*.

Marking verbs

In this book, a circle will be used to mark verbs.

One-word action verb

Maria (trimmed) her sister's hair.

Verb phrase

Snow (has been falling) since noon.

Many verbs show actions. Here are a few more examples. Each circled word is the verb of the sentence.

Pablo (will be eating) a hamburger and fries for lunch.

My brother (runs) his own business.

Last fall Hao Jin (was hurt) in an accident.

The next exercise contains sentences with action verbs. Practice finding the verbs in these sentences. If you run into trouble, ask yourself, "What's happening in this sentence?"

Exercise 1   Finding action verbs

Circle the **verb** in the following sentences.

Example

The treasurer (sent) her report yesterday.

1. Wanda laughs at all her jokes.

2. The apartments were being redone for new tenants.

3. The *Titanic* disaster in 1912 changed radio from a toy to an important means of communication.

4. "FM" stands for "frequency modulation."

5. Many of Professor Wang's students will succeed because of her help.

6. Last night's fire shocked the entire community.

7. Antonio's restaurant has been serving fresh fish daily.

8. David discovered a new shortcut to the campus.

9. No doubt the Lasowskis will be bringing their baby from the hospital tomorrow.

10. The entire bucket of roofing tar splashed into the pool.

Linking verbs

As noted earlier, not all verbs show actions. Some—the **linking verbs**—indicate existence or condition.

Linking verbs that show existence

The forms of the verb *to be* make up the main group of linking verbs that show existence. These forms include *am, are, is, was,* and *were.* Such words are called **verbs of being.**

One-word linking verb

My next class (is) in the biology lab.

The verb *is* tells us that the next class exists. The rest of the sentence tells us where it exists.

Sometimes verbs like *is* connect or link two words or ideas in an equivalent relation. In such cases, *is* and other forms of the verb *to be* function like equal signs.

Mr. Corbero (is) the instructor.

Mr. Corbero = instructor

Various forms of the verb *to be* can also connect the subject to a word that describes it.

The jazz concert (was) successful.

The two new houses (are) the fanciest on the block.

Other verbs in this group include phrases that end in *be, been,* and *being,* like *will be, has been,* and *was being.* The following sentence contains a linking verb phrase.

Verb phrase

Gloria (has been) absent for three days.

Verbs of seeming and sensation

Words like *seem* and *appear,* and sense words like *feel, smell, look, sound,* and *taste* can also be used as linking verbs, though some of them function as action verbs as well. *Become,* too, is a linking verb.

When verbs indicating seeming or sensation, or the verb *to become* are used as linking verbs, they often mean the same as the verb *to be.*

The child (appears) ill.

The child is ill.

The meal (tasted) good.

The meal is good.

She (became) a surgeon.

She was a surgeon.

Note, however, that some of the verbs in the categories mentioned above can also be action verbs, not linking verbs.

Carlos (tasted) all ten kinds of cookies.

Mariola (will appear) at the window precisely at nine.

Hans (felt) something sharp underfoot.

Exercise 2   Finding linking verbs

Circle the **verb** in the following sentences.

Example   The treasurer (is) very careful in her work.

    1. This book became required reading last year.

    2. The photograph looked better in black and white.

    3. Most of Gayle's answers are correct.

    4. Generally, the group's songs sounded alike.

    5. Brad Palmer is the youngest pledge at Eta Eta Pi.

    6. She looks unwell this morning.

    7. These comparisons seem inaccurate.

    8. The best rebounder was Larry Darwin.

    9. On first sight, the old man appeared stronger than before.

  10. The problems become more difficult later in the semester.

The next exercise contains sentences with both types of verbs, action and linking. Keep in mind that words like *appeared* and *looked* can be either action or linking verbs.

Exercise 3   Finding action and linking verbs

Circle the **verb** in each of the following sentences. Then write **action** or **linking** on the line provided.

Example   *linking*   The new manager (looks) tired.

_____   **1.** Byron showed great courage during his father's illness.

_____   **2.** Kurt is with his children every evening after work.

_____   **3.** Yesterday I saw Amy Perfito on her way to the beach.

_____   **4.** Earvin's suitcase weighed close to fifty pounds.

_____ 5. The Lakers played their best game last night.

_____ 6. Abdul looked everywhere in the theater for his watch.

_____ 7. The example appears on page 425.

_____ 8. Her magic tricks always delight the younger children.

_____ 9. The locket was in the drawer all the time.

_____ 10. This earthquake felt stronger than the last one.

_____ 11. The young singer sounded like his father.

_____ 12. A bad accident occurred on this street last week.

_____ 13. The sheets smell fresh.

_____ 14. For days afterward, I thought about her decision to leave school.

_____ 15. The bank opens for business at ten on Saturday.

The subject

Once you have found the verb of a sentence, it is usually easy to find its **subject.** Just ask "who?" or "what?" and then say the verb. This is the **subject question,** and the answer—usually one word—is the subject of that verb.

Most subjects appear before the verbs they are connected to. For example, let's find the subject of the following sentence:

The basketball players arrived by bus yesterday.

First find the verb of the sentence. In this case, the action of the sentence is *arrived.*

The basketball players (arrived) by bus yesterday.

Now use the subject question to find the subject. Ask "who?" or "what?" and then say the verb "arrived."

Subject question *who* arrived?
Answer (one word) *players*

Players is the subject. *Players arrived* is the core idea—the backbone—of the sentence.

Marking subjects

To show the subject, we will mark it with a double underline.

The basketball <u>players</u> (arrived) by bus yesterday.

Here are more examples of using the subject question. The verbs in these sentences have already been marked.

The local radio station (plays) progressive music.

Subject question *what* plays?
Answer (one word) *station*

Station is the subject. *Station plays* is the core of the sentence (subject + verb).

The local radio <u>station</u> (plays) progressive music.

The next example is a little harder.

Frank's history class (begins) at noon.

Subject question *what* begins?
Answer (one word) *class*

Class is the subject, not *Frank's* or *history*. Though these words might look like subjects, the sentence does not say "Frank's begins" or "history begins."

Frank's history <u>class</u> (begins) at noon.

Names as subjects

Find the subject in the following sentence:

Dean Rhea Park (gave) a lecture last week.

Subject question *who* gave?
Answer *Dean Rhea Park*

In this case, the subject is more than one word because "Dean Rhea Park"—a capitalized name and title—is what she is called in the sentence.

Dean Rhea Park (gave) a lecture last week.

If the capitalized name of a person or thing (like a book, a movie, or a town) is the subject, mark the whole name as the subject. If the name includes a capitalized title, include it as part of the subject also.

Exercise 4 Finding subjects

The verb of each sentence below is already marked. Find the **subject** by asking the subject question. Then underline it twice.
Unless the subject is a capitalized name, do not mark more than one word.

Example

The season (ended) with a victory.

1. The pass (landed) in the end zone.

2. The chair in the corner (needs) a new coat of varnish.

3. Mike's little brother already (has) his own bank account.

4. The science class (meets) at the planetarium today.

5. Last year's American history final examination (was) not very difficult.

6. Dr. Banning (answered) all of the questions from the audience.

7. Our local college just (held) its first commencement.

8. *Noises Off* (plays) all year at the Morris Civic Auditorium.

9. A good concert pianist (practices) almost every day.

10. Ruth Centini (spoke) to the class about nutrition.

Exercise 5 Finding subjects and verbs

In this exercise, the verbs are not marked. Mark each sentence by working in the following order:

1. Circle the **verb.**

2. Ask the **subject question.**

3. Underline the **subject** twice.

Example
The medicine <u>cabinet</u> (was) empty.

1. We agreed with all of her arguments.

2. The best comedian in the show was eleven years old.

3. The manager spoke highly of the team's talent.

4. Unlike the last president, Dr. Aaron places a high priority on research.

5. Commuters from the northern suburbs waited three hours for a train into town this morning.

6. The manual decarbing assistor needed replacement badly.

7. Chen's dancing instructor called in sick this week.

8. The puppy spent last night in a box in the basement.

9. The oldest student in the class looks like a bank president.

10. He is actually a prominent local sculptor.

11. WYKY's local weatherman guessed wrong this morning.

12. The victims reported the burglary themselves.

13. Wrecking Crew won the race by four lengths.

14. A painful limp slowed his walk.

15. The Consequential Insurance Company issued the policy last year.

The object and the complement

The last of the three main parts of a sentence is the **object** and the **complement.** Objects and complements are less essential than subjects and verbs. Every sentence must have a subject and a verb, but sentences do not need objects and complements to be complete. When an object or complement is present, however, it is part of the core idea of the sentence.

The object

The **object of the verb** (also called the **direct object**) receives the action of the verb. Since linking verbs do not show actions, it follows that only action verbs can have objects.

The normal position for objects, as you might have guessed, is after the verb.

The object question

It is as easy to find the object as it is to find the subject. Once you know the verb of the sentence, just ask the object question. Say the verb, and then ask "whom?" or "what?" The answer—usually one word like the subject—is the object. Here is an example:

The construction <u>company</u> (built) the library in eighteen months.

> **Object question** built *what?*
> **Answer (one word)** *library*

Library is the object of the verb *built. Company built library* (subject + verb + object) is the core idea of this sentence.

Marking objects

To show the object, underline it once.

The construction <u>company</u> (built) the <u>library</u> in eighteen months.

Let's look at another example.

<u>She</u> (answered) Sarah's letter immediately.

> **Object question** answered *what?*
> **Answer (one word)** *letter*

Notice that the object is *letter*, not *Sarah's. Sarah's* may look like an object, but the core of the sentence is *she answered letter.*

<u>She</u> (answered) Sarah's <u>letter</u> immediately.

Here is one more example:

The campus <u>bookstore</u> (opens) at noon today.

Object question opens *what?*

Answer *(We can't give an answer.)*

From what the sentence tells us, there is no answer to the object question. Therefore the sentence has no object. Notice that *at noon today* answers the question "opens when?" not "opens what?"

The campus <u>bookstore</u> (opens) at noon today. (NO OBJECT)

Names as objects

Follow the same rule for marking names as objects as you did in marking names as subjects.

My mother saw *Gone with the Wind* seventeen times.

Object question saw *what?*

Answer *Gone with the Wind*

Since *Gone with the Wind* is a capitalized name, we underline the whole name.

My <u>mother</u> (saw) <u>*Gone with the Wind*</u> seventeen times.

The complement

Since linking verbs (like *to be, to have,* and *to seem*) are not actions, they cannot have objects. But sometimes they are followed by words that look like objects and answer the object question. These words are called **complements.**

Complements following linking verbs always equal ("complete") or describe the subject. In this way they are very different from objects. Nevertheless, the object question can be used to find both objects and complements.

Remember that it is the *verb* that tells you whether the answer to the object question is an object or a complement, as shown in the following chart.

If the verb is	**The answer to the object question is**
an action verb	an object
a linking verb	a complement

The following example contains a complement:

The <u>instructor</u> (is) Dr. Andersen.

Object question is *who?*

Answer *Dr. Andersen*

Marking complements

Mark complements by underlining them once and writing COMP above them.

The instructor (is) Dr. Andersen. *[COMP marked over "Dr. Andersen"]*

Remember that even though *Dr. Andersen* looks like an object, it is a complement because of the linking verb *is*.

Descriptive words (adjectives) as complements

Many complements are nouns and pronouns (words like *car, book, it, we,* and *this),* but some complements are adjectives. **Adjectives** are words that describe or limit nouns and pronouns. For example, the cat looks *sick*, the rewards are *few*.

The following sentences show the difference between nouns and adjectives as complements.

Noun complement

Our new neighbor (is) a student at Penwicker College. *[COMP marked over "student"]*

Adjective complement

Our new neighbor (is) young. *[COMP marked over "young"]*

Names as complements

Mark names as complements in the same way as you marked them as subjects and objects, by marking the entire capitalized name.

For years our family physician (was) Dr. Andius. *[COMP marked over "Dr. Andius"]*

The following exercises will give you practice in finding both objects and complements.

Exercise 6 — Finding objects and complements

Find the **object** or **complement** in the following sentences by asking the object question. If the sentence has an object or complement, underline it once and write **COMP** over any complement.

Remember to look for linking verbs to find complements.

Examples

Francine (moved) the television to the living room.

Our television (is) a German brand. *[COMP marked over "brand"]*

1. Kelly's Bar offers a special every Monday night.

2. This morning the insurance examiner finally arrived.

3. This year's starting quarterback is Mark Williams.

4. The Democratic candidate was named honorary member of the club.

5. The distractions here are many.

6. Fortunately, no injuries occurred.

7. The final speaker of the evening appeared tired on the podium.

8. Sherlock Holmes is popular.

9. Sherlock Holmes is my favorite fictional detective.

10. The novel told yet another story of forbidden passion.

Exercise 7   Finding main sentence parts

In each of the following sentences, mark the

1. **verb,**
2. **subject,**
3. **object** or **complement,** if any.

Example

The store <u>manager</u> (is) <u>unhappy</u> with last week's sales report.
[*comp* written above unhappy]

1. Demonstrators swarmed through the European city.

2. The bookstore sells many historical novels.

3. In spite of examples, these instructions seem unclear.

4. It was sent yesterday.

5. This is the best college in the state.

6. The Knights of Columbus give charitable meals each year at this time.

7. Few governments are ready for tax reform.

8. The new camera operator's work was excellent.

9. The thunderstorm woke him up.

10. Carmen looked through the window at the street.

Review exercise

Mark the **verb, subject,** and **object** or **complement** of each sentence in the following paragraph.

The twentieth century saw the birth of a new form of storytelling. An ingenious combination of metal, celluloid, glass, and wiring produced a technological breakthrough. The result had a tremendous effect on the minds of millions. This art form, of course, is the motion picture. To many people it is the most important art form of the century.

Chapter 2 writing assignment

1. Write a good, one-sentence definition of the word *student*. Think about it; this may not be as simple as it sounds.
2. Using complete sentences, write a short paragraph (about half a page) in which you present and discuss your definition. Vary your sentences so that some include objects and some complements.
3. Go over what you have written and carefully add corrections where needed.

3. Reversed word order

In some sentences, the usual order of the main words—subject, verb, object or complement—is changed. Such changes occur most often in **questions** and in **emphatic sentences**, especially the **"Here is /There is . . ." sentences.**

Recognizing these situations will help you make subjects and verbs agree with each other. For example, you can choose correctly between the verbs *see* and *sees* only after you have found the correct subject. If the sentence is written in reversed word order, you might choose the wrong word as the subject and then use the wrong form of the verb.

Commands, too, deviate from normal word order and will be discussed in this chapter even though they do not show *reversed* word order.

Questions

To ask a question in writing, we usually change the order of the words in the sentence. The new sentence often has part or all of the verb in front of the subject. Verb phrases that begin with some form of the verbs *to be, to have,* and *to do,* or of *can* or *may* are most often used in questions.

Statement (normal word order)

Alma (is) treasurer this year.

Question (reversed word order)

(Is) Alma treasurer this year?

Notice that the question ends with a question mark, not a period.

Some sentences give an additional hint that they are questions; they *begin* with the words *who, whom, which, what, why, when,* or *how.*

In the following examples, the words *which, what,* and *whom* are the objects of the verb phrases *does like, did ask,* and *will see.* Notice that the answer to the question would supply the meaning of the words, *which, what,* and *whom.*

Which (does) she (like) best?

What (did) you (ask) me?

Whom (will) they (see)?

What and *who* are sometimes the subjects of questions. In such instances, the normal word order is not reversed.

Who (spoke) at the reception?

What (came) over you yesterday?

The other words that commonly begin questions—*when, where, why,* and *how* —usually are not the subject or object of the sentence. However, most questions that contain them also show reversed word order.

When (can) Nina (take) the test?

Why (are) you (looking) at me like that?

Exercise 1 Marking questions

Mark the **verb, subject,** and **object** or **complement** (if any) of each of the following sentences.

Example (Is) the answer on the worksheet?

1. Why was your worksheet late?

2. Is this your first philosophy course?

3. Who can answer my question?

4. Did this actress star in several musical productions?

5. When is the next train to Boston?

6. May Erica borrow your car?

7. Was corn also available in Europe?

8. How was your supper?

9. How do you spell her name?

10. Can Chris watch TV tonight?

Emphatic sentences

In many sentences, words are shifted to the beginning of the sentence to give them greater emphasis. The result is often a sentence written in reversed word order. Sentences beginning with *here* and *there* fall into this group.

Here is/There is . . . sentences

Here and *there* cannot be subjects of sentences. When a sentence begins with either of these words, the subject of the sentence often appears after the verb. Compare the following sentences. In both of them, the subject is *books*.

Reversed word order

There (are) your <u>books</u>.

Normal word order

Your <u>books</u> (are) there.

In the examples above, *there* suggests a specific place—a place you might be pointing to. However, even if *there* does not refer to a specific place but just indicates existence or presence, as in the following sentence, it still cannot be the subject.

Reversed word order

There (were) three <u>people</u> in your office earlier.

You can test this by putting the sentence into normal word order without the word *there*.

Normal word order

Three <u>people</u> (were) in your office earlier.

Sometimes other verbs are used with the emphatic *here* or *there*.

Here (goes) the <u>money</u>.

Exercise 2

Marking *Here is/There is . . .* sentences.

Mark the **verb** and **subject** of each of the following sentences.

Example

Here (are) the <u>answers</u> to the first ten questions.

1. There were other copies of my class notes.

2. Here comes the first customer.

3. There is a good example of lab technique.

4. Here are the extra diskettes for your computer.

5. Here stood the Old West Church.

Other emphatic sentences

Word order is reversed for the sake of greater emphasis in other sentences besides those starting with "Here is/There is . . ." The most common change is to bring a complement, a phrase, or a dependent clause to the front of the sentence to give it greater weight.

Here are two examples of this kind of sentence.

Reversed word order

A fine <u>doctor</u> <u>you</u> (are)!

Into the meadow (walked) a young <u>deer</u>.

Normal word order

<u>You</u> (are) a fine <u>doctor</u>!

A young <u>deer</u> (walked) into the meadow.

Exercise 3

Other emphatic sentences

Mark the **verb, subject,** and **complement** (if any) of each of the following sentences. If the sentence is in reversed word order, rewrite it in normal word order on the lines provided.

Example

On the blackboard (is) tomorrow's <u>homework</u> assignment.

Tomorrow's homework assignment is on the blackboard.

1. Into the room walked three players from the soccer team.

_____

_____

2. A blank page is the writer's worst enemy.

_____

_____

3. To Mr. Hogan went the last transceiver.

_____

_____

4. A fine student he became!

_____

_____

5. On the shelf sat the stack of newspapers.

_____

_____

Commands

Commands, sentences that contain requests or directions, sometimes differ from sentences that use normal word order. In these cases, though, words are not moved around but *removed.*

The word taken out is always the subject *you.* When *you* is missing from a command, it is "hidden" and still understood to be there. Omitting *you* gives the verb of the command more force since it now starts the sentence.

Mark the missing subject of a command as a "hidden word" by adding it above the sentence and underlining it twice.

Command

Stand next to the door.

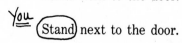

You (Stand) next to the door.

Exercise 4   Marking commands

Mark the **verb, subject,** and **object** or **complement** (if any) of each of the following sentences. If the subject is a hidden word, add it above the sentence and mark it correctly.

Example

You
(Return) your books to the library soon.

1. Please answer all questions on the examination.

2. Turn left at the next light.

3. Give the book to Ms. Abraham after class tomorrow.

4. Stop.

5. Look at the picture carefully.

The following exercise includes the various kinds of sentences you have been studying.

Exercise 5   Reversed word order

Mark the **verb, subject,** and **object** or **complement** (if any) of each of the following sentences.

Example

What (did) you (say)?

1. Is this the way to Beauville?

2. Here is a recent map of this region.

3. Who lives in the house now?

4. Read the article on the back page.

5. What was she doing near the safe?

6. One book disappeared each week of the last month.

7. There are no more copies of the essay.

8. Was she the first lawyer on the case?

9. Stop at the first apartment on the left.

10. There were ants in the kitchen this morning.

Review exercise

Mark the **verb, subject,** and **object** or **complement** (if any) of each sentence in the following paragraph. Watch for sentences with reversed word order.

Do you need a copy of one of your files? Here is the simplest method. Press the "F1" key. A list of files on the current disk will appear on the computer screen. Then move the cursor with the arrow keys. Once you have chosen a file for copying, press the "Enter" key. The computer automatically copies the marked file.

Chapter 3 writing assignment

1. Make a list of what you would like to do during an ideal vacation.
2. Arrange the list in order of preference.
3. Write a short paragraph (about half a page) in which you present your top two preferences and explain why they would make your vacation ideal.
4. Go over what you have written, making sure that your sentences are complete and varied. If necessary, add corrections.

4. Punctuating and capitalizing complete sentences

Sentences rarely appear alone. Usually they are part of paragraphs. Since it would be confusing to allow separate sentences to run together, we use punctuation to separate them. The first punctuation rule tells us how to punctuate separate sentences.

Punctuation Rule 1
Separating Independent Clauses

Separate independent clauses into sentences by using one of the following punctuation marks:

1. Period (.)
2. Question mark (?)
3. Exclamation point (!)

Periods, question marks, and exclamation points are called **end punctuation.**

Using the period

The punctuation mark most often used to separate complete sentences from each other is the **period.** Here is an example of a period used to separate independent clauses into simple sentences.

Independent clauses run together (INCORRECT)

The apartment has been empty for two months
the last tenants moved to Georgia.

Independent clauses separated with a period (CORRECT)

The <u>apartment</u> (has been) ^{comp}empty for two months.

The last <u>tenants</u> (moved) to Georgia.

It is an error (called a **run-on sentence**) to write independent clauses with no punctuation between them. Using a period to separate such clauses is one way to correct this error.

If a run-on sentence is to remain one single sentence, then the independent clauses can be separated by a colon (:) or a semicolon (;). You may recall that we already considered the semicolon in Chapter 1 (page 6). Colons and semicolons will be discussed later in this book, but here are two examples.

Do one chore before you go: wash the dishes.

Again we waited at the station; the train is always late.

Capitalizing complete sentences

Every complete sentence must start with a **capital letter.** Every sentence in the book you are reading, for example, starts with a capital letter, and all your sentences should begin that way, too.

Independent clauses run together (INCORRECT)

When the Jurgensens left, it started raining they did not have an umbrella.

Independent clauses separated with a period (CORRECT)

When the Jurgensens left, it started raining. They did not have an umbrella.

Exercise 1   Using periods

Some of the following items contain two or more independent clauses, and some do not.

1. Place a **period** after each independent clause.
2. **Capitalize** the first letter of each sentence.

Example   ^Wwe need more pictures in our dorm room. ^Iit looks empty without

them.

1. the Gatling Gun was invented in the 1800s many people thought it would change the West

2. their new album sold several million copies this includes sales in Europe as well

3. the store opened early the holiday season must be starting already

4. the contract clearly restricts the number of units available to discount buyers

5. surely the technical manual contains several solutions to the problem choose one of them

6. later we told Mrs. Gallagher about the snails in the garden she showed us a book on the subject

7. summer arrived yesterday few noticed it since the temperature stayed in the fifties

8. the bears discovered the garbage pile in the night this morning the entire area was a mess

9. books that have Dr. Hemming's signature on the title page are now worth over $1000 each

10. in the box on the stairs is a small yellow envelope get it for me please if you have the time

Using the question mark and exclamation point

In some cases the **question mark** or **exclamation point** is used instead of the period to end a sentence. If a sentence is asking a question instead of making a statement, a question mark MUST be used.

Incorrect

Did you see the Raiders' game on TV.

Correct

Did you see the Raiders' game on TV?

Unlike the question mark, the exclamation point is always optional. It is used instead of a period to give a sentence emphasis or to indicate an elevated tone of voice—usually a cry or shout or an expression of surprise.

I never expected such lovely flowers!
Julio yelled, "Get out of the way!"

Exercise 2   Using question marks

Some of the following items contain two or more independent clauses, and some do not.

1. Place a **period** or **question mark** after each independent clause.
2. **Capitalize** the first letter of each sentence.

Example

W̸e need more pictures in our dorm room. W̸ould you bring some back from home with you?

1. can you hear the speaker would you like to sit closer to the stage

2. those jackets look expensive they seem to be made of the finest leather

3. we need a film projector for today's class would someone get one from the AV closet in the main hall it isn't locked

4. most of the trainees in the forest service are hoping to spend the whole summer in the woods

5. why is that car on the sidewalk did something happen while I was gone

6. place the test tube in the rack and add three drops of solution

7. she wants to bet on one of the horses which do you think has a good chance of winning

8. is this the way to solve the problem I have trouble with anything involving trigonometry

9. the pistol fired accidentally no one was hurt

10. for him the war ended in a cold trench in Belgium he returned to England with the wounded two days later

Review exercise

The following paragraph lacks punctuation and only names are capitalized. Using **end punctuation** and **capital letters,** separate it into sentences. Remember that a complete sentence must have at least one independent clause.

Ellie Sena loves gardening last year she started her garden early she wanted to grow some peas before the hot weather set in the very next day rain started to fall it continued for a full week until all the gardens in the area looked like huge puddles all her seeds washed away Ellie's neighbor Joe Kawecki had put in some squash seeds but they rotted from all the wetness when the sun finally came out both Ellie and Joe prepared to start afresh they now knew the uncertainty that farmers must endure each year

Chapter 4 writing assignment

1. Do you think a six- or seven-year-old child should watch television? Ask yourself "Why?" and "Why not?" and list some positive and some negative aspects of TV viewing.
2. Write a short paragraph (about half a page) in which you present and discuss either one positive or one negative aspect and how it might affect the child. Vary your sentence structures as much as possible.
3. Go over what you have written, adding any necessary corrections.

Section II

Verbs

In Section I you learned that verbs were part of the core of the sentence. In this section you will learn more about verbs and verb phrases—how they are constructed, how they are used, and how to correct the most common errors in verb use.

5. Verbs and verb phrases

You have already worked with both one-word verbs and verb phrases in Section I. Here we will look more closely at **verb phrases**—groups of words that act like a single one-word verb.

Verb phrases

Using verb phrases allows us to tell more about an action than whether it occurred in the present or the past. With verb phrases, we can make four important changes in the way an action is presented.

1. We can change the TIME of an action, that is, the time when the action takes place. For instance, we can change the time of an action from the present to the future.

    Mr. Jefferson (**brings**) new uniforms.

    Mr. Jefferson (**will bring**) new uniforms.

    The verb phrase *will bring* tells us that the action occurs in the future instead of the present.

2. We can change the DIRECTION of an action by focusing on the receiver of the action. We do so by letting the receiver—rather than the performer—of the action be the subject of the verb.

    The referee (**postponed**) the game because of snow.

The game (has been postponed) because of snow.

In the first sentence, the referee did the postponing—he or she was the doer. In the second sentence, we don't know who did the postponing; the subject *game* is the receiver of the action and no doer is mentioned. When the doer of the action is the subject, the verb is said to be in the **active voice.** When the receiver of the action is the subject, the verb is said to be in the **passive voice.**

3. We can change the MODE of an action, that is, its state. For example, we can change a fact into a possibility.

Jeremy (plays) the trombone in this evening's concert.

Jeremy (might play) the trombone in this evening's concert.

The added word *might* changes the action from a fact to a possibility. Other added words change actions in other ways—for example, *should play, may play,* or *could play.*

4. We can indicate whether an action has reached COMPLETION. That is, we can show whether an action is finished or is still going on.

Grass (grows) in the garden.

Grass (has been growing) in the garden all spring.

Judy (worked) for Continental General last summer.

Judy (had worked) for Continental General last summer.

In the first sentence, we learn only that the action *grows* occurs right now. We don't know whether it is a new action or a continuation of an old one.

The second sentence, however, gives us this information. The verb *has been growing* tells us that the action started in the past and is still continuing.

In the third and fourth sentences, we find a similar situation. The third tells us simply that the working happened in the past. The fourth, with the verb phrase *had worked,* tells us that the work started in the past and is completed. *Had* is added to show completion; *have* or *has* is added to show a continuing action.

Structure of verb phrases

Verb phrases come in different lengths. But they all are similarly constructed. Each ends with an **action** or **linking word** (an action word shows action and a linking word shows existence, condition, or relationship), preceded by one or more **helping verbs**—the words that help make the changes we have just been discussing.

The action of the verb phrases—its meaning—is always carried by the last word in the phrase, the action or linking word. This word can be a verb, such as *run, see, appear,* or *own;* or it can be a verbal—a word made from a verb—like *running, seen, appeared,* or *owned.*

The helping verbs, which always come before the action or linking word, sim-

ply change the action word in the ways you have seen.
Here is a list of helping verbs.

Helping Verbs

1	2	3	4	5
shall	should	do	have	am
will	would	does	has	is
can	could	did	had	are
may	might		having	was
must				were
				be
				been
				being

Note that some of the words in columns 3, 4, and 5 can also be one-word verbs by themselves. To tell how such a word is being used, look at its position. If it is not the last word or the only word in a verb phrase, then it is a helping word. Let's look at an example:

I can have just a light lunch.

Here *have* is the action word and *can* is the helping word in the verb phrase.

Action and linking verb phrases

When verb phrases contain action ideas, most of us have little trouble recognizing them. But verb phrases that contain linking verb ideas sometimes cause difficulty.

Compare the following sentences:

Carol **will be arriving** by train.

Carol **will be** here soon.

The first sentence contains the three-word verb phrase *will be arriving. Arriving* is the main action of the sentence. Both *will* and *be* are used as helping verbs.

The second sentence, on the other hand, contains the two-word phrase *will be.* Notice first that this verb contains a linking, not an action, idea—*will be* is a form of the linking verb *to be.* Second, note that *here* is not an action either. In sentences like these, don't be tempted to mark words like *here* as part of the verb phrase.

Most linking verb phrases end in the following words:

be (example: *will be*)
been (example: *has been*)
being (example: *is being*)

Look carefully at verb phrases containing these words to see if the meaning is an action or a linking idea.

Marking verb phrases

Mark a verb phrase just like a one-word verb, by circling all the words of the phrase. All the verb phrases in this chapter have been marked in that way.

The exercises below will help you find verb phrases in sentences.

Exercise 1   Finding action verb phrases

Mark the **verb** or **verb phrase** in each of the following sentences. The list on page 40 can aid you in recognizing helping verbs.

All the verbs and verb phrases in this exercise are action verbs and action verb phrases.

Example   The class (has been moved) to the Science Hall.

1. The Barkleys will go to the Catskills this summer.

2. On weekdays I eat a small breakfast.

3. Wilma had done the best job possible.

4. Tonight's dinner was prepared by my daughter.

5. Kiley's girlfriend should bring extra plates.

6. The game has lasted over two hours.

7. We must read those novels for our last literature class.

8. Mr. Wilkes is leaving for Colorado.

9. The books should have arrived by now.

10. Tremaine, a transfer student, will be joining us in March.

11. The actors have been practicing since May.

12. The girls in the hall could have been listening.

13. The poem might have been recited more feelingly.

14. Sonya might have coped with her transportation problem

    differently.

15. The box had to be sent by courier mail.

Exercise 2

Finding linking verb phrases

Mark the **verb** or **verb phrase** in each of the following sentences. Refer to the list on page 40 for aid in recognizing helping verbs.
    All the verbs in this exercise are linking verbs.

Example

This sign (should have been) easier to see.

1. The garden will be ready for planting tomorrow.

2. The situation will look better in the morning.

3. Margaret has been class president for the last three years.

4. Professor Lin could have been ill last Monday.

5. This roast should taste better than the last one.

6. Walter is being difficult about lending the car.

7. Such a reaction might have seemed strange.

8. In this class the students are responsible for photographic developing fees.

9. The class list had been longer in past semesters.

10. You may have just one piece of cake.

The next exercise includes both action and linking verbs. In addition, it asks you to find and mark the helping verbs from the *have* and *be* groups (see columns 4 and 5 of the box on page 40).

Exercise 3

Finding action and linking verb phrases

1. Mark the **verb** or **verb phrase** in each of the following sentences. Use the helping verb list on page 40 to aid you.
2. Place an **X** over all the helping verbs from the *have* and *be* groups. (However, make sure they are helping verbs and not action or linking words.)

Examples

The fraternity (has been asking) for contributions to its scholarship

fund.

×
My parents (have been) in Idaho since May.

1. The clock had run several times already.

2. We should have ordered pizza.

3. Marcy's new job could be a wonderful opportunity.

4. The pie should have been left in the oven longer.

5. The dog had become irritated by all the fire alarms.

6. The computer system has been installed by a consultant from Lanfil Technologies.

7. She will have flown more than ten thousand miles by Tuesday.

8. Shea has been trying hard to win the councilman's seat.

9. The boss will be coming any minute.

10. Marv Murphy has been a broadcaster in this area for more than fifteen years.

11. Jim may have gone to the Coho Club.

12. She practiced the flute for years before performing in public.

13. The buses were running on a special schedule during the snowstorm.

14. The sauce might taste peppery.

15. The world has been made safe for democracy.

Adverbs, or words that can interrupt verb phrases

Sometimes a word that is not part of the verb phrase appears between words of the phrase, as in this example:

I (have) always (enjoyed) tennis.

The verb of this sentence is the phrase *have enjoyed*. We know this because *have enjoyed* follows the rules about verb phrases. It ends with an action word *(enjoyed)*, and includes a helping verb, *have*. The word *always* cannot be part of the verb phrase. *Always* describes the verb of the sentence by telling when the action occurred.

Words like *always* are called **adverbs**. Adverbs modify—that is, describe or limit—verbs, adjectives, and other adverbs. Let's look at some examples:

> I have **almost** reached my goal.
>
> The baby cries **almost** constantly.
>
> She has **almost** perfect features.

In the first example, the adverb *almost* modifies the verb *reached*. In the second example, the adverb *almost* modifies the adverb *constantly*, which in turn describes the verb *cries*. The third example shows the adverb *almost* modifying the adjective *perfect*. We will discuss adverbs more fully in Section IV. Right now let's focus on the use of adverbs with verbs.

The adverb questions

Adverbs can answer the following questions about the actions of verbs:

When?	I will **never** leave. She must return **today**.
Where?	Ms. Perrite has gone **out**. The bird flew **away**.
Why?	The game was canceled **because of rain**. (The adverbs in this group are usually phrases or clauses that begin with words like *because* or *since*.)
How?	Tom Hirsch had **quickly** hidden the letter. The accident must have happened **suddenly**.
Under what condition? (or yes or no?)	She will **not** come. He can **certainly** do a good job. Someone has **probably** found your bracelet. (Answers may include different degrees of certainty. Answers may also tell *yes* or *no* by indicating a condition or a relation to another action. You will encounter more adverbs that belong to this group in later chapters.)

As you can see from several of the examples we have been considering, not all adverbs interrupt verb phrases. The most common ones that *can* do so include the following:

Some Common Adverbs That Can Interrupt Verb Phrases

When?

now	often
always	seldom

never	usually
sometimes	frequently
once	occasionally

How?

quickly	well
slowly	poorly
easily	strongly
carefully	noisily

Under what condition? (yes or no?)

not	certainly
possibly	surely
probably	truly
perhaps	doubtlessly
also	nearly
only	somewhat
quite	mostly
almost	rather

The adverb *not*

The adverb *not* is commonly found in the middle of verb phrases.

We (could) not (find) the correct microscope.

Not is often contracted in verb phrases as follows:

We couldn't find the correct microscope.

Even though *not* is written as part of the verb (as in *couldn't*), it is still an adverb and not a helping verb. When you circle verbs in such sentences, leave *not* or *n't* out of the circle.

The following sentences contain examples of verb phrases with interrupting words. Review the adverb list on pages 44–45 and then do this exercise.

Exercise 4 — Verb phrases with adverbs

Mark the **verb** or **verb phrase** in each of the following sentences.

Example   Myron (had) never (been elected) to a class office.

1. They could not have married at a better time.

2. Myron has always wanted a career in the arts.

3. Problems like that are seldom resolved through anger.

4. This could possibly have been her greatest year.

5. Power once rested in his branch of the family.

6. The infantry had certainly won this battle.

7. These storms do not usually last more than three days.

8. We could also have bought the bonds.

9. The leading actress is often late.

10. Treatments for alcoholism are now advertised in this area.

Review exercise

1. Mark the **verb** or **verb phrase** in each of the following sentences. The helping verb list and the adverb list (pages 40 and 44–45) will help you. Some of the sentences in this paragraph have more than one clause and therefore more than one verb.
2. Place an **X** over all helping verbs from the *have* and the *be* groups. (Make sure, though, that they are helping verbs and not action or linking words.)

Example

Though he (can give) sound advice, it (has) seldom (been taken.)

   In my student days, I had always preferred serious drama, but my friends were usually much more drawn to musicals. I would sometimes go along with them to these shows. With all their stage activity, musicals had doubtlessly struck us as cheerful and exciting entertainment. Their glitter, too, must have strongly appealed to us, for it was such a contrast to the drabness of our small, industrial town. Could any of us, though, really appreciate the music? I do not recall. Still, it was fun to whistle all those tunes afterward. Even now, I smile when the radio plays a tune that I had once heard live on a stage.

Chapter 5 writing assignment

1. List several films you have seen recently, or TV programs you have watched, or books you have read.
2. Arrange your list in the order you would rank these films, programs, or books —from best to worst.
3. Write a short paragraph (about half a page) in which you focus on two films, programs, or books from your list and explain why you think one is better than the other.
4. Check what you have written carefully, adding corrections where needed.

6. Forms of verb phrases

You may have noticed that you cannot use just any helping verbs to form verb phrases. Let's take a look at why.

We will start by looking at the action or linking words in verb phrases.

The three principal parts of verbs

Each action or linking verb (always the last word in a verb phrase) has several forms. These forms are called its "parts." The verb *see*, for example, has the forms *see*, *to see*, *saw*, *seen*, and *seeing*, to name a few.

Three of these forms are especially important. They are called the **three principal parts** of a verb:

> Present tense form (see)
> Past tense form (saw)
> Past participle (seen)

The three principal parts and the *-ing* form, called the *present participle*, are used as action words in verb phrases. The present tense and past tense forms can stand alone, but the past participle and the present participle are always used with some form of the helping verbs *to have* or *to be*.

I (see) a hawk. Yesterday I (saw) an eagle.

I have seen many birds of prey around here.

Are there two eagles now, or am I seeing double?

Three principal parts of some common verbs are listed below.

Present tense	Past tense	Past participle
add	added	added
allow	allowed	allowed
apply	applied	applied
close	closed	closed
die	died	died
plan	planned	planned
postpone	postponed	postponed
study	studied	studied
work	worked	worked
become	became	become
bring	brought	brought
buy	bought	bought
go	went	gone
grow	grew	grown
hear	heard	heard
hit	hit	hit
run	ran	run
see	saw	seen
sit	sat	sat
teach	taught	taught

Regular verbs

The verbs in the first group above are called **regular verbs.** Most verbs belong in this group. Regular verbs make the past tense and past participle by adding -*d* or -*ed* to the present tense. Sometimes this involves doubling a consonant *(plan, planned)* or changing the final *y* to *i* (*apply, applied*). If at any point you are unsure whether to double a consonant or change the final *y* to *i*, refer to your dictionary.

Irregular verbs

The second group in the list above are called **irregular verbs.** They make the past tense and the past participle in a variety of ways. (Again, the dictionary will be your best aid.) Irregular verbs, though fewer in number, are among the most common.

Exercise 1   Three principal parts

Following is a list of twenty common verbs. Referring to the list on page 49 and to your dictionary, write the **past tense** and **past participle forms** next to the present tense form.

Example   work   _worked_   _worked_

Present tense	Past tense	Past participle
1. bid	_____	_____
2. teach	_____	_____
3. arrange	_____	_____
4. mean	_____	_____
5. delay	_____	_____
6. carry	_____	_____
7. die	_____	_____
8. learn	_____	_____
9. bring	_____	_____
10. hit	_____	_____
11. drive	_____	_____
12. know	_____	_____
13. prevail	_____	_____
14. give	_____	_____
15. rise	_____	_____
16. get	_____	_____
17. refer	_____	_____
18. wear	_____	_____
19. run	_____	_____
20. grow	_____	_____

Verb voice

As you may recall from Chapter 5, one of the qualities of a verb is its direction, or **voice**, which can be **active** or **passive**. It tells whether the subject is the *doer* of the action or its *receiver*.

If the subject is the doer of the action, the verb is in the **active voice.**

Active voice

<u>Sally</u> (wrote) an excellent history final.

The <u>department</u> (has asked) for more time to complete its report.

Both *wrote* and *has asked* are active voice verbs since their subjects are the doers. In the first sentence, Sally did the writing; in the second, the department did the asking.

If the subject is the receiver of the action, the verb is in the **passive voice.**

Passive voice

The <u>article</u> (was written) by the seniors.

That <u>question</u> (has been asked) every year.

The verbs here are both in the passive voice. In the first sentence, the article did not do the writing. The writing was done to it. The doer of the action was *the seniors*.

In the same way, the question in the second sentence did not do the asking. Notice that the second sentence does not mention the doer. In passive voice sentences, the doer does not have to be mentioned. Therefore, the passive voice is often used when the doer is unimportant and the receiver of the action is to get the emphasis.

Active voice, though, allows for a brisker, more forceful style. It is usually not necessary to use the passive voice even if the doer is much less important than the result of the doer's action. For instance, in the example above, "The question *has been asked* every year" could be changed to "The question *comes up* every year."

Exercise 2   Active and passive voice

1. Mark the **verb** and **subject** of each of the following sentences. If necessary, use the helping verb list on page 40.
2. Write **active** or **passive** on the line to show whether the subject is the doer or receiver of the action.

Example   *active*   The <u>manager</u> (has been working) all day.

_____   **1.** I love Passionella.

_____ **2.** _The Wizard of Oz_ is loved by millions.

_____ **3.** Jim Fiore has played many leading roles in college productions.

_____ **4.** The athletics storeroom was thoroughly searched.

_____ **5.** I have never worked with sculpting clay before.

_____ **6.** Amelia will be rewarded by the dean.

_____ **7.** In this case, Marcel should have asked permission first.

_____ **8.** Unfortunately, the door had been glued shut.

_____ **9.** The church deacon was fined four dollars for profanity.

_____ **10.** The essay gave Dinah a good idea for her physics research project.

_____ **11.** Their answer surprised even my father.

_____ **12.** His best suit was ruined by the cleaners.

_____ **13.** After a few minutes, Mrs. Benson calmed the crying child.

_____ **14.** Ms. Lynch owes us fifty dollars.

_____ **15.** Brad Palmer, to his regret, is used to rejection.

Verb tenses

Tense tells the time of an action. In addition, many verb tenses tell whether the action has been completed or not.

There are many tenses in English, including the following:

1. simple tenses—present
     past
     future

2. perfect tenses—present perfect
                   past perfect
                   future perfect
3. simple progressive tenses—present progressive
                   past progressive
                   future progressive
4. perfect progressive tenses—present perfect progressive
                   past perfect progressive
                   future perfect progressive

Each of these tenses has an active and a passive voice form.

Simple tenses

The three simple tenses are the present, the past, and the future.

The **present tense** is used to show an action that is happening now or that happens often.

Present tense—action happening now

Myron's sister (lives) in Morrison Hall.

Present tense—action that happens often

The store manager (writes) all policy letters herself.

The **past tense** shows an action that occurred in the past.

Past tense

Myron's sister (lived) in Morrison Hall last year as well.

The **future tense** shows an action that will happen in the future.

Future tense

From now on, the manager (will write) fewer policy letters herself.

The simple tenses of the verb *to see* follow.

Simple tenses

A. Active voice
  1. **Present:** present tense form used alone

Singular	*Plural*
I see	we see
you see	you see
he sees	
she sees	they see
it sees	

2. **Past:** past tense form used alone

Singular	*Plural*
I saw	we saw
you saw	you saw
he saw	
she saw	they saw
it saw	

3. **Future:** *shall* or *will* + present tense form

Singular	*Plural*
I will see	we will see
you will see	you will see
he will see	
she will see	they will see
it will see	

B. Passive voice

1. **Present passive:** *am, is,* or *are* + past participle

Singular	*Plural*
I am seen	we are seen
you are seen	you are seen
he is seen	
she is seen	they are seen
it is seen	

2. **Past passive:** *was* or *were* + past participle

Singular	*Plural*
I was seen	we were seen
you were seen	you were seen
he was seen	
she was seen	they were seen
it was seen	

3. **Future passive:** *shall be* or *will be* + past participle

Singular	*Plural*
I will be seen	we will be seen
you will be seen	you will be seen
he will be seen	
she will be seen	they will be seen
it will be seen	

Exercise 3   Writing simple tenses

Write the **three principal parts** of the verb on the first line. Then write the **correct form** of the verb on the second line. The instructions for each sentence will tell you which verb form is needed.

Example   *work, worked, worked*   Dr. Sommers ___*works*___ at
(to work)   (present active)
                                       Westlake Hospital today.

_____   **1.** Jeremy's parents always
(to consider)

_____ both sides of
      (present active)
an issue.

_____   **2.** That question _____
(to consider)   (present passive)
on page 177.

_____   **3.** Carol _____ in the
(to stand)   (past active)
bright light of the window.

_____   **4.** The briefcase _____
(to stand)   (past passive)
in the corner.

_____   **5.** I _____ Francine the
(to give)   (future active)
test papers.

_____   **6.** Francine _____ the
(to give)   (future passive)
test papers.

_____   **7.** We never _____
(to use)   (past active)
that brand before.

_____   **8.** I _____ the theater
(to suppose)   (present active)
is closed on Mondays.

_____   **9.** Dr. Corfu _____ an
(to find)   (past active)
important Indian archaeological site

near Penwicker Lake.

_____ **10.** She _____ more
(to discover)   (future active)
money if she looks in the bottom of

her purse.

_____ **11.** The sky _____ gray
(to turn)   (past active)
late this afternoon.

_____ **12.** Another assistant instructor
(to need)

                                     _____ shortly.
                                     (future passive)

_____ **13.** We _____ her
(to enjoy)
                             (past active)
                           performance very much.

_____ **14.** The believer in nonviolence
(to have)

                                   _____ faith in the
                                   (present active)
                           future.

_____ **15.** My interest in reading
(to awaken)

                                   _____ by this class.
                                   (past passive)

Perfect tenses

The three perfect tenses are the **present perfect,** the **past perfect,** and the **future perfect.** In general, the perfect tenses show actions that are completed ("perfected") in the present, past, or future.

The present perfect

The **present perfect tense** shows actions completed in the present.

The present perfect is like the past tense. Both show actions that started in the past, but the present perfect tense brings those actions closer to the present time. With the present perfect tense, the action either

1. is still happening or
2. has just occurred.

Compare the following sentences:

Past

Takeshi ⟨attended⟩ Penwicker College for two years.

Present perfect—action still happening

Takeshi ⟨has attended⟩ Penwicker College for two years.

In the first sentence, Takeshi probably isn't attending Penwicker any more. In the second sentence, he is still a Penwicker student—he hasn't stopped attending.

He (did) his work at home.

Present perfect—action just occurred

He (has done) his work at home.

In the first sentence we're not sure when the work was done. In the second, the action has just occurred.

The past perfect

The **past perfect tense** shows actions that

1. were completed in the past or
2. occurred before another action.

Present perfect—action still happening

Takeshi (*has* attended) Penwicker College for two years.

Past perfect—action completed in the past

Takeshi (*had* attended) Penwicker College for two years.

In the first sentence, Takeshi is still a student. In the second, he is not. Since the present perfect and the past perfect have opposite meanings, they cannot be used in place of each other.

The past perfect is often used with the past or the present perfect to show an action that was completed before another one was completed.

Niles (had found) the answer two weeks before we (did.)

The future perfect

The **future perfect tense** shows an action that will be completed in the future.

Future perfect

The manager (will have written) the policy letters by Tuesday.

The perfect tenses of the verb *to see* follow.

Perfect tenses

A. Active voice
   1. **Present perfect:** *have* or *has* + past participle

Singular	*Plural*
I have seen	we have seen
you have seen	you have seen
he has seen	
she has seen	they have seen
it has seen	

2. **Past perfect:** *had* + past participle

Singular	*Plural*
I had seen	we had seen
you had seen	you had seen
he had seen	
she had seen	they had seen
it had seen	

3. **Future perfect:** *will have* + past participle

Singular	*Plural*
I will have seen	we will have seen
you will have seen	you will have seen
he will have seen	
she will have seen	they will have seen
it will have seen	

B. Passive voice

1. **Present perfect passive:** *have been* or *has been* + past participle

Singular	*Plural*
I have been seen	we have been seen
you have been seen	you have been seen
he has been seen	
she has been seen	they have been seen
it has been seen	

2. **Past perfect passive:** *had been* + past participle

Singular	*Plural*
I had been seen	we had been seen
you had been seen	you had been seen
he had been seen	
she had been seen	they had been seen
it had been seen	

3. **Future perfect passive:** *will have been* + past participle

Singular	*Plural*
I will have been seen	we will have been seen
you will have been seen	you will have been seen
he will have been seen	
she will have been seen	they will have been seen
it will have been seen	

Exercise 4 Writing perfect tenses

Write the **three principal parts** of the verb on the first line. Then write the **correct form** of the verb on the second line. The instructions for each sentence will tell you which verb form is needed.

Example

choose, chose, chosen
(to choose)

The new coach *will have chosen* (future perf. active) his assistants by now.

_____
(to see)

1. We _____ evidence (pres. perf. active) of his good work.

_____
(to change)

2. The assignment _____ (past perf. passive) before last week.

_____
(to bring)

3. Byron _____ the (fut. perf. active) package by next Wednesday.

_____
(to deliver)

4. The package _____ (fut. perf. passive) already.

_____
(to become)

5. Drinking _____ a (pres. perf. active) political issue on this campus.

_____
(to make)

6. A suitable financial arrangement

_____.
(fut. perf. passive)

_____
(to be)

7. Her solutions _____ (past perf. active) successful in the past.

_____
(to stand)

8. Hershel _____ by his (pres. perf. active) position for the last few months.

_____
(to give)

9. This proposal _____ (pres. perf. passive) careful consideration.

_____
(to begin)

10. Finals week _____. (pres. perf. active)

Exercise 5   Using the perfect tenses

Each of the following sentences contains a blank line where the verb should be written. Additional comments follow some sentences.

On the line before the sentence, tell **which tense** should be used. Then *write* **the correct form** of that tense on the line in the sentence.

Use the charts in this section to help you. Be especially careful in choosing between verb phrases that begin with *has* or *have*.

Example

_____*past*_____
past or pres. perf.

They _____*returned*_____ the
                (to return)
letter two weeks ago.

_____
pres. perf. or
    past perf. (passive)

1. The track team _____
                        (to rank)
third in the nation. They lost that

ranking two weeks ago.

_____
pres. perf. or past perf.

2. The committee _____
                        (to hold)
its meetings in the Athletics Building.

They are still meeting there.

_____
pres. perf. or
    past perf. (passive)

3. The letter _____
                        (to sign)
before the meeting began.

_____
fut. perf. or
    pres. perf. (passive)

4. Your grades _____
                        (to mail)
by the time you leave on vacation.

_____
past or pres. perf.

5. The office manager _____
                        (to call)
last night.

_____
pres. perf. or past perf.

6. The attorney _____
                        (to announce)
his resignation from the committee by

the time the report became public.

_____
past perf. or past

7. Louie _____ his
                (to abandon)
psychology project.

_____ **8.** A good biography of the composer's

pres. perf. or
fut. perf. (passive)   life _____ recently.
                                        (to write)

_____ **9.** A new supervisor _____.

pres. perf. or   (to choose)
past (passive)   (The action just occurred.)

_____ **10.** Brian _____ the

pres. perf. or past   (to open)
                                  package yesterday.

Progressive tenses

There are six progressive tenses:

> present progressive
> past progressive
> future progressive
>
> present perfect progressive
> past perfect progressive
> future perfect progressive

The **progressive tenses** show actions that are still continuing ("progressing"). Though their names may sound complicated, these tenses are familiar to you.

Simple progressive tenses

The **simple progressive tenses** are common. They show continuing actions in the present, past, or future.

The present progressive is often used in place of the present tense to show the difference between an action that always or generally happens and an action that is actually going on now.

Present progressive—action happening now

Frank (is running) to work.

Present—action generally happens

Frank (runs) to work.

The present progressive also shows action that will be occurring.

Present progressive—action that will occur

For a change, Frank (is driving) to work tomorrow.

Perfect progressive tenses

The **perfect progressive tenses** show action that was continuing up to its completion. Here is an example:

Past perfect progressive tense

Until last week, Janine's brother (had been commuting) to his job by

train.

The progressive tenses of the verb *to see* follow.

Simple progressive tenses

A. Active voice

    1. **Present progressive:** *am, is,* or *are* + present participle (*-ing* form)

Singular	*Plural*
I am seeing	we are seeing
you are seeing	you are seeing
he is seeing	
she is seeing	they are seeing
it is seeing	

    2. **Past progressive:** *was* or *were* + present participle (*-ing* form)

Singular	*Plural*
I was seeing	we were seeing
you were seeing	you were seeing
he was seeing	
she was seeing	they were seeing
it was seeing	

    3. **Future progressive:** *will be* + present participle (*-ing* form)

Singular	*Plural*
I will be seeing	we will be seeing
you will be seeing	you will be seeing
he will be seeing	
she will be seeing	they will be seeing
it will be seeing	

B. Passive voice

    1. **Present progressive passive:** *am being, is being,* or *are being* + past participle

Singular	*Plural*
I am being seen	we are being seen
you are being seen	you are being seen
he is being seen	

she is being seen   they are being seen
it is being seen

2. **Past progressive passive:** *was being* or *were being* + past
   participle

Singular	*Plural*
I was being seen	we were being seen
you were being seen	you were being seen
he was being seen	
she was being seen	they were being seen
it was being seen	

3. **Future progressive passive:** *will be being* + past participle

   The future progressive passive is a very awkward construction: *I will
   be being seen, it will be being seen,* and so on. It is rarely used.

Perfect progressive tenses

A. Active voice

1. **Present perfect progressive:** *have been* or *has been* + present
   participle (*-ing* form)

Singular	*Plural*
I have been seeing	we have been seeing
you have been seeing	you have been seeing
he has been seeing	
she has been seeing	they have been seeing
it has been seeing	

2. **Past perfect progressive:** *had been* + present participle (*-ing*
   form)

Singular	*Plural*
I had been seeing	we had been seeing
you had been seeing	you had been seeing
he had been seeing	
she had been seeing	they had been seeing
it had been seeing	

3. **Future perfect progressive:** *will have been* + present participle
   (*-ing* form)

Singular	*Plural*
I will have been seeing	we will have been seeing
you will have been seeing	you will have been seeing
he will have been seeing	
she will have been seeing	they will have been seeing
it will have been seeing	

B. Passive voice

   The passive voice forms of these tenses are seldom used and will not be
   shown fully here. In general, they follow this pattern: *have been being
   seen, had been being seen,* etc.

Exercise 6   Writing progressive tenses

Write the **three principal parts** of the verb on the first line. Then write the **correct form** of the verb on the second line. The instructions for each sentence will tell you which verb form is needed.

Example   *choose, chose, chosen*   The new coach _will be choosing_
(to choose)   (future prog. active)
his assistants over the summer

vacation.

_____ **1.** Mr. Kalesta _____ the
(to type)   (pres. prog. active)
manuscript now.

_____ **2.** The department _____
(to begin)   (past prog. active)
its summer program in June.

_____ **3.** Tickets _____ at the
(to sell)   (past prog. passive)
Student Union.

_____ **4.** Professor James _____
(to read)   (future prog. active)
these essays over the Easter vacation.

_____ **5.** The data _____ into
(to enter)   (pres. prog. passive)
the report by hand.

_____ **6.** The bonfire _____ for
(to burn)   (pres. perf. prog. active)
eighteen hours.

_____ **7.** Before this year, the glee club
(to meet)

_____ in the Stepan
(past perf. prog. active)
Center.

_____ **8.** By next May, Dr. White
(to serve)

_____ as president
(fut. perf. prog. active)
for twelve years.

Exercise 7   Using the progressive tenses

Each of the following sentences contains a blank line where the verb should be written. Additional comments follow some sentences.

On the line before the sentence, tell **which tense** should be used. Then write the **correct form** of that tense on the line in the sentence.

Use the charts in this section to help you. Be especially careful in choosing between verb phrases that begin with *has* or *have*.

Example

_____*pres. prog.*_____   They _____*are running*_____ in the
(pres. or pres. prog.)   (to run)
marathon. (They don't usually run, but

they're doing it now.)

_____ 1. My parents _____ to
(pres. or pres. prog.)   (to respond)
every sweepstakes mailing they

receive. (They usually do.)

_____ 2. Our aunt and uncle _____
(pres. perf. prog. or   (to travel)
  past perf. prog.)   in South America for three weeks.

(They still are.)

_____ 3. The colonel _____
(pres. or pres. prog.)   (to say)
that his unit has the best safety record.

_____ 4. The class _____ the
(pres. or pres. prog.)   (to see)
film next Monday.

_____ 5. They _____ for several
(past perf. or   (to date)
  past perf. prog.)   months. (They dated continuously

during that time.)

Review exercise

Circle each verb in the following paragraph and write **active** or **passive** over it. Then change each passive verb to the active voice by rewriting the sentences involved on the lines provided below the exercise.

This button is the key to the mystery. It has been found by the library staff in the front garden. Ms. Cariosta discovered a shiny object among the geraniums and immediately brought it to me. It was thought by the police that some remnants of the burglar's coat had torn away with the button. The fabric will be analyzed by a local laboratory. If the suspect works at the college library, he or she will be identified by the police.

_____

_____

_____

_____

_____

_____

Chapter 6 writing assignment

1. Write a short paragraph (about half a page) in which you discuss a project, a hobby, or a job you are engaged in. Tell how you got started in it, what you have already accomplished, and what you expect to accomplish in it in the future. Try to be specific—that is, provide enough detail so that your readers will have a clear idea of your activity. You should also try to vary your tenses when appropriate.
2. Reread your paragraph, checking your tenses carefully and correcting any errors you find.

7. Subject-verb agreement

Certain verbs and verb phrases have forms that change depending on the subject. In the present tense, we say "I, you, we, or they *see*" but "he, she, or it *sees*," and "I, you, we, or they *have*" but "he, she, or it *has*." The verb *to be* has three forms in the present tense: "I *am*," "he, she, or it *is*," and "we, you, or they *are*." In contrast to other verbs, the verb *to be* also has two forms, instead of one, in the past tense: "I, he, she, or it *was*" but "we, you, or they *were*."

Matching verb forms to subjects is called **subject-verb agreement.** Making subjects and verbs "agree" means using the right verb form with the right subject. For example, *I see* is correct, and *I sees* is not.

The rules of subject-verb agreement are not always followed in speech. But speaking with our friends is different from writing a business letter, applying for a job, or composing a college essay. In college and business writing, the rules of subject-verb agreement should be followed carefully.

Let's look at situations that require subject-verb agreement.

Present tense verbs and the present tense rule

A present tense verb shows an action that is happening in the present time or an action that happens often. All present tense verbs can be expressed in one word, as in these examples:

Action happening now

I (see) your brother in the store.

Action that happens often

Uncle Wally (tells) good stories.

Except for the verb *to be*, all present tense verbs have two forms. The first is the **basic form.**

Present tense basic form

> run
> call
> dress
> apply

The second is the **-*s* form.**

Present tense -*s* form

> runs
> calls
> dresses
> applies

Notice that some verbs add -*s*, some add -*es*, and some that end in -*y* change the *y* to *i* before adding -*es*. The rules for spelling these forms correctly can be found in Chapter 22, "Spelling."

The **present tense rule** tells when these words should be used.

Present Tense Rule

For all one-word present tense verbs and present tense verbs that begin a verb phrase,

1. use the **-*s* form** when the subject has the same meaning as *he, she,* or *it.*
2. use the **basic form** in all other cases.

The present tense rule is the basic rule of subject-verb agreement. Remember that it applies only to a one-word verb and the first word in a verb phrase. Present tense forms like *would see* are not affected, since *would* is not a present tense verb.

Here are some examples:

Singular subject	Plural subject
I run	we run
you run	you run
he RUNS	
she RUNS	they run
it RUNS	

	Singular subject	Plural subject
	I dress	we dress
	you dress	you dress
	he DRESSES	
	she DRESSES	they dress
	it DRESSES	

Notice that the *-s* form of these verbs is used only with the subjects *he*, *she*, and *it*.

Exercise 1   Present tense verbs with pronoun subjects

Using the present tense rule, write the **correct form** of the verb given at left.

Example   *to fall*   it   _falls_

1. *to work*   I   _____

2. *to reply*   you _____

3. *to ask*   he   _____

4. *to remind*   they _____

5. *to force*   she _____

6. *to smile*   we   _____

7. *to pass*   it   _____

8. *to arrange*   you _____

9. *to interview*   they _____

10. *to hunt*   it   _____

11. *to see*   she _____

12. *to enroll*   we   _____

13. *to marry*   she _____

14. *to sympathize*   I   _____

15. *to choose*   he   _____

Exercise 2   Present tense verbs with pronoun subjects

Using the present tense rule, write any **correct pronoun subject** chosen from the following list. Use each of the pronouns at least once.

Singular	**Plural**
I	we
you	you
he	they
she	
it	

Example   _____He_____ remembers.

1. _____ rings.

2. _____ find.

3. _____ protect.

4. _____ wake.

5. _____ eats.

6. _____ relies.

7. _____ play.

8. _____ drives.

9. _____ search.

10. _____ classify.

11. _____ hopes.

12. _____ fixes.

13. _____ thank.

14. _____ bleaches.

15. _____ dig.

The verbs *to be* and *to have*

Two verbs that have special uses are *to be* and *to have*. These verbs also have irregular present tense forms. In addition, *to be* has irregular past tense forms.

The present tense forms of *to be* are *am, is,* and *are.* Its past tense forms are *was* and *were.* These forms are used as follows.

Singular subject	Plural subject
I am	we are
you are	you are
he IS	
she IS	they are
it IS	

Singular subject	Plural subject
I WAS	we were
you were	you were
he WAS	
she WAS	they were
it WAS	

Notice that even though *to be* doesn't have regular present tense forms, it is like other verbs in one respect. The *-s* form is used with *he, she,* and *it.*

Notice also that, except in commands, *be* is not a verb by itself.

The verb *to have* has two present tense forms—*have* and *has.* They are used as follows:

Singular subject	Plural subject
I have	we have
you have	you have
he HAS	
she HAS	they have
it HAS	

Exercise 3

To be and *to have* with pronoun subjects

Write the **correct form** of the verb given at left. The tense you should use for each verb *to be* is stated in parentheses.

Example   *to be*   (present tense)   it   _____*is*_____

1. *to be*   (present tense)   I   _____

2. *to have*   you   _____

3. *to be*   (present tense)   he   _____

4. *to be*   (present tense)   they _____

5. *to have*   she _____

6. *to be*   (past tense)   we _____

7. *to be*   (past tense)   he _____

8. *to be*   (past tense)   I _____

9. *to have*   I _____

10. *to have*   he _____

11. *to be*   (present tense)   we _____

12. *to be*   (past tense)   it _____

13. *to be*   (present tense)   she _____

14. *to have*   they _____

15. *to be*   (past tense)   you _____

Present tense verbs in sentences

So far we have been looking at subject-verb agreement in the simplest possible situations: one pronoun subject and one verb. Now let's see how subject-verb agreement works in complete sentences.

The proper matching of subject and verb is a major step toward making a sentence clear and precise. That is important, for when we write, we want the reader to understand exactly what we mean. To achieve good communication, we need first of all to connect the subject and the verb properly; as you recall, they are the very core of a sentence.

Sentences with personal pronoun subjects

You remember from our discussion earlier in this chapter that you should check for subject-verb agreement in sentences containing

1. one-word present tense verbs.
2. verb phrases that start with present tense forms.

The following sentences all have one-word verbs and personal pronoun subjects—*I, you, he, she, it, we,* or *they.*

Exercise 4   Sentences with one-word verbs and
personal pronoun subjects

Mark the **subject** of each verb. Then, on the blank line, write the correct **present tense form** of the verb given in parentheses. Be sure to follow the present tense rule.

Example   She often __watches__ late movies on TV.
                           (to watch)

  1. We _____ in the all-Greek glee club.
         (to sing)
  2. I usually _____ to work on photography projects.
              (to prefer)
  3. He frequently _____ in the morning.
                (to run)
  4. She _____ working at the Computer Center.
         (to enjoy)
  5. We really _____ very little about the moons of
             (to know)
     Jupiter.

  6. They _____ every piece of mail they _____.
          (to answer)   (to receive)
  7. He _____ his work has improved.
         (to find)
  8. It _____ from place to place during the winter.
         (to wander)
  9. We _____ to the office manager.
         (to report)
 10. It _____ to help her become less tense during exam
         (to seem)
     week.

Exercise 5   Sentences with one-word *to be* and
to have verbs and pronoun subjects

Each of the sentences in this exercise contains a blank line where a present tense verb belongs. Mark the **subject** of each sentence. Then complete each sentence with the correct **present tense form** of the verb given in parentheses. Use the chart on page 71 to help you.

Example   She _____is_____ one of the candidates for treasurer.
                        (to be)
  1. I _____ in town for just this weekend.
         (to be)
  2. She _____ an excellent employee.
           (to be)

3. They _____ one of the finest examples of Indian
        (to have)
beadwork in the Southwest.

4. He _____ in the market for a BMW.
        (*was* or *were*)

5. It _____ time for another evaluation.
        (to be)

6. You _____ not what the coach expected.
        (to be)

7. She _____ only a few weeks to finish her report.
        (to have)

8. You _____ already a candidate for the promotion.
        (*was* or *were*)

9. They _____ never critical of my efforts.
        (to be)

10. He usually _____ enough quarters for the washing
            (to have)
machines.

Exercise 6   Correcting sentences with present tense verbs and pronoun subjects

Each of the sentences in this exercise contains a present tense verb.
Mark the **verb** and **subject** of each sentence. Then correct any incorrect present tense forms. If the sentence contains no errors, write **OK**
in the margin.

Examples

                      works
        She (work) every Saturday.

   OK   We (find) this class challenging.

1. We washes dishes every evening.

2. Most evenings she walks by the lake after supper.

3. Usually they teaches that course in the spring.

4. He do whatever will help.

5. I knows you need someone to work evenings.

6. The rest of the week she ride with her sister early in the

morning.

7. You vote the same in every election.

8. He never ring the bell.

9. It classify those documents for us.

10. I refer to the items in folder one, of course.

Exercise 7   Correcting sentences with *to be* and *to have* verbs and pronoun subjects

Each of the sentences in this exercise contains a *to be* or *to have* verb. Mark the **verb** and **subject** of each sentence. Then correct any incorrect verb forms. If the sentence contains no errors, write **OK** in the margin.

Examples
                                is
                    She (be) my best teacher.

            ok   He (has) a day off.

1. We is on her list of available applicants.

2. She have a copy in her desk.

3. He be luckier than most.

4. I is nowhere near a solution to this problem.

5. You has a color television in your room.

6. It were hard enough without Byron's help.

7. We have several examples of her art in stock.

8. I never were a student in his upper division course.

9. He has an answer for everything.

10. They was not pleased.

Sentences with noun subjects

Now let's look at sentences with nouns as subjects. The key to doing these sentences is a process called **pronoun substitution.**

If you are in doubt about which present tense form to use with a noun subject, do the following:

1. Find the subject of the verb.
2. Choose the personal pronoun that expresses the meaning of that subject.

3. Choose the verb that goes with that pronoun subject by following the present tense rule.

As you know by now, the personal pronoun subjects are

Singular	Plural
I	we
you	you
he	they
she	
it	

In the following examples, the pronoun substitute has been written above the subject.

     she
My <u>mother</u> speaks fluent German. (Present tense rule: *she speaks*)

      they
These <u>commuters</u> work at the Penwicker Building. (Present tense rule: *they work*)

        they
Both <u>Frank</u> and his <u>father</u> watch football every Sunday. (Present tense rule: *they watch*)

Exercise 8

Sentences with present tense, *to be,* and *to have* verbs and noun subjects

Each of the sentences in this exercise contains a blank line where a present tense verb belongs. Mark the **subject** of each verb and above the subject write its **pronoun substitute**. Then complete each sentence with the correct **present tense form** of the verb given in parentheses.

Be sure to follow the present tense rule.

Example

      she
<u>Marylynn</u> __wants__ one of the vases for herself.
       (to want)

1. The new government _____ every citizen to vote.
                 (to require)

2. The players _____ Sondra and Michele.
          (*was* or *were*)

3. My left eye _____ a touch of green in the pupil.
           (to have)

4. A dollar _____ less than it did.
       (to buy)

5. The cruise _____ a good vacation idea.
       (to be)

6. Careful planning _____ many mistakes.
        (to eliminate)

7. The tests _____ some surprise questions.
   (to have)
8. Life _____ easier now.
   (to be)
9. The janitors _____ the trash every other day.
   (to remove)
10. Brian _____ happy with his test results.
    (to appear)

Present tense forms in verb phrases

The rule about present tense verbs also applies to the first word in a verb phrase—the present tense forms of the helping verbs *to be, to have,* and *to do.*

> Bill and Simon **have** been receiving his mail.
>
> The university **is** building a new radio station.

The past tense forms of the verb *to be, was* and *were,* must also agree with the subject.

> Henry **was** decorated for bravery in the Vietnam War.

This rule applies only to the *first* word in a verb phrase. Verb phrases like *would see* or *could take* are not affected.

Note that *be* should not be used as the first word in a verb phrase.

Exercise 9 Correcting sentences with present tense verbs in verb phrases

Mark the **verb, subject,** and **pronoun substitute** of each sentence. Then correct any incorrect present tense forms. If the sentence contains no errors, write **OK** in the margin.

Examples

They   *have*
Tessie and Kurt (has eaten) supper early tonight.

         he or she
OK   My teacher (is scheduling) conferences.

1. The horse have escaped through the break in the fence.

2. The singer are often asked about concert tickets.

3. Balcony seats have been available for months.

4. Mario be looking for Ben Garetski.

5. The two faculty members has responded to their complaints.

6. The film is being shot in Brooklyn.

7. The shirt are made in Taiwan.

8. The chicken is cooking in the outdoor grill.

9. Jim and Annette is not attending the concert this evening.

10. The restaurants on this block has offered to support the station.

Problem sentences

Some sentences are more difficult to correct for subject-verb agreement than others. They include sentences with

> reversed word order
> widely separated subject and verb
> more than one subject or verb

Reversed word order

As you recall from Chapter 3, the usual order of the main words is changed in questions and emphatic sentences, including the "Here is/There is ..." sentences. Often all or part of the verb precedes the subject. In speech people tend to use the -s form of the verb in all reversed word order sentences, regardless of subject. This is especially true in sentences starting with *here is* and *there is*.

Sentences with reversed word order must be watched carefully for subject-verb agreement.

> Here **is** your test score.
>
> Here **are** your test scores.

The form of the verb depends on the subject. If the subject is plural, like *tools* or *blankets*, it would be incorrect to write "Here is your tools" or "There is your blankets."

Widely separated subject and verb

Many sentences have phrases or clauses placed between the subject and its verb. These phrases or clauses sometimes contain words that are confused with the real subject of the verb.

In the first sentence below, for example, the verb must agree with *cars*, not *train*, since *cars* is the real subject of the sentence. In the second, it must agree with *box*, which is the subject, and not with *pencils*.

The <u>cars</u> on that train (**are**) air-conditioned.

This <u>box</u> of pencils (**has** been sitting) here all day.

It is incorrect to say "The *cars* on that train *is* air-conditioned" or "This *box* of pencils *have* been sitting here all day."

More than one subject or verb

When two or more subjects are connected by *and*, the pronoun substitute is plural. On the other hand, if the connecting word is *or* or *nor*, the verb agrees with the subject nearest to it.

<u>Ms. Williams</u> *they* and <u>Mr. Hanson</u> (**have**) night classes. (Present tense

rule: *they have*)

he
Neither the <u>students</u> nor <u>Mr. Hanson</u> (**works**) on Tuesday night.

(Present tense rule: *he works*)

When one clause contains more than one verb, each verb must agree with its subject.

Sentences with more than one verb in one clause

She
<u>Serena</u> (**works**) at the health club and (**goes**) to school at a nearby

community college.

He
<u>Herb</u> (**runs**) in the morning, (**plays**) tennis and (**swims**) at noon, and

still (**has**) energy for a walk at evening.

It's easy to overlook the second or third verb in a sentence, but you should make sure that *all* verbs agree with their subjects.

If a sentence contains more than one clause, check the subject-verb agreement in the individual clauses.

Sentences with more than one clause

it *they*
The <u>theater</u> (**looks**) full, but <u>tickets</u> (**are**) still available.

Exercise 10 Problem sentences

Mark the **verb, subject,** and **pronoun substitute** of each sentence. Then correct any incorrect present tense forms. If the sentence contains no errors, write **OK** in the margin.

                                             it   *is*

The <u>probability</u> of getting several job offers (are) small.

                     they

OK The <u>events</u> of the last few days (have saddened) me.

1. The ladies in the laundry room is running a football pool.

2. Mr. Vanagan, one of my sister's neighbors, like to tell war stories.

3. Here is the prizes that you ordered.

4. The water in these glasses has been standing for three days.

5. The film looks good but sound terrible.

6. It seem like the whole week were wasted.

7. Are this your lab examination book?

8. Neither Mr. Brandt nor his students is coming back on the bus.

9. Either the dogs or the raccoon keep getting into the garbage cans.

10. The Calieris and their daughter is returning from vacation tomorrow.

Review exercise

Correct all errors in subject-verb agreement in the following paragraph by writing the correct verb form above any incorrect verb form. You may mark these sentences if you wish.

    The idea that there exist a basic building block of nature called the "atom" go back to the early Greeks. Atoms are the fundamental unit of all chemical elements, but they is not the most elementary particles of matter. All atoms contains protons and electrons, as well as other particles. Especially interesting be the fact that regardless of what element they comes from they all

looks alike.

Chapter 7 writing assignment

1. Write a paragraph (about half a page long) describing your worst weekend of the past year. Try to vary your sentences, subjects, and verb forms.
2. Reread your paragraph, paying special attention to your tenses and to the agreement of subject and verb. Add any necessary corrections.

8. Regular verbs

Many verbs have past tense and past participle forms that are created by adding *-d* or *-ed* to their basic present tense forms. These verbs are called **regular verbs.**

Past tense and past participle

The **past tense** is a simple one-word form that shows past time action. The **past participle** is combined with helping verbs to make verb phrases. You may want to review Chapter 6 to have information about constructing verb phrases freshly in mind.

Regular verbs form the past tense and past participle by adding the endings *-d* or *-ed* to the basic present tense form.

The three principal parts of some common regular verbs appear below.

Present tense	Past tense	Past participle
close	closed	closed
work	worked	worked
add	added	added
die	died	died
occur	occurred	occurred
play	played	played
apply	applied	applied
plan	planned	planned

Notice that some verbs that end in *y* change the *y* to *i* before adding *-ed*. Compare *play* and *apply* from the above list.

Some verbs double the final letter before adding the *-ed* ending. See *occur* and *plan* in the above list.

See Chapter 22, "Spelling," to learn more about spelling the past tense and past participle of regular verbs.

Using the Past Tense and Past Participle of Regular Verbs

For regular verbs, add *-d* or *-ed* to

1. one-word past tense verbs.
2. past participles in verb phrases.
3. past participles used in other ways (for example, as subjects, objects, or adjectives)

Let's look at these situations one at a time.

Past tense verbs

The following sentence contains a one-word past tense verb. Note the absence of helping verbs.

Correct

The author (visited) the scene of the crime.

The following sentence contains a verb with the correct past tense ending left off.

Incorrect

The messenger (return) the package last Friday.

The verb *return* is clearly wrong for this sentence. First, the meaning of the sentence is past time, since the action happened *last Friday*. Second, even if the verb were meant to be a present tense verb, *return* does not agree with the subject, *messenger*. (*Messenger* [he] *returns*.)

The correct past tense verb for this sentence is *returned*.

Correct

The messenger (returned) the package last Friday.

Exercise 1   Regular past tense verbs

Mark the **subject** of the following sentences. Then complete each sentence with the correct **past tense verb**.

Example   Sheila ___*received*___ their latest offer yesterday.
                    (to receive)

1. Yesterday he _____ first trombone in the band
                    (to play)
   concert.

2. I know he _____ to go to college last fall.
                    (to want)

3. The registrar _____ the spring catalogue already.
                    (to publish)

4. She _____ herself well for her new career.
                    (to prepare)

5. Stanley _____ every question he could think of.
                    (to ask)

6. The dean _____ making the error.
                    (to admit)

7. The big man _____, and tears filled his eyes.
                    (to frown)

8. Michael's Buick _____ away from the stop sign.
                    (to roar)

9. They _____ in the afternoon and studied at night.
                    (to play)

10. Mr. Wagner _____ his students to compete in the na-
                    (to urge)
    tional science contest.

Exercise 2   Past tense and present tense

Each of the following sentences contains a regular one-word verb. Some of the verb forms are correct, and some are not. Either the past or the present tense might be needed.

   Write **present** or **past** on the line to show which tense is required. Correct any incorrect verbs. If the verb is already correct, write **OK** over any correct verb.

Examples   ___*past*___   Then Alice ~~pick~~ *picked* a card from the deck.

          OK ___*present*___   Jim often smiles when embarrassed.

          _____   **1.** Susan play records all yesterday afternoon.

          _____   **2.** On weekends he like to drive to the farm.

_____ **3.** Renata learn too late about the deadline.

_____ **4.** Robert Fulton invented the steamboat in the 1800s.

_____ **5.** People call it "Fulton's Folly."

_____ **6.** Our friends usually offer either soup or salad before dinner.

_____ **7.** Mr. Dahlberg replace the picture tube for $150.

_____ **8.** The Founding Fathers of our country never want one branch of government to become too strong.

_____ **9.** Their son always ask for ice cream after a meal.

_____ **10.** Sandro repair the antenna broken in the storm.

Exercise 3 Past tense regular verbs

Mark the **verb** and **subject** of the following sentences. Correct any incorrect verbs. If the verb is already correct, write **OK** in the margin.

Example

Barry's <u>boss</u> ⟨move⟩ into the corner office.
moved

1. The gentlemen like the restaurant, but their wives don't.

2. The Harrises invite us to go skiing with them soon.

3. He just remembered that he promise to submit an article for the school newspaper.

4. After much discussion, the judges declare Another Horse's Color the winner.

5. The band receive an invitation to return.

6. Careless campers cause forest fires.

7. Last night the president appear on television.

8. This man seem ready to go back to work.

9. Brenda correct the error in the computer yesterday.

10. This time, the local politicians allow the company's engineers

to draft their own policy.

Past participles in verb phrases

When a verb phrase contains a *have-* or *be*-group helping verb, the action word must be either an *-ing* word (a present participle) or a past participle.

If the past participle ending (*-d* or *-ed*) is dropped, the sentence seems to contain an incorrect present tense form. Present tense verbs cannot be used with helping verbs from the *have* or *be* group.

Study the following sentences.

Wilma (**has fulfilled**) her fondest ambition.

The faculty (**is housed**) in Lambert Hall.

Both of the action words end in *-ed* or *-d* because they are regular verbs and the verb phrases contain a *have-* or *be*-group helping verb.

Exercise 4   Regular past participles in verb phrases

Place an **X** over each *have-* or *be*-group helping verb. Then complete each verb phrase with a correct **regular past participle.**
NOTE: Do not use any verb twice.

Example

         X
should be *answered*

1. could have been _____

2. could _____

3. did _____

4. should be _____

5. was _____

6. will be _____

7. might have been _____

8. had _____

9. will _____

10. is _____

11. were _____

12. has _____

13. can be _____

14. may have _____

15. does _____

Exercise 5   Regular past participles in sentences

Mark each **verb phrase** in the following sentences, and place an **X** over any *have-* or *be-*group helping verb. Then correct any incorrect verb phrase. If the verb is already correct, write **OK** in the margin.

Example

X reflected

Sean's image (was reflect) in the mirror.

1. Several pieces of wood were place on the worktable.

2. The last bell has already sound.

3. This game should be play by more than three players.

4. That question was never ask.

5. The infected organs will be remove Wednesday.

6. Three men were arrest yesterday for the Lucky's Liquor Barn holdup.

7. We could serve them fried eggs and ham for breakfast.

8. The arbitrator's ruling was appeal to the governing board.

9. Despite the blizzard, the mail was deliver all week.

10. A new benefit program was announce by the board of directors.

11. Each of the senators has benefit from the passage of the pension bill.

12. The request for noncompressive widgets will be process by the accounting clerks as soon as we receive a purchase order.

13. The mechanic's accident was probably cause by a worn gasket.

14. Your film will not be develop until Wednesday.

15. Professor Nettelbaum will probably cancel next week's class.

Past participles used as adjectives

Past participles are not used just in verb phrases. They can also function like adjectives. You remember that in talking about complements in Chapter 2 we defined adjectives as words that describe or limit nouns and pronouns. In the following examples, past participles play a similar role.

> The film, **edited** for television, was shown on Sunday.
> The **wrecked** car sat by the freeway.
> She spoke about her **renewed** hopes.

Edited, the past participle of the verb *to edit*, describes *film; wrecked*, the past participle of the verb *to wreck*, describes *car;* and *renewed*, the past participle of the verb *to renew*, describes *hopes.*

Notice that these words, even though they are not used as verbs, clearly refer to actions that have happened. The film has been *edited*, the car has been *wrecked*, and the hopes have been *renewed.*

Past participles like these are often spelled incorrectly, even by some professional writers. If you doubt that, ask yourself how many times you have seen the word *old-fashioned* spelled *old-fashion.* (The verb *to fashion* means *to make. Old-fashioned* means *fashioned,* or *made,* in the old way.)

Exercise 6   Regular past participles used as adjectives

Circle the **verb** in each sentence. Then write the correct **participle** on the line.

Example   The ___*cornered*___ senator (would say) nothing.
(to corner)

1. The soldiers gave a _____ account.
(to muddle)

2. The _____ organs will be removed Wednesday.
(to infect)

3. _____ foods don't sit well on my stomach.
(to fry)

4. The highway to the left is marked as a _____ area.
(to restrict)

5. That sounds like the opinion of a _____ person.
(to prejudice)

6. The school building program, _____ by budgetary
(to plaque)

problems, will be greatly reduced.

7. Sheila suffers from a slightly _____ spine.
(to compress)

8. My younger brother wants to enter the field of _____
(to apply)

electronics.

9. For most people, washing dishes is a _____ chore.
(to hate)

10. _____ boots are coming back into style.
(to lace)

Exercise 7   Regular past participles used as adjectives

Each of the following sentences contains a past participle used as an adjective.

Circle the **verb** in each sentence. Then correct any errors in past participles NOT used in a verb phrase. If a sentence contains no errors, write **OK** in the margin.

Unanswered
Example   ~~Unanswer~~ letters (sit) on my desk.

OK I (love) fried food.

1. Their act is performed with specially treat clothing.

2. The police looked for signs of force entry.

3. The Meyers asked about our special price on recently repaired vehicles.

4. The fluid flowed faster through previously heat pipes.

5. Please place all previously check baggage on the floor in front of you.

6. The varnish, apply in layers, produces a nice surface shine.

7. Angelica learned about his alter plans only yesterday.

8. A confuse mayor spoke to the town council last night.

9. The cleaners returned a wrinkle pair of pants.

10. The open door revealed a surprise young boy.

Used to and *supposed to*

Use and *suppose* are two regular verbs that deserve special attention. When either of them is followed by an infinitive—a verb phrase made from the word *to*, plus the simple present tense form of a verb *(to go, to study)*—they present a special spelling problem.

Hubert **used to** love reading mysteries.
Jerline was **supposed to** wake us at dawn.

Notice the *-d* on the end of *used* and *supposed* in these sentences. Every time these words are followed by *to*, they must end in *-d*. There is no other way to spell these phrases.

used to
supposed to

Even the best students sometimes misspell these phrases. Because of the *t* in *to*, no one hears the *-d*. To spell these words correctly, learn to see the *-d*.

Exercise 8   *Used to* and *supposed to*

Correct any errors in the use of **used to** or **supposed to** in the following sentences. If a sentence is already correct, write **OK** in the margin.

Example

supposed
Juan is ~~suppose~~ to call us soon.

1. I use to like writing.

2. Brenda is suppose to solve the last three problems by herself.

3. This medicine was supposed to help, but it didn't.

4. The game did not end as it was suppose to.

5. The dollar is not worth as much as it use to be.

6. Walking is suppose to be good exercise.

7. Is Simon use to the cold weather here?

8. This store used to be a bakery.

9. You are suppose to have the article ready for the next edition.

10. When was the concert suppose to start?

Review exercise

In the following paragraphs, correct all errors in verb forms by crossing out the error and writing the correction above it.

Jim Pruitt call Brad Bradford this morning to have him look at his refrigerator. Jim want Brad's opinion about whether to repair or replace it. He knew that Brad use to work on refrigerators and air conditioners all through high school. The refrigerator just stop working sometime during the night. There were an electrical storm at two in the morning, and Jim were concern that there might have been an electrical overload that damage the refrigerator.

Jim did not want to buy a new one if he did not need to, since his daughter was suppose to go to college in the fall and Jim could not afford the add expense. Brad look at the refrigerator carefully but could not find any real damage—just a switch that had become burn. He replace it easily and charge Jim nothing.

Chapter 8 writing assignment

1. Imagine that a stranger knocks on your door, tells you she is ill, and asks to use the phone. What would you do and why? List your reactions and the reasons for them.
2. Choose two or three points from your list and discuss them in a paragraph (about half a page). Be sure to explain the reasons for the reactions you are discussing. Try to vary your sentence structure and your verbs, but rely as much as possible on the active voice.
3. Go over your paragraph carefully, checking for errors and making any needed corrections.

9. Irregular verbs

This chapter will help you write correct verb phrases by showing you how to choose among the present tense, the past tense, and the past participle forms of irregular verbs—among words like *see, saw,* and *seen,* for example.

Helping verbs

First of all, though, you need to be able to find verb phrases correctly. Helping verbs from the *have* and *be* groups are particularly important in this regard, for they tell you whether the past tense or the past participle should be used. As you recall from Chapter 6, irregular verbs make the past tense and the past participle in a variety of ways, and sometimes (as with the verb *to see*) the past tense form and the past participle form differ *(saw, seen).* Helping verbs can act as a clue that the past participle, and not the past tense, is needed.

The list of helping verbs that you used in Chapter 5 is reprinted on page 94. Refer to it when you do Exercise 1.

Exercise 1 Finding verb phrases

Mark all **verbs** and **subjects** in the following sentences. Then place an **X** over all *have-* and *be*-group helping verbs.

Example The Ford is being repaired at New Castle Auto.

93

1. Next week's game is played at Shaughnessy Stadium.

2. Loud noises from the new mining operation have been frightening the children.

3. Has the money arrived yet?

4. The chair was thrown away last winter.

5. Rain has been falling for several weeks now.

6. Medical supplies have already been flown into the stricken area.

7. I have never worn that tie.

8. Colonel Stroud has been busy for several hours.

9. This will just take a minute.

10. The birthday cake could have been made this morning.

Helping Verbs

1	2	3	4	5
shall	should	do	have	am
will	would	does	has	is
can	could	did	had	are
may	might		having	was
must				were
				be
				been
				being

The three principal parts of verbs

The main verb forms are known as the three principal parts. We have already been dealing with all three:

present tense
past tense
past participle

The **past tense** form is always used by itself. It expresses past time actions.

The **past participle,** on the other hand, is always used with helping verbs from the *have* and *be* groups.

All verbs have these three principal parts. For **regular verbs,** the past tense and the past participle are identical. They are formed by adding a *-d* or *-ed* ending to the present tense.

Irregular verbs, as we have already seen, make their past tense and past participle forms in a variety of ways, and the past participle of the same verb may look different from its past tense *(saw, seen; gave, given; threw, thrown).*

To walk is an example of a regular verb. Its principal parts are

Present	**Past**	**Past participle**
walk	walked	walked

To see, to give, and *to throw* are examples of irregular verbs. Their principal parts are

Present	**Past**	**Past participle**
see	saw	seen
give	gave	given
throw	threw	thrown

Learning the three principal parts of irregular verbs is important. It does no good to know when to use the past tense if you don't know which word *is* the past tense. When in doubt, consult the dictionary. If the past participle of a verb differs from its past tense, you will find it listed right after the past tense.

Using the past tense

The past tense must be used *by itself.* It is never used with helping verbs. The following sentence contains the past tense form of the irregular verb *to go* (principal parts: *go, went, gone*).

We **went** to Texas on our vacation.

Notice that *went* is a one-word verb, and since it is the past tense form of *to go*, it is used correctly in the example.

Unlike present tense verbs, past tense verbs have only one form. The form *went* agrees with all subjects, both singular and plural. (The one exception to this rule is the verb *to be: she was, they were.*)

Exercise 2   Choosing past tense verbs

Write on the first line the **three principal parts** of the verb given in parentheses. Then write the correct verb form on the line within the sentences. Refer to your dictionary as needed.

Example   *write, wrote, written*   They _____*wrote*_____ to Mr.
(to write)

Kania for his advice.

1. _____   No snake can _____
(to bite)

through a tire.

2. _____   What _____ of
(to become)

Hank Corso?

3. _____   The horse _____
(to die)

yesterday afternoon.

4. _____   Her first album _____ in
(to sell)

the millions.

5. _____   Dr. Cerruti _____ to
(to choose)

give his final on April 27.

6. _____   Simonetta _____
(to hurt)

her hand during the second quarter

of the game.

7. _____   I know he always
(to do)

_____ his best.

8. _____   The dog _____
(to eat)

before noon.

9. _____   How much farther do we
(to have)

_____ to go?

10. _____   The old tree _____
(to fall)

during the storm.

11. _____ The train _____
(to leave)

several hours ago.

12. _____ Selma _____ me
(to write)

about her mother's success.

13. _____ I _____ under the
(to stand)

tree until the rain stopped.

14. _____ The equipment director
(to tell)

_____ us to begin

taking inventory on Tuesday.

15. _____ Our library staff
(to keep)

_____ a record of

visitors during open house.

Exercise 3 Correcting past tense verbs

Circle the **verb** in each of the following sentences. Write its **three principal parts** on the line. Then correct any incorrect past tense forms.

Example _See, saw, seen_ I ~~seen~~ James on my way to the park.
                                        saw

_____ **1.** The opening of the pier drawed a

large crowd.

_____ **2.** The customers spent most of their

money at the kissing booth.

_____ **3.** Misha lost several of his best poems

during the move.

_____ **4.** Steve took an incomplete in the

course.

The three principal parts of verbs **97**

_____ 5. Dr. Ali spoken to him about complet-

ing his final essay by June 24.

_____ 6. The weatherman gone to a meteoro-

logical convention.

_____ 7. The phone rang three times before

breakfast.

_____ 8. Phil meeted every challenge presented

to him.

_____ 9. She teached herself to enjoy oysters.

_____ 10. The manager drived to the warehouse

himself.

Using the past participle with helping verbs

In contrast to the past tense, the past participle cannot be used alone as a verb. It must be used with the helping verbs from the *have* and *be* groups. For that reason—as we noted at the beginning of this chapter—helping verbs can be a signal that the past participle, and not the past tense, is needed.

Consider these examples:

Michael could **have broken** the program's access code.

The story **was written** in 1897.

Each verb phrase above contains at least one helping verb from the *have* or the *be* group. That tells you that the next word of the verb phrase after the helping verb must be a past participle. The past tense (*broke* and *wrote*) would have been incorrect here.

Note that in the second sentence the verb *was written* agrees with the subject *story*. *Story* (it) *was written*, not *story were written*.

Exercise 4   Choosing past participles

Write the **three principal parts** of the verb in parentheses on the first line. Place an **X** over any *have*- or *be*-group helping verb. Then write the **correct verb form** on the line within the sentence. Consult your dictionary as needed.

Example

choose, chose, chosen
(to choose)

The coach will have

$\overset{X}{}$

_____ *chosen* _____ his

assistants by now.

1. _____
(to forget)

I had _____ that it

was a true story.

2. _____
(to lead)

The children were

_____ to safety by

the police sergeant.

3. _____
(to speak)

Several students have

_____ to the dean

about his proposed grading changes.

4. _____
(to begin)

She has already

_____ to send out

her scripts.

5. _____
(to wear)

A dress like this was

_____ at the ball.

6. _____
(to spend)

Several thousand dollars were

_____ redecorating

his office.

7. _____
(to cost)

The cabinets could have

_____ twice as

much.

8. _____
(to take)

Three senators have

_____ full

responsibility for the disclosure.

9. _____ Traffic has _____
   (to grind)
to a halt.

10. _____ Raymond might have
    (to give)
_____ us more

warning.

11. _____ Our house was
    (to find)
_____ by the real

estate agent.

12. _____ Their trust in the government has
    (to break)
been _____.

13. _____ The Essenes had
    (to make)
_____ their home

in this valley.

14. _____ The men who had
    (to write)
_____ the scrolls

hid them in those caves.

15. _____ We were never
    (to teach)
_____ how to

clean test tubes.

Exercise 5   Correcting past participles

Circle each verb in the following sentences. Place an **X** over any *have*-
or *be*-group helping verb. Write the **three principal parts** of the verb
on the line. Then correct any incorrect past tense forms.

Example

run, ran, run Mr. Hicks (has)[×] often (ran)[run] for county treasurer.

_____ 1. Three hundred and sixty dollars were spended on the awards banquet.

_____ 2. None of the villagers could be found.

_____ 3. The statue was broke in shipping.

_____ 4. My instructor has wrote his own textbook.

_____ 5. Martin's knee was tore in the auto accident.

_____ 6. Who has never did a research paper before?

_____ 7. My father has grew roses for the last fifteen years.

_____ 8. Alexander has hitted a single in his last seventeen games.

_____ 9. She had known his secret for a few months.

_____ 10. The skin was cutted in two places.

Past tense and past participle forms

Irregular verbs are not really that irregular. They fall into a small number of easily learned groups.

Irregular verbs can form their principal parts in any of these ways:

1. They can add an -*n* sound to the past participle.
2. They can change the sound of the main vowel of the present tense form in the past tense and past participle.

3. They can imitate regular verbs by changing the last sound of the past tense and past participle to -d or -t.
4. They can change in more than one of the above ways or they can change not at all.

In the following sections, these possibilities are organized for you in logical groups, with a simple descriptive code printed above each group. In this code, the letters X, Y, and Z stand for the main vowel sound inside the verb, and the endings -n, -d, and -t are used to show when these sounds are added to the past tense and past participle forms. Don't worry about learning this code. Instead, spend your time learning the words within the groups.

Verbs that add -n

The first three groups add an -n sound to the past participle. These words are divided into three groups because of the ways they change their main vowel sounds.

Group 1 changes only the main vowel sound in the past tense. Group 2 changes it the same way in both the past tense and the past participle. Group 3 changes the main vowel sound in two different ways: one for the past tense and one for the past participle.

Group 1	X	Y	XN
to bid	bid	bade	bidden
to eat	eat	ate	eaten
to fall	fall	fell	fallen
to give	give	gave	given
to grow	grow	grew	grown
to know	know	knew	known
to see	see	saw	seen

Group 2	X	Y	YN
to bite	bite	bit	bitten
to break	break	broke	broken
to choose	choose	chose	chosen
to speak	speak	spoke	spoken
to wear	wear	wore	worn

Group 3	X	Y	ZN
to arise	arise	arose	arisen
to do	do	did	done
to drive	drive	drove	driven
to ride	ride	rode	ridden
to rise	rise	rose	risen
to write	write	wrote	written

Exercise 6   Correcting verbs that add -n

Circle each verb in the following sentences. Place an **X** over any *have*- or *be*-group helping verb. Then correct any incorrect one-word verb or the action verb in any incorrect verb phrase.

Example

         X   bitten
This dog (has) often (bit) newsboys.

1. The ice in the bucket was froze before morning.

2. Professor Grolle should never have gave his keys away.

3. Our pilot has flown many hours in worse weather than this.

4. Three speakers were chose to represent the college.

5. The cart was drew by several large horses.

6. Herman already threw the ball to second base.

7. Many of us had already knew what was on the test.

8. The Dutch ambassador spoken to one of the waiters.

9. The letter was wrote in a hurry.

10. Have you ever rode horses bareback?

Verbs that change to -d or -t

The next two groups imitate regular verbs by changing the last sound to -*d* or -*t*. Some of these verbs keep the same main vowel, and some change the main vowel.

For all these verbs, the past participle is the same as the past tense.

Group 4	X	XD/T	XD/T
to build	build	built	built
to have	have	had	had
to make	make	made	made
to spend	spend	spent	spent

Group 5	X	YD/T	YD/T
to bring	bring	brought	brought
to buy	buy	bought	bought
to hear	hear	heard	heard
to keep	keep	kept	kept

to leave	leave	left	left
to lose	lose	lost	lost
to mean	mean	meant	meant
to say	say	said	said
to teach	teach	taught	taught
to tell	tell	told	told
to think	think	thought	thought

Exercise 7   Correcting verbs that change to -*d* or -*t*

Circle each verb in the following sentences. Place an **X** over any *have*- or *be*-group helping verb. Then correct any incorrect one-word verb or the action verb in any incorrect verb phrase.

Example

        x bought

The exercise equipment (can be ~~buyed~~) on credit.

1. Has anyone brought mayonnaise?

2. Alexander soon made plans to invade Greece.

3. Buddy never meant to talk that loud.

4. He had builded these three houses.

5. Had you heared about John's scholarship?

6. He spended his last dollar on that beer.

7. The boys in the back had told her not to bother them.

8. The sisters founded another reason to avoid going to Aunt Mattie's.

9. Will could sent the letter for you.

10. The groceries were brung into the house by the neighbor's son.

Verbs that do not add endings

The next four groups change vowel sound without adding endings or show no changes at all.

Group 6	**X**	**X**	**X**
to cost	cost	cost	cost
to cut	cut	cut	cut

to hit	hit	hit	hit
to hurt	hurt	hurt	hurt
to let	let	let	let
to shut	shut	shut	shut

Group 7	X	Y	X
to become	become	became	become
to come	come	came	come
to run	run	ran	run

Group 8	X	Y	Y
to bind	bind	bound	bound
to dig	dig	dug	dug
to feed	feed	fed	fed
to fight	fight	fought	fought
to find	find	found	found
to hang*	hang	hung	hung
to hold	hold	held	held
to lead	lead	led	led
to meet	meet	met	met
to read	read	read**	read**
to sit	sit	sat	sat
to stand	stand	stood	stood

Group 9	X	Y	YN
to begin	begin	began	begun
to drink	drink	drank	drunk
to ring	ring	rang	rung
to swim	swim	swam	swum

Very irregular verbs

Two important verbs have very irregular forms. They are the verbs *to be* and *to go*.

Group 10			
to be	am, is, are (be)	was, were	been
to go	go	went	gone

Exercise 8   Correcting verbs that do not add endings

Circle each verb in the following sentences. Place an **X** over any *have-*

---

* *To hang* has the forms *hang, hanged, hanged* when it means "put to death by hanging."
** Though there is no change in spelling from the present tense form, the sound of the past tense and past participle *read* changes to rhyme with *led*.

or *be*-group helping verb. Then correct any incorrect one-word verb or the action verb in any incorrect verb phrase.

Example

          X swum

Jorbelle (has ~~swam~~) across the river.

1. Several of the scarves were torn and cutted.

2. The package from Ohio State had came in the afternoon mail.

3. He drunk the last of the wine with dinner.

4. The most aristocratic senators won every vote.

5. Kenny smiled when his son become a cub scout.

6. Ms. Springler digged several mysterious holes in the garden recently.

7. We had came to see the cardinal.

8. They leaded him by the hand to the side of the well.

9. The chimpanzee hung upside down for over an hour.

10. Their meals had cost less than fifteen dollars.

Review exercise

Correct all verb errors in the following paragraphs by crossing out the error and writing the correction above it.

A. When we arrived at the other end of the valley, we seen that the British soldiers was already camped across river. Captain Wainwright had receive orders from General Latrobe not to surrender the valley, so he sended me and Will Jennings to scout their position. He also told us to find out how many of them there was. Night had just fell, and we left immediately. Neither Will nor I had ate any supper.

B. We gone by foot to the river's edge and had no trouble until we tried to cross. We thought that there might be several small boats by the water's edge, but the Redcoats had sank them. If we wanted to cross, it would have to be by swimming. I turned to Will and I seen a strange look in his eyes. Then I remembered. Will had growed up in the back country and never learn to swim. I looked at the water. It had rose almost to its yearly high, thanks to the melting spring snow from the mountains. I looked again at Will. He say he wanted to try, and without looking at me, he bended down to remove his boots. I prayed briefly and set to work on mine.

Chapter 9 writing assignment

1. Think about a person you admire or esteem. List the qualities you particularly value in that person.
2. Choose two of the qualities you listed and write a short paragraph (about half a page) in which you discuss them in some detail. Be sure to make it clear to the reader *why* you value these qualities. In presenting your ideas, try to vary your sentence structures and your verbs and subjects.
3. Carefully go over your paragraph, paying special attention to your tenses and to irregular verbs. Make any corrections that might be needed.

Section III

Nouns and pronouns

Nouns are words that stand for persons, places, things, and ideas. *Father, Lisa, hill, truck,* and *goodness* are examples of nouns. **Pronouns** are words that stand for nouns and can take the place of nouns in sentences. In fact, the word *pronoun* means "for noun" (*pro* means "for").

10. Nouns

Nouns are naming words. **Common nouns** name members of a group or category—*car, house, city, friend*. **Proper nouns** name specific things, places, or people—*Buick, White House, New York, Karla Jones*. Notice that proper nouns are capitalized.

Nouns can be grouped in other ways. Some nouns, called **concrete nouns**, name physical objects, like *sugar, child,* or *river*. Others, called **abstract nouns**, name qualities, ideas, and emotions, like *talent, belief,* or *love*.

Finding nouns

There are several ways to find nouns. One is to look for sentence clues. Another is to use your knowledge of sentence structure.

Words that point to nouns

The words *a, an,* and *the* often point to nouns. These words are a special group of adjectives called *articles*. (As you recall from Chapter 2, adjectives are words that describe or limit nouns and pronouns.) The articles *a, an,* and *the* are generally used with nouns. Therefore they can serve as clues when we are looking for nouns.

In many cases, the noun is not the first word after *a, an,* and *the*. In English, other adjectives that describe the noun often come before the noun. Study the following sentence.

The last Democratic presidential candidate came from Arizona.

The word *the* points to a noun. Can you find it?

The last Democratic presidential **candidate** came from Arizona.

The points to the noun *candidate*. The words *last, Democratic,* and *presidential* are adjectives, and they describe the noun *candidate*.

Some other words point to nouns just as *a, an,* and *the* do:

this	my
that	your
these	his
those	her
	its
	our
	their

Exercise 1

Words that point to nouns

Place an **X** over all words that point to **nouns**. Then draw an arrow from those words to the nouns they point to.

Example

X
the harbor police

1. an ideal solution to the problem

2. between two of my best friends

3. this meal

4. the first sensible suggestion

5. those beautiful stuffed chairs

6. a colorful maze

7. answering her classified ad

8. their new dress design

9. our English essays

10. its long, bushy tail

Cues from sentence structure

Of course, not all nouns have words like these preceding them. You'll need to use your sentence structure skills to find all the nouns in sentences.

Recall that nouns name persons, places, things, and ideas. So any word that names a person, place, thing, or idea in a sentence is a noun. The word *watches* is a noun in the following sentence.

He saw several **watches** that he liked.

Notice, however, that words that look like nouns in a sentence can be used in other ways. In the next example, the word *watches* is a verb.

Bert Ling **watches** "The Mating Game" every afternoon.

In the following sentence, the word *building*, which is often used as a noun, is used as an adjective to describe the noun *permit.*

She was granted a **building** permit last week.

Exercise 2   Finding nouns

Place an **X** over all **nouns** in the following sentences.

Example
$$\overset{X}{\text{The police}} \overset{X}{\text{inspector noticed footprints}} \text{ in the rose } \overset{X}{\text{garden.}}$$

1. The harbor police are investigating a recent theft.

2. Scotty now has full control of the project.

3. The audit has not been going very well.

4. One of the university's trustees asked for a full report.

5. The van needs a new motor.

6. Maybe those gray mushrooms had something to do with it.

7. Michael's boss sent him back to the clerk's room for another

   copy of the contract.

8. The old television in the garage could be repaired.

9. The highway took a sharp turn to the right.

10. The salesperson in the paint store said these colors will make the room come alive.

Singular and plural nouns

Most nouns do more than name a person, place, thing, or idea. They also tell how many persons, places, things, or ideas they are referring to.

Singular nouns show that only one person, place, thing, or idea is referred to. **Plural nouns** refer to more than one person, place, thing, or idea. *Girl, book,* and *thought* are examples of singular nouns. *Girls, books,* and *thoughts* are examples of plural nouns.

Most singular nouns become plural by adding endings. Sometimes these endings are not pronounced in speech. But they must still be present in writing. This chapter will show you how and when to make nouns plural.

Nouns with -*s* or -*es* plural endings

The plural form of most English nouns is created by adding -*s* or -*es* to the singular form. Other ways of making plural nouns will be discussed later.

Some examples of nouns that have -*s* or -*es* plurals appear below.

Singular	Plural
actor	actors
idea	ideas
fortune	fortunes
Pontiac	Pontiacs
sidewalk	sidewalks
Wilson	Wilsons

Nouns that end in an *s, x, z, sh,* or *ch* have -*es* added to form the plural.

	Singular	Plural
S:	boss	bosses
X:	ax	axes
Z:	Perez	Perezes
SH:	ash	ashes
CH:	church	churches

Some nouns that end in *o* also add -*es*. Many nouns that end in *y* change the *y* to *i* before adding -*es*.

	Singular	Plural
O:	potato	potatoes
but	radio	radios

Y:	ally	allies	
	library	libraries	
	story	stories	
but	alley	alleys	
	key	keys	
	Henry	Henrys	

These rules are covered in more detail in Chapter 22, "Spelling."

Exercise 3   Singular and plural nouns

Write the correct **singular** or **plural form** for each noun.

Examples

Singular	Plural
chart	*charts*
feeling	feelings

	Singular	Plural
1.	writer	_____
2.	saying	_____
3.	kiss	_____
4.	box	_____
5.	Benedict	_____
6.	applesauce	_____
7.	video	_____
8.	story	_____
9.	push	_____
10.	marble	_____
11.	alley	_____
12.	tomato	_____
13.	_____	boats
14.	_____	dresses

15. _____ essays

16. _____ cities

17. _____ rodeos

18. _____ drivers

19. _____ fairies

20. _____ Germanys

Sentence signals pointing to singular or plural nouns

These pages will show you how to use **sentence signals** to choose noun forms. Nouns are not always preceded by these signals, but when they are, you can tell whether a singular or a plural form is needed.

Adjectives that tell how many

The first group of sentence signals are adjectives that tell how many. As you recall, adjectives describe or limit nouns. The following adjectives will always tell you which noun form to use.

Singular adjectives (describe a singular noun)	Plural adjectives (describe a plural noun)
this that	these those
one	two, three (and so on)
a, an	
another each, every much	other few, several, many

Many adjectives can be used with either singular or plural nouns—*any, some, the,* and so on. But the ones above must be used as the chart shows.
Study the following examples:

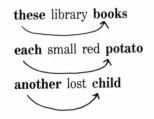

Exercise 4   Adjective signals indicating singular or plural nouns

Place an **X** over the **adjective signals** in the following phrases. Then write the correct **noun form** on the line.

Example

    X
an embarrassing <u>moment</u> (moment)

1. those telephone _____ (bill)

2. a farewell _____ (dinner)

3. Scott's other wonderful _____ (quality)

4. these small _____ (inconvenience)

5. another blue _____ (carpet)

6. an unopened _____ (envelope)

7. four unfortunate _____ (trade) in a _____ (row)

8. every small single-family _____ (home)

9. much _____ (activity) in the store

10. few _____ (student) in the class

Exercise 5   Adjective signals indicating singular or plural nouns

Place an **X** over the **adjective signals** in the following phrases. Draw an **arrow** to the noun it describes. Then correct any incorrect nouns.

Example

    X   drapes
these green ~~drape~~

1. many cousin

2. five new pen

3. a few used carburator

4. several neighborhood friend

5. a large stone library

6. several unused classroom

7. those wicker baskets

8. several printing press

9. one of a few letter

10. Barry's last twelve game

Exercise 6   Adjective signals in sentences

Place an **X** over any **adjective signals** in the following sentences. Then write the correct **noun form** on the line.

Example   She has borrowed thr^Xee _books_ that belonged to Brad. (book)

1. The newspaper made several _____ in reporting the Loyola game. (mistake)

2. Both of my two _____ are at the cleaners. (sweater)

3. Many _____ like to do business over lunch. (client)

4. Two _____ stood slightly open. (door)

5. A sudden _____ overwhelmed Franklin. (fear)

6. Those _____ were set by lightning. (fire)

7. Another local _____ will go on the air soon. (network)

8. Several _____ were fired. (shot)

9. This _____ should have been plural. (noun)

10. Much _____ had gone into this project. (work)

Phrases that tell how many

Certain phrases can also help you choose the correct noun forms. Phrases like the following must end in a plural word.

each of the **books**
one of his **answers**
two of my mother's good **sandwiches**

several of the best railroad **stocks**

a pair of **socks**

a bunch of **grapes**

Only the last word in the phrase must be plural. In the fourth phrase, for example, *railroad* looks like a noun, but the phrase talks about several *stocks*, not several *railroads*. *Railroad* just tells what kind of stock. In fact, *railroad*, which is usually a noun, functions here as an adjective, describing *stocks*. (You can probably think of many nouns that are also used as adjectives, for instance "*library* books," "*tax* laws," or "*ice* water.")

Notice the *of* in these phrases. *One of my sweaters* is not the same phrase as *one sweater*.

Exercise 7 Phrase signals

Write the correct **noun form** on the line.

Example

each of the _ _answers_ _ (answer)

1. a pair of _____ (earring)

2. each of the _____ (guy) from the neighborhood

3. two of these _____ (desk)

4. several of the _____ (teen-ager)

5. one _____ (motor)

6. one of the _____ (motor)

7. a bunch of _____ (flower)

8. each _____ (box)

9. two of Martin's _____ (friend)

10. a few of those _____ (glass)

Exercise 8 Phrase signals in sentences

Cross out any **incorrect noun** in the following sentences and replace it with the correct noun.

Example

Two of the ~~chart~~ *charts* were missing from the shelf.

1. Fifteen of those dollar came from the poker game.

2. The doctor found two possible sources of the infection.

3. Two of my friend will be waiting for us.

4. The book has several of its page missing.

5. We bought a few inexpensive picture frame.

6. Steve Sutton founded the mission on three principle.

7. Two of the recipe were better than the others.

8. We wrote both of the college on the list.

9. He replaced a window with a sheet of plywood.

10. The program had all these flaw.

Verbs that tell how many

Some verbs have forms that must match the subject. You may remember from Chapter 7 that this matching of subjects and verbs is called **subject-verb agreement.** Verbs that must follow the rules of subject-verb agreement often tell whether a noun subject is singular or plural.

The <u>waiter</u> *he or she* (wears) a bright red bow tie.

The <u>waiters</u> *they* (wear) bright red bow ties.

The <u>waiter</u> *he or she* (has worn) a bright red bow tie.

The <u>waiters</u> *they* (have worn) bright red bow ties.

Verbs that must agree with their subjects include

1. all one-word present tense verbs.
2. *was* and *were*.
3. verb phrases that begin with these words.

Exercise 9   Verb signals

Mark each **verb** in the following sentences. Then write the correct **subject** on the line. Finally, write the **pronoun substitute** above the subject.

Example

The <u>donuts</u> *they* (donut) (sizzle) in the pan.

1. The bright _____ (light) shine across the highway.

2. Chao Li's best _____ (friend) are looking for an apartment.

3. The science writers' _____ (convention) has been scheduled for June in Atlanta.

4. The new _____ (delegate) want to hold the meeting here.

5. _____ (Essay) were assigned yesterday.

6. His _____ (car) was parked in a garage around the corner.

7. The last _____ (note) echo in the theater.

8. Their _____ (story) sounds interesting.

9. The _____ (college) needs a new law library.

10. The neighborhood's newest _____ (store) have sales going on right now.

Exercise 10   Verb signals in sentences

Mark each **verb** and **subject** in the following sentences. Then correct all **subjects** that don't agree with the verb.

Example

The ~~bumper~~ bumpers (need) to be replaced.

1. The sandwich need more mustard.

2. His reputation follows him everywhere.

3. The representative from the union speak on Tuesday.

4. Mario's essay are being published in *Rising Tide,* the school's literary magazine.

5. My work schedule leave me more time for studying this semester.

6. Another victory for the football team always makes news in this town.

7. The answer are printed on the instructor's last handout.

8. His dream are ambitious and a little bit frightening.

9. The regular customer of this tavern know each other well.

10. The referee are discussing their decision now.

Nouns with unusual plurals

Some nouns have unusual plural forms. Their final consonant may change when the -es ending is added; their vowel sound may change and they may have a different plural ending than -es; or they may have the same form in both the singular and the plural.

Nouns ending in -f or -fe

Most nouns that end in an f-sound form their plural by changing the f to v and adding -es.

Singular	Plural
knife	knives
self	selves
wife	wives

Some nouns, however, retain the f in the plural, for instance, *chief, chiefs,* or *belief, beliefs.*

Nouns that change vowel sounds

Some nouns change in the way they are pronounced and spelled. A few of them also have the ending -en or -ren in the plural.

	Singular	Plural
No *n:*	die	dice
	foot	feet
	goose	geese
	mouse	mice
	tooth	teeth
	woman	women
	man	men
Add *n:*	child	children
	ox	oxen

Nouns that do not change

A few nouns have the same singular and plural form.

Singular	Plural
deer	deer
fish	fish
sheep	sheep

Forming plurals of letters and numbers

Numbers and letters can form plurals either with or without an **apostrophe**—that is, by adding either *s* or *'s*.

Many people prefer the form *without* the apostrophe since the apostrophe usually shows possession. We recommend that you use this form in your own work.

Plural

We have several IBM PCs in the office.

These students worked very hard for their B.A.s.

The song you heard comes from the 1920s.

Possessive

There is something wrong with the PC's microprocessor.

Route 41's surface is being repaired.

Exercise 11   Nouns with unusual plurals

Correct any incorrect **nouns** in the following sentences.

Example
Hilda keeps all her ~~knife~~ knives on the kitchen shelf.

1. Several goose have started using the pond at my father's farm.

2. He keeps goats and sheeps most of the year and raises a few cash crop.

3. The woman in this company are all eligible for promotion.

4. I spoke to the childs yesterday about their behavior.

5. The office was visited by several salesmans.

6. Barry bought three new fishes for his home aquarium—all guppy.

7. Janet received several 93s on her physiology exams.

8. Rita received three 87 on her recent quizzes.

9. The members of the commission decided the issue for themselfs.

10. She broke two of her tooth in the fall.

Review exercise

Correct all errors in **singular** and **plural nouns** in the following paragraphs.

Some evenings both of Jenny's parent had to work. One such evenings, when her favorite baby sitters was putting her to bed, Jenny asked her, "Why does Santa live at the North Pole?" It was just two week before Christmas. The baby sitter was afraid to tell Jenny the truth, for Jenny could then spoil this Christmases for her two little brother. Finally, the women smiled at the little girl, showing a gold teeth, and told her how Santa's several allergy forced him to move north with his many elf.

The next morning Jenny shared this stories with both her parent. They were amused and asked themself what they would have told this sharp little girl in answer to such a questions.

Chapter 10 writing assignment

1. Write one sentence that summarizes the physical appearance of your campus or town library.

2. Jot down a list of physical details that support your statement.
3. Choose an order in which to present these details. Remember that the picture you paint with your words must be a clear one.
4. On a new sheet of paper, turn these notes into a one-page descriptive paragraph, paying special attention to nouns and making sure that all of them are in the correct form.
5. Go over your description carefully and make any corrections you think are needed.

11. Pronouns

Pronouns are words that stand for nouns. Like nouns, pronouns refer to persons, places, things, and ideas. But although nouns already have specific meanings, most pronouns get their specific meanings by referring to a noun that has been mentioned or will soon be mentioned. The pronoun becomes a kind of shorthand for the noun.

The sharing of meaning between noun and pronoun is called **pronoun reference.** The noun referred to is called the pronoun's **reference word** or its **antecedent.**

In this chapter you will learn how to choose correct pronoun forms and how to make pronoun references clear and correct.

Kinds of pronouns

Pronouns can be divided into several groups.

Personal pronouns: *I (me, mine), you (yours), he (him, his), she (her, hers), it (its), we (us, ours), they (them, theirs)*

Demonstrative pronouns: *this, that, these, those*

Interrogative pronouns (used in asking questions): *who (whom, whose), which, what*

Indefinite pronouns: *each, all, everyone, everybody, some, none, any, either, neither, one* (referring to a person), *someone, other, another, several, nobody, somebody*

Relative pronouns (used in dependent clauses): *who (whom, whose), what, which, that, whoever,* and so on

Numerical pronouns (used in counting): *one, two, three,* and so on

Notice that several of these pronouns have alternate forms—all of the personal pronouns (*I, you,* and so on) and the pronoun *who.* You will learn when to use these forms shortly.

Pronouns can be used as a subject, object, or complement. (At this point, you may want to review the parts of Chapter 2 that discuss subjects, objects, and complements, and tell you how to mark them.)

Since many words that look like pronouns may actually be used to describe or limit nouns (that is, used as adjectives), you must be careful in marking sentences that contain these words. Compare the following sentences.

One used as a pronoun (to replace a noun)

Several students looked for the answer. Only <u>one</u> (found) it.

One used as an adjective (to describe a noun)

Several students looked for the answer. Only one <u>student</u> (found) it.

In the first example, the word *one,* a numerical pronoun, is the subject of the verb *found.* In the second example, the word *one* limits the subject *student.*

Exercise 1   Pronouns as subjects, objects, and complements

Mark the **verb, subject,** and **object** or **complement** (if any) of each of the following sentences.

Example   <u>Some</u> (bring) their <u>children</u> to school.

1. This was next to the swing.

2. One does not say such things.

3. She lifted herself onto the window ledge.

4. They know everyone here.

5. None of the children has brought a ball.

6. The dog buried it in the yard.

7. I wrote that article for the newspaper.

8. Paolo found these under the kitchen sink.

9. Two of his cousins have graduated already.

10. We examined each carefully.

Forms of pronouns

Many pronouns are spelled the same no matter how they are used. The pronoun *each*, for example, has only one form for both subjects and objects.

Subject   <u>Each</u> of the brothers (agreed) with Sam.

Object   Wanda (marked) **each** of her books.

But several important pronouns—the personal pronouns (*I, you,* etc.) and the pronoun *who*—have different subject and object forms. When the pronoun *she* is used as a subject, for example, the correct form is *she*. But when it is used as an object, *her* is correct.

Subject   <u>She</u> (spoke) to the dean for me.

Object   Stanley (saw) **her** at the administration center.

The **subject form** (also called the **subjective case**) is used for

1. subjects.
2. complements following linking verbs.
3. appositives following subjects and complements.

(You will study appositives in Chapter 14.)
   The **object form** (also called the **objective case**) is used for

1. objects of action verbs.
2. objects of prepositions (*prepositions* are words such as *of, with, to, from,* and *about;* they will be discussed more fully in Chapter 12) and verbals (words made from verbs, which will be discussed more fully in Chapter 14).
3. appositives following these objects.

In addition, every pronoun has a third form, called the **possessive form** or the **possessive case**, which shows possession or ownership.
   The following list shows the subject, object, and possessive forms of the personal pronouns and the pronoun *who*.

Subject form	Object form	Possessive form
I	me	my, mine
you	you	you, yours
he	him	his
she	her	her, hers
it	it	its
we	us	our, ours

Subject form	Object form	Possessive form
they	them	their, theirs
who	whom	whose

The pronoun *who* deserves special attention. In speech, the form *whom* is almost never used. Many people assume that *whom* is British or a more formal version of *who*.

But *whom* is simply the object form of *who*, just as *him* is the object form of *he*. Use *whom* wherever an object is required.

Exercise 2

Pronouns as subjects, objects, and complements

Complete the sentence with the correct **pronoun form**. Then tell whether the pronoun is used as a **subject, object,** or **complement.**
Mark the sentences, if you like, to help you find their main parts.

Example

_____*object*_____   _____*Whom*_____ are you seeking?
(Who/Whom)

_____ 1. Mary consulted Michael and _____
(I/me)
about the project.

_____ 2. Her father and _____ went fishing
(she/her)
during the holidays.

_____ 3. The dean told her sister and _____
(he/him)
about the test results.

_____ 4. The real leaders of the band are

_____.
(they/them)

_____ 5. The right answer surprised _____.
(we/us)

_____ 6. As soon as possible, Wendy, her brother, and

_____ are leaving for Tulsa.
(I/me)

_____ 7. _____ has Marilyn asked about her
(Who/Whom)
promotion?

_____ 8. _____ are visiting his family now.
(They/Them)

_____ **9.** I met her nieces and _____ at the

(she/her)

gallery yesterday afternoon.

_____ **10.** _____ is at the door?

(Who/Whom)

Exercise 3 Correcting pronoun forms

Correct any **pronoun** errors in these sentences. If a sentence contains no errors, write **OK** in the margin.

Mark the sentences, if you like, to help you find their main parts.

Example The first president of the club was ~~him~~ he.

1. Who plays tennis here?

2. The foreman knows both my brother and I.

3. Only her, Dr. Werley's daughter, had both the motive and the

   opportunity for murder.

4. It was him on the phone again.

5. Another winter storm will hit us tonight.

6. Whom can help you the most?

7. Only you and us can tell the difference.

8. Whom did you hear on the phone?

9. The least guilty person is him.

10. I have a candy bar to divide between you and I.

Pronoun reference

As we noted at the beginning of this chapter, pronouns often get their meaning from their **reference words,** or **antecedents.**

The relationship between the pronoun and its reference word, or antecedent, must have two important qualities—clarity and agreement. That is, it must be clear which word is being referred to, and the pronoun and its reference word must agree in gender and number.

Most reference words are nouns, though some are phrases or other pronouns.

Clarity of pronoun reference

There must be no doubt about which word a pronoun refers to. If several references are possible for the same pronoun or if a pronoun refers to a complicated sentence instead of a simple phrase, the reader could become confused.

The following sentences contain examples of clear and unclear pronoun references.

Clear

Judith Swanson is an excellent actress. **She** will star in the next community theater production.

(*She* = Judith Swanson)

Unclear

Judith Swanson and Maria Galvez are excellent actresses. **She** will star in the next community theater production.

(*She* = Judith Swanson? Maria Galvez?)

Clear

Walking to work makes me feel relaxed. I should do **it** more often.

(*It* = walking to work)

Unclear

The French recolonized Vietnam after World War II, when Ho Chi Minh fought on the side of the Allies against the Japanese. **That** created a complicated situation.

(*That* = French recolonizing Vietnam? Ho Chi Minh fighting for the Allies? both ideas together?)

Confusion of reference is particularly likely with the following pronouns:

demonstrative pronouns *this, that, these, those*
relative pronouns (used to introduce adjective clauses) *who, which, that*
interrogative pronoun (used in asking questions) *who*

If the meaning of a pronoun is unclear in any sentence, it is best to replace the pronoun with a noun or a phrase that makes our sentence clear. After all, we want others to grasp exactly what we are saying and not misunderstand us.

Agreement of pronouns and reference words

If a pronoun's reference word (or antecedent) has a plural meaning (like *cars*), the pronoun must also be plural; if the reference word is singular, the pronoun must be, too. This link between the pronoun and its reference word is called **agreement in number.** Similarly, if the reference word has a masculine meaning (like *man*), the pronoun must also be masculine. A feminine reference word requires the pronoun to be feminine, and a neuter reference word requires the pronoun to be neuter—that is, have no sexual characteristics. This relationship between the pronoun and its reference word is called **agreement in gender** (sexual reference).

Of course, not all pronouns have separate singular and plural forms, and most do not have separate masculine, feminine, and neuter forms. But for those that do, the correct form must always be chosen.

This rule also applies when possessive pronouns, like *his* and *their*, are used as adjectives (*his* coat, *their* friends).

Be careful when using the pronouns *he, she,* and related words to refer to a member of a group. Many people object when writers and speakers assume that all members of an occupation or group are either male or female. This sentence, for example, assumes that all dentists are male:

> Look for a dentist who does his own lab work.

The sentence can be corrected as follows:

> Look for a **dentist** who does **his or her** own lab work.
>
> OR
>
> Look for **dentists** who do **their** own lab work.

Exercise 4   Pronoun reference

Many of the items in the following exercise contain errors in pronoun reference—they lack clarity or agreement.

1. If the pronoun reference is unclear or cannot be found, rewrite the pronoun to correct this error.
2. If the pronoun and the reference word do not agree, correct the pronoun by crossing out the error and writing the correct form above it.
3. If the sentence is already correct, write **OK** on the lines.

Example

Sophie and Gloria were both invited to the audition. I hope she gets the part.

Sophie and Gloria were both invited to the audition. I hope Gloria gets the part.

1. We asked for the dean's opinion. She gave a surprising answer.

_____

_____

2. Let's spend a day at the beach. They always relax me.

_____

_____

3. Place an X over every pronoun and correct them if they are wrong.

_____

_____

4. Every car dealer in the country has his own way of providing service.

_____

_____

5. Solitary stars and solar systems make up our galaxy. There are certainly many of them.

_____

_____

6. Fred saw the ad in the newspaper. It was the thing he looked at in the morning.

_____

_____

7. Everyone should carry their own equipment.

_____

_____

8. A good secretary knows how to keep her boss organized.

_____

_____

9. Cleaning windows and ironing shirts are my least favorite jobs. I don't want to do it.

_____

_____

10. Did you enjoy attending the workshop on journalism and the new obscenity law? I'm looking forward to reading about it.

_____

_____

_____

Review exercise

Correct all errors in pronoun form or reference in the following paragraph.

Roweena has been working with small computers and computer systems for years. For her it started as a hobby. In her junior year at Joliet State College, she entered the local science fair. All of them showed interesting projects. Roweena's project about computer codes won first prize, and she received a fellowship for graduate school. This meant a lot, both to her mother and she. Their adviser, Ms. Christiansen, was proud of them all. But most of all he was proud of Roweena.

Chapter 11 writing assignment

1. We all have chores that must be done no matter how we feel about them. Make a list of some of the chores you enjoy doing and another list of those you dislike.

2. Select one chore from your two lists and write down all your reasons for liking or disliking it.
3. Arrange your reasons in an order that will let you present them effectively.
4. Write a short paragraph (about half a page) in which you describe the chore in some detail and discuss why you like or dislike it. In presenting your ideas, try to vary your sentences and pay particular attention to pronouns.
5. Go over your paragraph carefully. Make sure that all your verbs agree with their subjects and that there are no pronoun errors. Make any corrections needed.

Section IV

Adjectives, adverbs, verbals, and appositives

We have seen that subjects and verbs are the basic parts of every sentence and that many sentences also have an object or a complement. But most sentences have other words in them as well.

Some of these words describe subjects and objects. As you recall from Chapters 2 and 10, words that describe nouns and pronouns (the words that act as subjects or objects) are called **adjectives.** Other words describe verbs. Such words are called **adverbs.** You remember from Chapter 5 that adverbs can also describe adjectives and other adverbs. This section will look at adjectives and adverbs more closely.

This section will also look at **verbals,** words made from verbs. Some verbals act as adjectives and adverbs; some act as nouns.

Finally, this section will look at **appositives,** nouns that complete or explain other nouns.

12. Adjectives and adjective phrases

In addition to one-word adjectives, there are phrases and clauses that function like adjectives—that is, they describe or limit nouns and pronouns. This chapter will discuss adjective words and phrases. Clauses that act like adjectives will be considered in Chapter 16, "Subordination."

The adjective questions

We can locate adjectives by using the four **adjective questions.** Every adjective—word, phrase, or clause—answers one of them.

Adjective questions
which?
what kind?
how many (or how much)?
whose?

Mark adjectives in sentences, except those used as complements, by drawing an arrow from the adjective to the word it describes.

"Which?"

Some of the adjectives that answer the question "which?" are

a	this
an	that
the	these
	those

The following sentence contains two adjectives—*the* describes the subject and *those* describes the object.

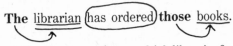

The librarian (has ordered) those books.

Adjective question *which* librarian?
  Answer *the* librarian

Adjective question *which* books?
  Answer *those* books

The tells us that a particular librarian is being discussed, not just any librarian. *A* and *an* also tell "which," but they are less specific. If we say "**A** librarian has ordered those books," we generally mean "one librarian out of many" and we don't necessarily know which one. To distinguish between *the* and *a* or *an*, it helps to remember that *the* is also called the **definite article** and *a* and *an* are called **indefinite articles.** Consider this example:

Mike (needs) **a** car.

Mike needs car is the core of this sentence (subject + verb + object). The adjective *a* answers the question "which car?" by showing that no particular car is being considered at the moment.

"What kind?"

Adjectives that answer the question "what kind?" are a large group. The following sentence contains an adjective that tells "what kind."

A new store has opened in the mall.

By finding the verb and using the subject and object questions, we discover the core of this sentence: *store has opened.*

A new store (has opened) in the mall.

But the sentence tells us more. It tells us what kind of store.

Adjective question *what kind* of store?
  Answer: a *new* store

New is an adjective describing *store.*

A **new** store (has opened) in the mall.

Many adjectives tell "what kind." They include words that reveal the color of something or its sound, feel, smell, taste, size, or condition. Words like *happy, definite, simple,* and *beautiful* are also adjectives that tell "what kind."

"How many?" or "how much?"

A third group of adjectives tells "how many" or "how much."

> The dean canceled three classes already.

The core of this sentence is *dean canceled classes* (subject + verb + object).

> The <u>dean</u> (canceled) three <u>classes</u> already.

Now we can look for adjectives.

> **Adjective question**   *how many* classes?
> **Answer**   *three* classes

Three is an adjective answering the question "how many?"

> The <u>dean</u> (canceled) **three** <u>classes</u> already.

Adjectives that tell "how much" are similar to those telling "how many."

> Asa needs more time for his project.

> **Adjective question**   *how much* time?
> **Answer**   *more* time

More is an adjective telling "how much."

> <u>Asa</u> (needs) **more** <u>time</u> for his project.

Adjectives that tell "how many" or "how much" include numbers (like *one*, *two*, and so on) and words like *some*, *many*, *much*, *more*, *all*, and *few*.

Note that many of these words can also be used as nouns and as pronouns. (Review the list of pronouns on pages 125–126.) Caution is needed here. Such words are adjectives only if they describe a noun or a pronoun nearby in the same sentence. When these words are used by themselves, they are nouns or pronouns.

> ***Three* as a noun**

> <u>Three</u> (is) my lucky number.

> ***Three* as an adjective**

> The <u>dean</u> (canceled) three <u>classes</u> already.

> ***Three* as a pronoun**

> <u>Three</u> (got canceled) already.

> The <u>dean</u> (canceled) three already.

The sentences with *three* used as a pronoun would have to follow a sentence such as "How many classes did the dean cancel?" so that you would know what *three* referred to.

"Whose?"

Adjectives that answer the question "whose?" are called **possessive adjectives.** They show possession, ownership, belonging, or relatedness. As you have already seen in Chapter 11, pronouns have possessive adjective forms. Possessive adjectives can also be formed from nouns.

Forming possessive adjectives from nouns

Adjectives that answer the question "whose?" are usually formed by adding an **apostrophe** (') or an **apostrophe** and *s* (*'s*) to the ends of nouns. The general rule is that an apostrophe and *s* are added to all singular nouns and to all plural nouns that do not end in *s* but that only an apostrophe is added to plural nouns that do end in *s*. Let's look at some examples:

Singular nouns (apostrophe and *s*)
her mother's success
the actress's part
a child's toy
the dog's owner

Plural nouns that do not end in *s* (apostrophe and *s*)
men's shoes
three sheep's tails
children's problems

Plural nouns that do end in *s* (apostrophe alone)
my two uncles' homes
these heiresses' fortunes
the birds' nests

Possessive adjectives from nouns that are names of people and animals are formed in similar fashion: apostrophe and *s* for the singular nouns and just the apostrophe for the plural nouns:

Piccolo's bark
Bess's parents
the Smiths' daughter
the three Jameses' predicament

Possessive adjectives are not made only from nouns that denote people or animals. They can be made from nouns that denote things as well. The same rules that apply to possessive adjectives made from names of people and animals also apply to possessive adjectives made from names of things.

the book's pages
the shirt's hem

eight days' wages
all of the jars' contents

Finding possessive adjectives in a sentence

To find possessive adjectives in a sentence, we ask the question "whose?"

Olaf's friends are happy about the promotion.

The core of the sentence is *friends are happy* (subject + verb + complement). Notice that the verb is a linking verb.

Olaf's friends are happy about the promotion.

Now look for possessive adjectives.

Adjective question   *whose* friends?
Answer   *Olaf's* friends

Olaf's friends are happy about the promotion.

The word *Olaf's* is an adjective made from the noun *Olaf,* and it describes the subject of the sentence, *friends.*

Forming possessive adjectives from pronouns

The indefinite pronouns *one, someone, somebody, nobody, anybody, anyone, everybody, everyone, another,* and *other* form possessives like singular nouns—with an apostrophe. The possessive adjective form of *someone,* for example, is *someone's,* and the possessive adjective form of *other* is *other's.* Except for *other,* these pronouns do not have plural forms. The possessive of *others* (the plural form of *other*) is made by adding just an apostrophe—*others'.*

Some of the other indefinite pronouns that you recall from Chapter 11—*none, several, each,* and *all*—normally are not made into possessive adjectives. We never say "each's pens" or "all's books." To indicate possession, we would have to say "the pens of each" and "the books of all."

The personal pronouns and the pronoun *who* have special possessive forms. The following chart shows the possessive adjective forms of these common pronouns.

Possessive Adjectives from Pronouns

Pronoun	Adjective
I	my

Pronoun	Adjective
you	your
he	his
she	her
it	its
we	our
they	their
who	whose

Confusing adjectives and nouns

A word of caution is in order about adjectives made from nouns. Many such adjectives are spelled just like the nouns they are made from.

> The chapter assignment begins on page 27.

The subject of the second sentence is *assignment*, not *chapter*. Even though *chapter* looks like a noun, it is an adjective here, answering the question "what kind of assignment?"

> The chapter assignment begins on page 27.

Some possessive adjectives contain names, and it may be tempting to mark these adjectives as subjects or objects. Of course, to do so would be wrong.

> John's coat was left in the cafeteria.

The subject of this sentence is *coat*, not *John's*. John was not left in the cafeteria —his coat was.

> John's coat was left in the cafeteria.

Exercise 1   One-word adjectives

The verb, subject, and object or complement, if any, have been marked for you in the following sentences. Mark each **adjective** by drawing an arrow from it to the word it describes.

Example

Adolph saw the new show with me.

1. The key chain saved my life.

2. She is a model student.

3. The old boxes were inhabited by mice.

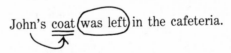

4. These librarians take their work seriously.

5. The largest <u>set</u> (was) not available. [Comp above "available"]

6. The broken <u>statues</u> (can be fixed).

7. His <u>inventory</u> (includes) several new microprocessor <u>chips</u>.

8. Our <u>minivans</u> (are) an excellent <u>bargain</u>. [Comp above "bargain"]

9. The Croton daily <u>newspaper</u> (declared) bankruptcy yesterday.

10. Several recent <u>videos</u> (have featured) famous film <u>actors</u>.

Exercise 2   Marking sentences with adjectives

Mark the **verb, subject,** and **object** or **complement** (if any) in the following sentences. Then draw an arrow from each **adjective** to the word it describes.

Example

The new <u>computer</u> (will be) available soon. [Comp above "available"; arrow from "new" to "computer"]

1. The grocery store never reduces its meat prices.

2. Mr. McRae's children bought Grandpa's car.

3. Soon the downtown theaters will close.

4. The mailbox contained these three utility bills.

5. Septima answered the door for us.

6. The dark cemetery frightened the two children.

7. Your father's order is ready.

8. Their karate instructor offered several free lessons.

9. Those bananas are not ripe yet.

10. Each new announcement increased our surprise.

Prepositional phrases as adjectives

Just as there are verb phrases—group of words that act like one-word verbs—there are also **adjective phrases,** or groups of words that act like one-word adjectives. The most common adjective phrases are prepositional phrases.

Prepositional phrases are descriptive phrases that act as adjectives or adverbs. They are usually short, and they are all constructed in the same way. Each one begins with a **preposition**—a word like *to* or *from*—and ends with a noun or pronoun, called the **object of the preposition.**

Prepositional phrases often contain adjectives that describe the object. These adjectives are optional, however.

A few sample prepositional phrases appear below.

Preposition	+	(adjectives)	+	object
to				Lisotte
for				me
in		the		car
on		his new		desk
over		the		rainbow

An object of a preposition is similar to an object of a verb. Both are found in the same way—with the **object question.** However, instead of saying the verb, say the preposition and then ask "whom?" or "what?"

In the following sentence, *radiator* is the object of the preposition *under*.

Prepositional phrase

under the old radiator

Object question	*under* what?
Answer	*radiator*

A short list of common prepositions

To help you find prepositional phrases in the following exercises, a list of common prepositions is printed below.

Some Common Prepositions

about	beneath	inside	throughout
above	beside	into	to
across	between	like	toward
after	beyond	near	under
against	by	of	underneath
along	despite	off	until
among	down	on	up
around	during	out	upon
at	except	outside	with
before	for	over	within
behind	from	through	without
below	in		

Two- and three-word prepositions

along with	in spite of
because of	next to
except for	out of

___

Exercise 3   Prepositional phrases

Tell which of the following are prepositional phrases by writing **YES** or **NO** on the line. For each prepositional phrase you find, place an **X** above the preposition and underline its object.

Example

    <u>YES</u>   in the <u>store</u>   (X above "in")

1. _____ to Joseph

2. _____ my bank account

3. _____ with Marilyn and me

4. _____ for the coming symposium

5. _____ in chains

6. _____ above the village walls

7. _____ behind her back

8. _____ describing the magazine cover

9. _____ Doug's latest record

10. _____ despite their anxiety

Pronouns in prepositional phrases

    You recall from Chapter 11 that for some pronouns the object form differs from the subject form: *me, him, her, us, them,* and *whom.* That is important to remember because pronouns used as objects of prepositions must be in object form.

    When checking for errors with pronouns, look carefully at prepositional phrases with more than one object joined by *and, or, but,* or *nor.*

Pronoun in prepositional phrase

to Michael and **me** *(object form)*

Exercise 4   Pronouns in prepositional phrases

Complete each prepositional phrase with the correct form of the **pronoun** in parentheses.

Example   to _____me_____ (I)

1. with _____ (she)

2. from _____ (it)

3. through _____ (he)

4. for _____ (who)

5. above _____ (that)

6. between mother and _____ (I)

7. behind Jack, Vincent, and _____ (she)

8. except for Brian and _____ (we)

9. to _____ (who)

10. toward Anni and _____ (they)

Exercise 5   Pronouns in prepositional phrases

Place parentheses around each **prepositional phrase** in the following sentences. Then correct any **pronoun** errors.
   Notice that you do not need to know how a phrase is used to correct errors within it.

Example   The letters for (Jack and ~~I~~ me) have arrived.

1. The foreman is a good friend of you and I.

2. Sister Alicia gave the letter to Mrs. Radola and she.

3. To who did you give copies of the contract?

4. Each of us wanted to go on the trip.

5. For who was this gift purchased?

6. The briefcase was brought to her by the manager and he.

7. Several new albums were previewed at the reception.

8. You bought your books from who?

9. The cabinet's decision was overturned by the president and him.

10. By who was the note to her sister and she written?

Prepositional phrases used as adjectives in sentences

As noted a few pages back, prepositional phrases are used as adjectives or adverbs. This chapter focuses on prepositional phrases used as adjectives; Chapter 13 will deal with prepositional phrases used as adverbs.

Here is an example of a prepositional phrase used as an adjective in a sentence:

> The horse in the third stall is mine.

In this sentence, the prepositional phrase *in the third stall* answers the adjective question "which horse?"

> **Adjective question**   *which* horse?
> **Answer**   the horse *in the third stall*

Marking prepositional phrases

Mark prepositional phrases by

1. placing **parentheses ( )** around each phrase.
2. drawing an **arrow** to the word the phrase describes.

The parentheses group the phrase so you can treat it as one word. The arrow shows that the phrase is an adjective.

This sentence, by the way, is the equivalent of a five-word sentence, if you count the prepositional phrase as a one-word adjective.

Prepositional phrases in a series

Prepositional phrases occasionally come one after another. When this occurs, look at the second phrase carefully. Sometimes it describes the object of the prepositional phrase before it, and sometimes not.

Compare the following sentences. In each one, notice which word the second prepositional phrase describes.

The gentleman (on the left)(with the money)(is making) a deposit.

The gentleman (with the money)(in his hand)(is making) a deposit.

Exercise 6   Prepositional phrases in sentences

In the sentence below, the verb, subject, and object or complement, if any, have been marked for you. Mark each **adjective prepositional phrase** with parentheses and an arrow.

Example

The sign (on the lawn)(is) new. [comp]

1. The men from his department (will arrive) soon.

2. A bracelet of gold beads (was shown) Saturday.

3. The answers to these questions (will be discussed) tomorrow.

4. Mr. O'Connor just (changed) the schedule of deliveries.

5. The lamp by the couch in the living room (needs) a new bulb.

6. One of the graduate students (will help) you.

7. The paper (has printed) most of her letters.

8. The life of the party (has left) a calling card.

9. Two of these new tennis rackets from Grossen's (are) [comp] defective.

10. One of us (should answer) the letter from Dr. Watusi.

Confusing prepositional phrases and subjects

Many words inside a prepositional phrase look like subjects and objects of verbs.

To avoid mistakes when marking these sentences, mark prepositional phrases with parentheses *before* looking for subjects and objects. Then you can be sure that the true subject and object of the verb are outside the parentheses.

For example, what is the subject of this sentence?

The color of my brother's tennis shoes is brown.

By noticing first that *of my brother's tennis shoes* is a prepositional phrase, we can find the true subject, *color*, more easily.

The <u>color</u> (of my brother's tennis shoes) (is) ^{comp} <u>brown</u>.

As you recall from Chapter 7, which discussed subject-verb agreement, finding the right subject will help you use the right verb.

The above sentence is the equivalent of a five-word sentence.

1 2   3   4 5

The <u>color</u> (of my brother's tennis shoes) (is) ^{comp} <u>brown</u>.

A special problem arises with sentences that have pronouns like *one* as subjects. Compare the following sentences.

> One of the students has brought the tickets.
>
> One student has brought the tickets.

Since *of the students* is a prepositional phrase, the subject of the first sentence is *one*.

<u>One</u> (of the students) has brought the tickets.

The subject of the second sentence is *student*, and *one* acts as an adjective describing *student*.

One <u>student</u> has brought the tickets.

Marking sentences completely

For the rest of this course, when you are asked to **mark a sentence completely,** mark what each *word or major phrase* does in the sentence. You do not need to show what words inside phrases do. Just show what the phrase itself is doing.

When marking sentences completely, it is best to work in the following order:

Sentence Marking Order

1. Group **prepositional phrases** with parentheses
2. Mark the **verb, subject,** and **object** or **complement**
3. Starting at the beginning of the sentence, draw arrows to show what each **adjective** and **adverb** word or phrase describes

---

This list will be updated from time to time as you learn about other sentence structures (like verbal phrases and dependent clauses).

Exercise 7   Prepositional phrases in sentences

Mark each sentence completely.

Example

The sign (on the lawn) is new. [comp]

1. The focus of this discussion has shifted.

2. She suggested the film at the NuArt.

3. Several of these envelopes have been opened.

4. We played the team from Argentina.

5. The manager of the store on the corner suggested several of these.

6. Ari has received two of the tickets.

7. The game of the week is being televised.

8. The men in the front office have spent millions of dollars.

9. Her friend in Alabama wrote another of her long letters.

10. We need a new committee chairman.

Review exercise

Mark each sentence completely.

The evening of the ninth day of April fell, and the rain began. Loud explosions of thunder frightened Pablo. Everything inside the house rattled slightly. A dog near the stable behind the house yelped again and again. When he heard the terror in that dog's bark, Pablo felt more afraid.

Suddenly the sound of the thunder stopped. Pablo slowly

opened the curtain of a window in the library. The faint lights of the stars twinkled overhead, and the air outside the window smelled fresh and cool. The lawn around the house was a deep, wet combination of grass and dandelions. Pablo could just see the dark shape of the eastern slope of the mountains. The sight of those mountains was a welcome relief.

Chapter 12 writing assignment

1. What kind of area would you like to live in: city, suburb, small town, or rural community? Write a sentence stating your preference, and then make a list of your reasons.
2. Decide on the best order in which to present your reasons and rearrange your list accordingly.
3. Write a short paragraph (about half a page) discussing and justifying your preference. Vary your sentences and try to include in them several different prepositional phrases.
4. Reread your paragraph and correct any errors.

13. Adverbs and adverb phrases

Adverbs are words that modify (describe or limit) verbs, adjectives, and other adverbs. To mark adverbs, draw arrows, as you did for adjectives in Chapter 12. Here are two examples using the adverbs *yesterday* and *usually*. The arrow is drawn from the adverb to the word it describes.

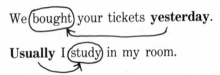

We (bought) your tickets **yesterday**.

Usually I (study) in my room.

Both adjectives and adverbs are marked with arrows because they both describe other words. You can tell the difference between them by looking at the word the arrow points to. Adjective arrows point to nouns and pronouns. Adverb arrows point to verbs, adjectives, and other adverbs.

The adverb questions

As you may recall from Chapter 5, adverbs that modify verbs can be identified by using the five **adverb questions.** To ask an adverb question, first say the verb and then ask:

> when?
> where?
> why?
> how?
> under what condition? (or yes or no?)

Before we look at these questions one at a time, you may want to review the discussion of adverbs in Chapter 5 (pages 43–45).

"When?"

The first group of adverbs tells when the action takes place. It includes such words as *today, never, now, often, seldom,* and *yesterday.* Any word or phrase that tells when an action happens is an adverb.

They will return home tomorrow.

Adverb question return *when?*
Answer *tomorrow*

They will return home **tomorrow.**

Another way to answer the question "when?" is to tell "how often" something occurs. *Twice, seldom, never,* and *frequently* are a few of the many words in this group.

I never eat breakfast.

Adverb question eat *when?*
Answer *never*

I **never** eat breakfast.

"Where?"

Words that tell where an action takes place are another group of adverbs.

The Drama Fraternity meets here.

Here and *there,* two very common adverbs, are members of this group.

Adverb question meets *where?*
Answer *here*

The Drama Fraternity meets **here.**

Another way to tell "where" is to say in what direction an action occurred.

She laid the book down.

Adverb question laid *where?*
Answer *down*

She laid the book **down.**

Adverbs that tell "where" include *far*, *near*, *somewhere*, and *nowhere*. Adverbs that tell "in what direction" include *north*, *south*, *up*, *in*, and *out*.

"Why?"

As noted in Chapter 5, most adverbs that tell why an action occurred are phrases and clauses beginning with words like *because*, *since*, *so that*, and the like. These words will be considered later. Don't forget, though, that "why?" is one of the adverb questions.

"How?"

The adverbs that make up the largest group tell how an action occurs. This group contains most of the adverbs that end in *-ly*.

> Moira answered the questions easily.
>
> The cat moved quietly through the streets.

These sentences contain adverbs that tell how the action happens.

> **Adverb question**   answered *how?*
> **Answer**   *easily*

> **Adverb question**   moved *how?*
> **Answer**   *quietly*

Moira answered the questions **easily**.

The cat moved **quietly** through the streets.

Almost any adjective that tells "what kind" can be made into an adverb with the ending *-ly*, as the following brief list shows.

Adjective ("what kind?")	Adverb ("how?")
awkward	awkwardly
beautiful	beautifully
easy	easily
generous	generously
high	highly
real	really
weak	weakly

In fact, only a few adjectives have adverb forms that are spelled differently, aside from the *-ly* ending. The most common among them is *good*.

Adjective ("what kind?")	Adverb ("how?")
good	well

The question "under what condition?" may be answered in several different ways.

The first group of adverbs that answers this question consists of phrases or clauses that begin with words like *if*.

He will sing if we plead with him.

Adverb question   will sing *under what condition?*
Answer   *if we plead with him*

The clause *if we plead with him* acts as an adverb modifying the verb *will sing*.

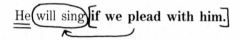

Adverb clauses will be discussed more fully in Chapter 16.

The second group of adverbs that answers this questions tells *yes* or *no*. These adverbs are located more easily if we actually ask the question "yes or no?" instead of "under what condition?"

Bobby does not want another piece of pie.

Adverb question   does want *yes or no?*
Answer   does *not* want

Note that *not*, the adverb here, occurs in the middle of a verb phrase. When we mark this adverb, an arrow should be drawn to the *action* word in the verb phrase.

Bobby (does) **not** (want) another piece of pie.

Here is another adverb that tells *yes* or *no*.

He certainly knows a lot of people.

Adverb question   knows *yes or no?*
Answer   *certainly*

Certainly modifies the verb *knows*.

He **certainly** (knows) a lot of people.

The third group of adverbs that answers this question indicates a relationship or a degree. Sometimes these adverbs are located more easily if we ask "under what condition?" and sometimes they're located more easily if we ask "yes or no?" Be sure to try both questions to make sure you've found all of the adverbs in this group.

Jamie is also a father.

Adverb question   is *under what condition?*

     Answer   *also* (indicates a relationship)

Maybe I passed the test.

Adverb question   passed *yes or no?*

     Answer   *maybe* (indicates a degree somewhere between *yes* and *no*)

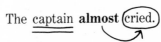

The captain almost cried.

Adverb question   cried *yes or no?*

     Answer   *almost* (indicates a degree somewhere between *yes* and *no*)

The captain **almost** cried.

    Use the following list of common adverbs to help you do the exercises that follow. Keep in mind, though, that it is not complete. A complete list would probably fill this chapter.

Some Common Adverbs

When?

yesterday	always	early
today	never	late
tomorrow	sometimes	earlier
now	often	later
once	seldom	
usually	frequently	
soon	occasionally	

Where?

here	in	north
there	out	south
anywhere	up	east
somewhere	down	west
nowhere	downstairs	near
everywhere	upstairs	far

Why?

This group contains mostly adverb phrases and clauses, like those starting with *since* and *because.*

How?

quickly	fast	commonly
slowly	well	noisily
easily	slow	narrowly
carefully	slowly	

Under what condition? (or *yes or no?*)

phrases and clauses beginning with words like *if*

not	certainly	perhaps
also	possibly	doubtlessly
too	almost	nearly
probably	maybe	mostly

Some adverbs in the "when" and "how" lists, like *early, late, earlier, later, fast,* and *slow* can also be used as adjectives.

Exercise 1   One-word adverbs

Each of the following simple sentences contains only one adverb. Mark each **adverb** and tell which adverb question it answers.

Example

<u>When</u>   Many citizens never (vote.)

_____ **1.** Herman seldom opens his junk mail.

_____ **2.** The coach threw down his bat.

_____ **3.** She easily answered all his questions.

_____ **4.** The dog raced downstairs.

_____ **5.** I never expected this promotion.

_____ **6.** Yesterday one of the English faculty retired.

_____ **7.** Professor Brandt speaks well.

_____ **8.** Cautiously, the children entered the dark house.

_____ **9.** Now Evelyn likes him.

_____ **10.** They have not filled the prescription.

Adverbs modifying adjectives and other adverbs

Adverbs can also modify (describe or limit) adjectives and other adverbs.

> A very old man walked into the store.
>
> This boy is uncommonly bright.
>
> Selma spoke too quickly.

In the first two sentences, *very* and *uncommonly* describe the adjectives *old* and *bright*. In the third, *too* describes the adverb *quickly*.

> A **very** old man walked into the store.
>
> This boy is **uncommonly** bright.
>
> Selma spoke **too** quickly.

All three answer the adverb question "how?"

Adverb question	*how* old?
Answer	*very* old

Adverb question	*how* bright?
Answer	*uncommonly* bright

Adverb question	*how* quickly?
Answer	*too* quickly

When adjectives are used as complements, the words that describe them are adverbs.

> The children were **unusually** quiet.
> comp

Here, the adjective *quiet* is a complement following the linking verb *were*, and *unusually* is an adverb describing *quiet*.

Adverbs that describe adjectives and adverbs may occasionally look like nouns or adjectives. For example, the word *hardware* is often used as a noun. But in the phrase *hardware store*, *hardware* is an adjective describing the noun *store*.

> **hardware** store

And if *store* becomes an adjective describing the noun *owner*, for example, *hardware* then becomes an adverb.

> **hardware** store owner

Exercise 2   One-word adverbs

All subjects, verbs, and objects or complements have been marked in the following sentences. Mark each **adverb** by drawing an arrow from it to the word it describes.

Example

I never (met) a totally stupid person.

1. A very tired little girl (climbed) upstairs.

2. We always (considered) the fat man's questions carefully.

3. The house (is) strangely *comp* quiet.

4. Too many delegates (disliked) the minister's proposal.

5. Her remarkably fine singing (moved) us deeply.

6. The dean's estimates (were) a hotly debated *comp* subject.

7. Canada (possesses) really large oil reserves.

8. Perhaps a few deep breaths (will calm) you.

9. They (are) also *comp* hungry.

10. The newly named chairperson (spoke) yesterday.

Prepositional phrases as adverbs

In Chapter 12, we discussed prepositional phrases and saw how they function as adjectives. Prepositional phrases can also function as adverbs.

Adverb prepositional phrases are marked like adjective prepositional phrases —with parentheses (to show that they act as one word) and an arrow pointing to the words or phrases they describe.

Prepositional phrases

Parliament (passed) the Mining Act (**for the wrong reasons**. (answers

the question "why?")

We (stood) (**in the rain**) (**during the inspection**. (*In the rain* answers

the question "where?" *During the inspection* answers the question

"when?")

Notice that when a long prepositional phrase (or group of phrases) begins a sentence, it is set off by a comma.

At the end of the boring biology lecture, we ran for the door.

Exercise 3   Adverb prepositional phrases

Mark each sentence completely.

Example

1. The mail is usually delivered at my house in the morning.

2. These papers fell from your desk.

3. Without any warning, our new teacher canceled all her classes for the rest of the week.

4. Henriette shared her news in a confidential whisper.

5. For his bravery, Melbar received a medal at the banquet.

6. Harold admitted the theft with a sly grin.

7. At the children's party, Ms. Pelotti gave our daughter a very costly present.

8. With great determination, Leon walked toward the door.

9. The darkness keeps the secret well in this tunnel.

10. Did you go to the bookstore by the new route?

"Hidden" prepositions in adverb phrases

Some prepositional phrases that tell "when" are often written without a preposition. This is simply an abbreviation. We read these sentences as though the missing preposition were present—just as, you may recall from Chapter 3, the subject *you* in commands is "hidden," that is, omitted but understood (for example "Turn off the TV!").

Phrases can be shortened in this way because the missing word is obvious and easily understood. The following sentences contain "hidden" prepositions.

(On) **Christmas Eve** our neighbors celebrated their fiftieth wedding anniversary.

(During) **Last weekend** Anya worked on her taxes.

If you have trouble recognizing these phrases as adverbs, look for groups of words that tell "when."

Adverb phrases with missing prepositions are marked like other adverb prepositional phrases—with parentheses (to show that they act as one word) and an arrow pointing to the word or phrase they describe.

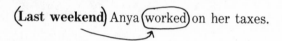

(**Last weekend**) Anya (worked) on her taxes.

Indirect objects

Another kind of adverb phrase with a missing preposition is called the **indirect object.** Indirect objects look like objects of the verb, but they are really objects of a missing preposition like *to, for,* and *of.*

Indirect object

Mrs. Morescu gave (to) him a big kiss.

To find indirect objects, say the verb and ask "to (or *for* or *of*) whom or what?" Indirect objects are marked with parentheses and an arrow, like other adverb phrases. In addition, the missing prepositions are written above them. (This will help you notice them more easily.)

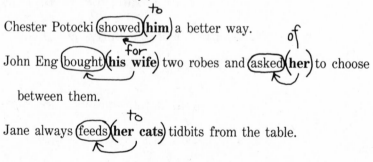

Chester Potocki (showed)(him) a better way.

John Eng (bought)(his wife) two robes and (asked)(her) to choose

between them.

Jane always (feeds)(her cats) tidbits from the table.

Exercise 4 Missing prepositions in adverb phrases

Mark all **indirect objects** and **other adverb phrases with missing prepositions** in the following sentences. Write in the missing preposition. (This exercise will be easier to do if you circle all verbs first.)

Example

They (gave)(him) their complete attention (that day).

1. He asked us several unusual questions.

2. The old colonel brings the birds sunflower seeds day and
   night.

3. This month Maureen is giving her vacation in Ireland a lot of thought.

4. Our math instructor awarded each of his students high grades.

5. The youngsters sent their mother some roses.

6. Last summer we wrote the district manager a strong letter of protest.

7. Tuesday an award will be given the production company for finishing on time.

8. The owner offered them a fair settlement.

9. Fritz works weekends as well as weekdays.

10. She found him exactly the jacket he wanted.

Review exercise

Mark each sentence completely. Add any missing prepositions in adverb phrases.

Yesterday I stayed inside the house and gave it a good cleaning. This morning all of the rooms sparkled, but I felt very irritable. I needed a change from my daily routine. I walked out of my front door and immediately felt better. I was in a really energetic mood, so I roamed around my neighborhood for hours. The noise of the traffic and the crush of the crowds seemed oddly exhilarating today.

I went down an unfamiliar street and stumbled into Kaminsky's Produce Shop. Mrs. Kaminsky sold me a huge bunch of carrots with feathery green tops and three pounds of seedless grapes. I got equally good bargains at the hardware store and the bakery on the same street. I walked back to the house with bags under each

arm. My legs were tired, but I was humming a little tune. Maybe I

will explore new territory tomorrow morning.

Chapter 13 writing assignment

1. Suppose that you must give someone directions on how to get from your home or school to a store, a library, a scenic spot, a theater, or a relative's or friend's home. Jot down these directions, making them as clear and specific as possible.
2. Expand your list into a short paragraph (about half a page) in which you first state your main idea and then present the details of the route. Be sure to describe the significant landmarks that the person following your directions should watch for.
3. Reread what you have written, and correct any errors.

14. Verbals and appositives

Verbals are words that are made from verbs but do not act as verbs. They may occur alone or as part of a phrase. **Appositives** are nouns or pronouns that help explain other nouns or pronouns but never act as subjects or objects in themselves. They also may occur alone or as part of a phrase.

Verbals

Verbals are not complete verbs, and so a verbal can never be the verb at the core of a sentence. Verbals most often act like nouns, adjectives, and adverbs in a sentence. There are three kinds of verbals:

1. **-ing words,** like *raining* and *seeing* (also called **present participles** or **gerunds,** depending on how they're used in a sentence)
2. **infinitives,** like *to rain* and *to see*
3. **past participles,** like *rained* and *seen*

The **-ing** form is made by adding *-ing* to the present tense form, sometimes doubling the final letter.

The **infinitive** is made by adding the word *to* to the present tense form.

The **past participle** is made in a variety of ways. The most common is to add *-ed* or *-d* to the present tense form.

Verbs that add *-ed* or *-d* to make the past tense form and the past participle are called **regular verbs.** Other verbs, called **irregular verbs,** make the past participle by changing the main vowel sound of the verb and/or by adding *-d, -t,* or *-n.* You may find it helpful to review Chapter 9, "Using Irregular Verbs."

Exercise 1   Verbals

Write the **verbal** forms of the following verbs. If need be, look up the verb in a dictionary.

Example

	-ing word	Infinitive	Past participle
write	writing	to write	written

	-ing word	Infinitive	Past participle
1. sing	_____	_____	_____
2. arrange	_____	_____	_____
3. see	_____	_____	_____
4. run	_____	_____	_____
5. plan	_____	_____	_____
6. try	_____	_____	_____
7. pass	_____	_____	_____
8. buy	_____	_____	_____
9. teach	_____	_____	_____
10. find	_____	_____	_____
11. edit	_____	_____	_____
12. calculate	_____	_____	_____
13. dance	_____	_____	_____
14. organize	_____	_____	_____
15. become	_____	_____	_____

Verbal phrases

Phrases built around verbals are called **verbal phrases.** Here are examples of verbal phrases made from the three kinds of verbals we have been looking at.

Verbal phrases

playing the trombone well

to find the answer quickly

seen at the birthday party

Notice that the words in a verbal phrase may

1. describe the verbal.
2. act as the object or complement of the verbal.
3. describe the object or complement.

In the first phrase above, *well* describes *playing,* and *trombone* is the object of *playing.*

Object question   *playing* what?
Answer   *trombone*

The, as you know, is an adjective describing *trombone.*
   The other two phrases, *to find the answer quickly* and *seen at the birthday party,* can be analyzed in the same way. (Notice that the prepositional phrase *at the birthday party* acts like one word describing the verbal *seen.*)
   In other words, the verbal is the key word in a verbal phrase. It doesn't describe other words in the phrase—other words describe it. For comparison, the following phrase is NOT a verbal phrase, even though it contains a verbal.

NOT a verbal phrase

the dancing teacher

The verbal *dancing* is not the key word in this phrase. The key word is *teacher.* The verbal *dancing* merely serves as an adjective describing *teacher.* We know that *teacher* could not be an object of the verbal because it doesn't answer the object question.

Object question   *dancing* what?
Answer   (There is no answer.)

Exercise 2   Verbal phrases

Tell which of the following are **verbal phrases** and which are not by writing **YES** or **NO** on the line. In addition, place an **X** over any object of a verbal.

Example

_____YES_____ to play cards in the evening

_____ 1. answering letters

_____ 2. the basketball court

_____ 3. skiing with the instructor

_____ 4. to play tennis this afternoon

_____ **5.** seen after church

_____ **6.** another jogging book

_____ **7.** finished yesterday

_____ **8.** smiling proudly

_____ **9.** to the bank

_____ **10.** gone with the wind

Verbals and verbal phrases in sentences

Both verbals and verbal phrases can be used as nouns, adjectives, and adverbs in sentences.

Verbals and verbal phrases as nouns

To forgive requires generosity. (subject of verb _requires_)

My sister loves **to entertain.** (object of verb _loves_)

You must stop **nagging.** (object of verb _stop_)

Dancing after midnight at the Zig-Zag Club made him tired. (subject of verb _made_)

They should start **studying for a test.** (object of verb _start_)

Verbals and verbal phrases as adjectives

Our **typing** teacher lives in Oakwood. (describes _teacher_)

Janine, **dancing in the chorus,** was noticed by Mr. Birnbock, a New York producer. (describes _Janine_)

Verbals and verbal phrases as adverbs

Romero spends his mornings **writing.** (modifies _spends_)

Mrs. Rittenbaum came home **to rest.** (modifies _came_)

Brian wasted an hour **talking on the telephone.** (modifies _wasted_)

Anna-Maria drove ten miles **to see a movie.** (modifies _drove_)

To reach my house, take the next left. (modifies _take_)

Remember that verbals are words _formed from_ verbs; they are never the core verb of a sentence. _Dancing_ is not a verbal in the following sentence; it is part of the verb _is dancing._

Janine (is dancing) in the chorus. (This sentence contains no verbal phrases.)

Marking verbals and verbal phrases

Mark all one-word verbals according to the way they're used—as subjects, objects, complements, adjectives, or adverbs. Mark verbal phrases by placing each phrase in **square brackets [ ]**. Then mark it as a subject, object, complement, adjective, or adverb in the usual way. Here are some examples:

Verbals and verbal phrases as subjects, objects, and complements

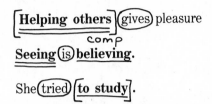

She (tried) [to study].

Verbals and verbal phrases as adjectives and adverbs

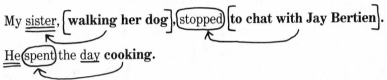

He (spent) the day **cooking**.

We can now revise our sentence marking order as follows.

Sentence Marking Order
(Revised)

1. Group **verbal phrases** in square brackets.
2. Group remaining **prepositional phrases** in parentheses.
3. Mark the **verb, subject,** and **object** or **complement**.
4. Starting at the beginning of the sentence, draw arrows to show what each remaining **adjective** and **adverb** word or phrase describes.

Remember that you don't have to mark a phrase within another phrase. Just treat the largest phrase as one word, no matter what other phrases it contains. The phrase *to chat with Jay Bertien* in the last set of examples is such a phrase. Let's look at a longer example.

General Abrams (spends) his evenings [playing ball with all the

children from the neighborhood].

In this sentence, the long verbal phrase describes the verb (by telling *how* the general spends his time).

The following exercise contains simple verbal phrases used as nouns and adjectives in sentences.

Exercise 3   Verbal phrases in sentences

Mark each of the following sentences completely. Do not mark phrases within other phrases.

Example

Answering questions is an occupational hazard (for politicians.)

1. She refused to give up her place in line.

2. Meta has no desire to get married.

3. He found a dollar stuck to the floor of the cafeteria.

4. Jim discovered the dog rummaging through the garbage can.

5. Opening the presents was my favorite part of Christmas.

6. The outside of the house really needs to be painted.

7. A coil in the heating unit was replaced yesterday.

8. Ben prefers to eat rare meat.

9. The need to work overwhelmed Barry.

10. Written at the last minute, the story had to be revised.

Punctuating verbal phrases in sentences

Sometimes verbal phrases are separated from the rest of the sentence with commas, and sometimes they are not. When to punctuate verbal phrases with commas depends on two things:

1. their position
2. the kind of information they contain

Introductory verbal phrases

If a verbal phrase that acts as an adjective or adverb introduces (begins) a sentence, it is usually set off by a comma, as in these examples:

> **Seeing her brother,** Mrs. Mendoza broke out in tears.
>
> **To pay for his car,** John worked overtime.

Seeing her brother is an introductory verbal phrase that acts like an adjective. It describes *Mrs. Mendoza*. *To pay for his car* is an introductory verbal phrase that acts like an adverb. It modifies the verb *worked*, telling *why* John worked overtime.

Note, however, that such introductory verbal phrases are set off by commas only if they act as adjectives or adverbs. If they function as the *subject* of a sentence, no comma is used. Consider these examples:

Becoming a doctor is her aim.

To daydream about a job may not lead to one.

Becoming a doctor and *To daydream about a job* are the subjects of their sentences. Therefore no commas are used.

Exercise 4   Punctuating introductory verbal phrases

The verbal phrases in the following sentences are printed in boldface type. Draw an **arrow** from each verbal phrase that acts as an adjective or adverb to the word it describes. If it is an introductory phrase, add a **comma** whenever necessary (remember that introductory verbal phrases acting as subjects do not need commas). If a sentence requires no additional punctuation, write **OK** in the margin.

Example

To rescue the children, we cut several holes in the roof.

1. She imagined Rosemary **arriving at the station.**

2. **To see her brother this summer** Stacia will have to go to the farm.

3. **Hoping to be considered for a promotion** Martinez has registered for night courses at City College.

4. A man **answering that description** works at the restaurant.

5. **Stuck in the elevator** the professor used the time to grade papers.

6. **Looking at his hand** the boy noticed a small paper cut.

7. **Finding all that money** was just luck.

8. **Getting help from the French artillery** General Washington launched his assault in Yorktown.

9. We watched Lena's balloon **rising through the clouds.**

10. **To buy the farm** my family borrowed from three banks.

"Necessary" and "extra" adjective verbal phrases

Adjective verbal phrases that do not begin a sentence are punctuated according to the information they contain. Some adjective verbal phrases contain information that is needed to provide identification or narrow down the meaning of the nouns they describe.

Verbal phrases that are "necessary" in this sense require no additional punctuation. Any verbal phrase that is not "necessary" is considered "extra" because the information it provides is not *essential* to the meaning of the sentence, even though it may be important information. These extra phrases are set off by commas.

To help you understand the difference between necessary and extra adjective verbal phrases, look at the following sentence.

Necessary verbal phrase

People **wearing jeans** are not allowed in this restaurant.

You can see that *wearing jeans* is a very necessary part of the sentence. The restaurant does not turn away all people, only people *wearing jeans*. Since this phrase is necessary, it is not separated from the rest of the sentence by commas. Let's look at another sentence.

Necessary verbal phrase

Parties **organized by Ferdie** are always successful.

The phrase *organized by Ferdie* narrows down the meaning of *parties*. Not all parties are successful, only those *organized by Ferdie*. Again, no commas are necessary.

On the other hand, extra verbal phrases can usually be removed from a sentence without changing the sentence's meaning.

Extra verbal phrase

His mother, **sitting in that chair,** wants a little attention.

The phrase *sitting in that chair* just provides some extra information about *his mother*. Therefore, this verbal phrase is set off from the rest of the sentence by commas. (Notice that *two* commas are needed to set off the extra verbal phrase when it is in the middle of a sentence. One comma, whether placed at the beginning or the end of the phrase, would not be enough.)

Let's look at another extra adjective verbal phrase.

Extra verbal phrase

Larry, **dressed in his best clothes,** went to the bank.

Once again, commas separate this nonessential piece of information from the rest of the sentence, which carries the core idea—*Larry went to the bank.*

You will need to distinguish between necessary and extra verbal phrases in your own writing. Compare the following sentences.

The nurse walking by the door heard what I said.

The nurse, walking by the door, heard what I said.

You would write the first sentence if your readers did not know which nurse you were talking about; you're making it clear that you're talking about the particular nurse who was walking by the door. You would write the second sentence if you had already explained exactly which nurse you're describing; you're simply telling your readers what she was doing when she heard you. You can see how important punctuation is to the meaning of what you write.

Exercise 5   Punctuating verbal phrases

All verbal phrases in the following sentences are printed in boldface type. Add **commas** where necessary. If a sentence needs no additional punctuation, write **OK** in the margin.

Remember that only verbal phrases containing extra, or nonessential, information should be separated with commas from the rest of the sentence.

Example

Our baseball team, worn out by yesterday's game, observed a ten

o'clock curfew.

1. **Hoping to meet women** Kurtis stayed in the library every

evening.

2. I have two pairs of jeans. The pair **thrown into the corner**

needs to be washed.

3. **Discovering new skills** has changed Marissa's life.

4. The soloist **playing in tonight's concert** has never performed

the Brahms sonata before.

5. Zeta Melbourne **giving a one-woman show next week** regu-

larly performs in this auditorium.

6. Arnie VanDerKellen **watching the fireworks** was as delighted

as his children with the display.

7. Melba served lunch to some ladies **canning tomatoes in the basement.**

8. The prince spoke the words **written for him by the archbishop.**

9. The old family dog **resting by the fire** looks as tired as Grandpa **sleeping in a chair beside him.**

10. Several of the governors **invited to the reception** have publicly refused to attend.

Combining sentences to create verbal phrases

All rough drafts contain unnecessary words. One of the major goals of revising and editing is to refine sentences and paragraphs so that they are concise ("concise" means "to the point" or "not wordy,") and so that your sentence structures show some variety. You want to be clear *and* interesting in the way you express yourself.

Combining two sentences or clauses so that one becomes a verbal phrase within the other helps bring variety to sentences and might make them more concise as well.

Uncombined

Mr. Bramble was looking for his grade book. He discovered his lost answer sheets instead.

OR

Mr. Bramble was looking for his grade book when he discovered his lost answer sheets instead.

Combined

Mr. Bramble, **looking for his grade book,** discovered his lost answer sheets instead.

OR

Looking for his grade book, Mr. Bramble discovered his lost answer sheets instead.

There is nothing wrong with the uncombined examples, and sometimes they may be the best choice. But the combined versions give you another option—an option that could be very useful if you have too many short sentences or if you need to tighten some longer sentences.

Making a clause or a sentence into an adjective verbal phrase carries some risk, however. It is possible to attach the phrase to the wrong word and to end up with a dangling phrase. A **dangling phrase** is a phrase incorrectly positioned next to a word it does not modify. Here's an example of this error:

Wearing a red shirt, the bull attacked the man.

The verbal phrase is an adjective that clearly describes *man*, not *bull*.

The bull attacked the man **wearing a red shirt.**

Many dangling phrases are less obvious than this. Find them by finding the words they actually describe.

Holding hands, their hearts filled with joy.

If this sentence were correct, the phrase *holding hands* would have to be an adjective describing *hearts*. Obviously hearts cannot hold hands. One way to correct this example would be to revise the sentence as follows:

Holding hands, the couple felt their hearts fill with joy.

Let's look at one more example:

Going out of business, the store's furnishings went on sale.

This sentence, too, tells us a piece of nonsense—that the furnishings went out of business. It could be revised this way:

Going out of business, the store put its furnishings on sale.

As you add variety to your sentence structure by using verbal phrases, make sure that all adjective verbal phrases describe the right words and do not dangle.

Do exercises like the following in the spirit of discovery. You are practicing writing options that will help you produce your own best work.

Exercise 6   Combining to create verbal phrases

Combine each of the following to create at least one verbal phrase. Be sure that the verbal phrase is punctuated correctly and that it does not dangle.

Example   The student is raising his hand. He has discovered the solution to

problem seventeen.

The student, raising his hand, has discovered the solution to problem seventeen.

1. Someone finally repaired the old rocker. It was broken by the children.

_____

_____

2. The program was ranked highly in the ratings. It was canceled anyway.

_____

_____

3. The deficit has not been reduced in twelve years. It was supposed to be temporary.

_____

_____

4. Mrs. Serota funded the project herself. She was responding to pleas of the conservationists in her district.

_____

_____

5. The paintings are a recent acquisition. They have been displayed at the Abrahms Gallery.

_____

_____

6. Samuel Beckett was born in Ireland. He spent many years in Paris.

_____

_____

7. An attendant saw the robbery. The attendant was working alone at the Gasexx station.

_____

_____

8. The report was recently filed with the district alcohol commission and was discussed almost immediately in the press.

_____

_____

9. Their cat purrs constantly. She must be looking for attention.

_____

_____

10. The television station released a list of its owners. This action was in response to critics.

_____

_____

Appositives and appositive phrases

Sometimes a noun is followed by another noun that completes or explains it.

These second nouns are called **appositives.** If the appositive is accompanied by adjectives or adjective phrases, the whole group of words is called an **appositive phrase.**

The following sentence contains an appositive phrase that explains _sister,_ the object of the verb.

We visited Ann's sister, a registered nurse.

The word _nurse_ refers to the same person as _sister._ It acts like a second object of the verb, and when we read this sentence we understand this.

Single words can also be appositives. In the following sentence, the subject _cousin_ is not capitalized. It is therefore a one-word subject, not part of a name, and _Bertha_ is an appositive describing it.

My cousin **Bertha** recently moved here.

Occasionally, verbal phrases that act like nouns appear as appositives. Consider this example:

Moral behavior, **doing what is right,** sometimes causes conflicts.

This verbal phrase is an appositive describing the subject.

Marking appositives and appositive phrases

An appositive is marked like other phrases. One mark groups it. Another shows that it is an appositive. A third shows that word it describes or explains. Only the mark that shows it to be an appositive is new to you.

Marking Appositive Phrases

1. **Group** the appositive phrase with parentheses.
2. **Mark the appositive** within the phrase by
   a. **underlining** it once,
   b. writing **App** above it.
3. Draw an **arrow** from the appositive to the word or words it explains.

We can mark some of the sample sentences as follows.

We visited Ann's sister, (a registered <u>nurse</u>).
APP

My cousin (<u>Bertha</u>) recently moved here.
APP

Exercise 7 Appositives

Mark each appositive in the following sentences.

Example

They received Cardinal Alphonso, (the papal <u>messenger</u>), in the
APP

palace garden.

1. The Shadow Warriors, a local street gang, have recently

   joined with another gang, the Snow Kings, in a neighborhood

   cleanup drive.

2. Michael's brother, a medical technician, has promised to pay his tuition this semester.

3. His brother the medical technician has promised to pay Michael's tuition this semester.

4. One of the advertisements was placed by my uncle the writer.

5. Only one thing, poverty, prevented him from being rich.

6. A detective by nature, Terry Hruska immediately reconstructed the events of last night.

7. Our great ambition, to win the game, made us practice daily.

8. We recently bought one of the better accounting programs, ProRate.

9. His friend Ben wrote it.

10. Georgina is saving money, a few dollars each day.

Pronouns as appositives

As you know, the personal pronouns and the pronoun *who* change form, depending on how they are used. This applies especially to pronouns used as appositives. Use the **subject form** for all appositives following

1. subjects
2. complements

Use the **object form** for appositives following objects.

Appositive following subject

His two best friends, **Bill and I,** have known each other since high

school.

Appositive following complement

The winning players will be the guests—**we.**

Appositive following object

We voted for the best candidate—**her.**

Take a look back at pages 127–128 for a list of all subject and object forms.

Exercise 8   Pronouns as appositives

Correct any **pronoun** errors in the following sentences. If a sentence has no errors, write **OK** in the margin.

Example

The hypnotist's subjects, Jennifer and ~~me~~ $\overset{I}{}$, were asleep in minutes.

1. The soup was prepared by the fraternity's favorite cooks, Marco and I.

2. A solution was provided by the best chemistry student in the class—she.

3. These are the new class officers, Mr. Macy, Mr. Hsing, and she.

4. Another young couple—them—used the tickets instead.

5. Both patients, Henry and he, recommended this doctor.

Punctuating appositives

Appositives are set off by commas unless they contain information that is needed to identify a specific person or thing—the same sort of information we considered in studying adjective verbal phrases. Appositives that contain such essential information should not be separated from the rest of the sentence by commas.

Appositives containing needed information.

My friend **the actor** is now working in New York.

The poet **T.S. Eliot** was also a banker.

In the first sentence, the appositive *the actor* tells us which friend the writer is talking about (we assume he or she has more than one friend). In the second, the name identifies *the poet*, which is the subject. In both cases, then, the appositives provide information needed to identify the subjects.

Appositives containing extra information

His latest film, **a western,** is about an aging marshal.

Lenore Maseda, **one of the theology faculty,** is traveling in Ethiopia this spring.

Like verbal phrases, extra appositives and appositive phrases used in the middle of a sentence require two commas, one at each end of the appositive phrase.

Sometimes appositives introduce a sentence. When they do, they are followed by a comma, just like introductory verbal phrases.

Appositive in introductory position

A student of history, my mother recalled the incident easily.

Exercise 9   Punctuating appositives

The appositives in the following sentences are printed in boldface type. Supply **commas** where necessary. If a sentence needs no additional punctuation, write **OK** in the margin.

Example

A new dress material, **Plexicloth,** was used in this stunning creation.

1. He placed the order with his uncle **Bill.**

2. The cause of the conflict **a disagreement over land reform** was soon forgotten.

3. The gun **a battered .38** was recovered from the lake.

4. He said the social welfare system punishes its beneficiaries **the poor.**

5. The city council plans to rewrite a bylaw **the one against loitering.**

6. Jamaal is studying the quark **a subatomic particle.**

7. **A poet of sorts** he wants to have its name changed to something more pleasing.

8. Consequential Insurance **our auto insurance company** waits three months and then pays its claims promptly.

9. She ended the set with her best saloon song **a slow version of "Torchie."**

10. I finally got the whole story from my friend **the hotshot lawyer.**

Combining sentences to create appositives

Like verbal phrases, appositives can add variety to your sentences. You can combine sentences so that one becomes an appositive within another.

Uncombined sentences

English is one of the Germanic languages. English also contains many French and Latin words.

Combined sentences

English, **one of the Germanic languages,** also contains many French and Latin words.

By combining these two sentences, the most important information is saved. Only the weak verb *is* and the repeated subject *English* are lost. The writing is tighter and more sophisticated, and the sentence structure is more interesting.

Of course, not all sentences are improved by combining. As always, use your own judgment. But you should consider the opportunities for combining sentences.

Exercise 10 Combining to create appositives

Combine each of the following groups of sentences to create at least one appositive. Be sure that the appositive is punctuated correctly.

Example

Kane is a candidate for city attorney. He will be speaking at the college on Wednesday.

Kane, a candidate for city attorney, will be speaking at the college on Wednesday.

1. One senator appeared in the commercials. The senator was Henry White.

_____

_____

_____

2. The fraud was eventually uncovered. It was a scandal involving military recruitment.

_____

_____

_____

3. The local review officer had been bribing high school students to enlist. The officer was named Sergeant Raggs.

_____

_____

_____

4. The dream centers on Ben's childhood hero. In his youth he idolized King Arthur.

_____

_____

_____

5. The wood of that tree burns very well. I'm talking about the heart ash.

_____

_____

_____

6. Elaine works at the ministry. She told me about this job.

_____

_____

_____

7. We entered Howard because of its political science department. Howard has one of the finest political science departments in the country.

_____

_____

_____

8. The academic gown is worn on Regent's Day. Regent's Day is a traditional holiday of the college.

_____

_____

_____

9. Simple revenge is a common motive for murder. It was the reason behind the Marietta case.

_____

_____

_____

10. His sisters were named Andrea and Claudia. He received no sympathy from his sisters.

_____

_____

_____

Review exercise 1

Add commas where needed in the following paragraphs.

Sitting on the grass Louis glanced at the sky. The sun shining brightly warmed his face. His gaze returned to a book lying open beside him and to the letter placed within it.

Vacationing in an out-of-the-way spot he had forgotten school entirely. His two best friends Marcel and Carolyn had been a distant memory. Now they had decided to get married and he had to attend the wedding a fancy affair probably. Thoroughly disgusted he reread the letter written on pale blue paper. The wedding was to be in Dayton Carolyn's hometown in September a month from now.

Gathering up his knapsack Louis strode toward a speck in the distance the general store with the island's only telephone. Leaving the island would be hard but it was time to get back to the world of his friends and the world of work.

Review exercise 2

Edit the following paragraphs by combining sentences to create verbal phrases and appositives. Make sure your new verbal phrases and appositives are punctuated correctly.

Thomas Haney wrote his short stories between 1953 and 1971. They are accounts of his life in New Orleans. One of his recurring characters is clearly based on his mother. His mother's name was Doris. The character's name is Mildred Patou.

Mildred is a tough, appealing character. She works at a diner to support her three children and her sister. Mildred devotes her life to her family, but she does have one wish for herself. She wants to buy a pink Cadillac with purple velour seats. Her children laugh at her when she talks about her dream car. They try to tease her out of this embarrassing notion. But Mildred holds firm to her wild hope. Readers can see that she is an optimistic woman.

Haney's stories are filled with characters like Mildred. His characters are vivid and unpredictable people. They remind us of men and women we really know.

_____

_____

_____

_____

_____

_____

_____

_____

_____

_____

_____

_____

Chapter 14 writing assignment

1. Jot down a few of the plans you have for next year. Arrange them in the order of importance. Write a good, concise sentence telling why your top plan is so important to you.
2. Write a short paragraph (about half a page) discussing this plan and how you intend to carry it out. Try to add variety to your sentences by using some verbal phrases and appositives.
3. Go over your paragraph and see if there are any sentences that would benefit from being combined. Make any corrections you think necessary.

Section V

Coordination and subordination

The next chapters deal with two ways of combining sentence elements—coordination and subordination. You'll also learn how to spot sentence fragments and how coordination and subordination can help correct them.

Coordination means combining elements so that the reader knows they are *equal*. It involves linking two or more independent clauses, dependent clauses, subjects, verbs, objects, adjectives, and adverbs.

Subordination means combining elements so that the reader knows they are *unequal*. The relationship between a noun and its adjective, for example, is an unequal, or subordinate, relationship, and so is the relationship between a verb and its adverb. The adjective describes the noun, and the adverb describes the verb.

Coordination and subordination are sentence-combining and editing techniques that can greatly improve your writing by making it clearer and more concise.

15. Coordination

Coordination means combining *equal* sentence elements—either equal parts of one clause or equal clauses.

The result is called **compounding.** A sentence with more than one subject, for example, has a **compound subject.** A sentence with more than one verb has a **compound verb.** And a sentence with more than one independent clause is a **compound sentence.**

Let's look at compound parts within a clause first.

Compound sentence parts

Any sentence element can be compounded through coordination. A sentence can have more than one subject, verb, or object. A noun can have more than one adjective. A verb can be described by several adverbs. A preposition can have several objects.

Compounding sentence parts does not change the structure of a sentence. For example, two subjects, when attached to one verb, act like one subject, and so on.

Coordinating conjunctions

A **conjunction** is a connecting word that joins words or groups of words in a sentence. The kind of conjunction that allows two or more sentence parts to act as one is the **coordinating conjunction.** Coordinating conjunctions join equal parts of a sentence to each other—subject to subject, verb to verb, and so on.

The most commonly used coordinating conjunctions are listed below.

Coordinating Conjunctions

and	yet**
or*	so**
but	for**
nor*	

* *Or* and *nor* are sometimes used with the adjectives *either* and *neither*.
** *Yet, so,* and *for* are not always used as conjunctions.

Learn this list, especially *and, or, but,* and *nor.*

The following sentences show how one of these conjunctions can be used within a clause.

Two subjects

The prime minister **and** parliament reached an agreement yesterday.

Three subjects

The prime minister, the foreign secretary, **and** parliament reached an agreement yesterday.

Two verbs

I raced home **and** did the laundry.

Two objects of a verb

Janine bought a dress **and** a coat.

Two adjectives

A close **and** careful look at the lock showed that it had been tampered with.

Two adverbs

She spoke gently **and** kindly to the crying child.

Two objects of a preposition

I wrote to the dean **and** the college president.

Marking compound sentence parts

Sentences with compound parts are not difficult to mark. If there are two subjects, simply mark them both with double underscores. If there are two verbs, circle them both. If a prepositional phrase has two objects, include both objects in the parentheses.

Two subjects

The <u><u>prime minister</u></u> and <u><u>parliament</u></u> (reached) an agreement yesterday.

Three subjects

The <u><u>prime minister</u></u>, the <u><u>foreign secretary</u></u>, and <u><u>parliament</u></u> (reached)

an agreement yesterday.

Two verbs

<u><u>I</u></u> (raced) home and (did) the laundry.

Two objects of a preposition

I (wrote) (to the dean and the college president).

If the conjunction joins words that are widely separated, you can add a looping line that touches the conjunction and the joined sentence elements. This sometimes helps make clear what elements a given conjunction joins.

Three verbs

I (raced) home, (did) the laundry, and (relaxed) for the rest of the

evening.

Exercise 1   Sentences with compound parts

On the lines below, tell what is joined by each conjunction—for example, *3 verbs, 2 subjects,* and so on.

Example

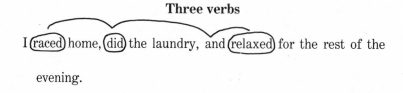

<u>3 subjects</u>   Marcie, Alicia, and Larae won radios in the

bookstore contest.

_____   1. Steve brought the camera and set up the light-

ing equipment.

_____ 2. The second and third cars in the race are driven by brothers.

_____ 3. Neither the diplomat nor his assistant was aware of the contents of the letter.

_____ 4. This semester I am taking accounting and math.

_____ 5. We drove behind the bank and the shoe store.

_____ 6. The announcement was made quietly but firmly.

_____ 7. Three teams, Oakland, Philadelphia, and West Los Angeles, made the play-offs.

_____ 8. The networks have promoted the event and sold most of their advertising time.

_____ 9. Stan seems shy yet confident.

_____ 10. The system is efficient, economical, and easy to maintain.

Using commas with a list

Sentences with compound sentence parts sometimes require special punctuation. To illustrate this, let's take another look at two examples we considered earlier.

Two subjects

The prime minister and parliament reached an agreement yesterday.

Three subjects

The prime minister, the foreign secretary, and parliament reached an agreement yesterday.

Each of these sentences contains a **list,** or **series,** of items—in these cases, a list of subjects. A list of two items does not need to be punctuated.

List of two items

The prime minister and parliament. . . .

A list of three or more items is punctuated with commas.

List of three items

The prime minister, the foreign secretary, and parliament. . . .

Punctuating sentences with a list of items (compound sentence parts) is easy if you know how many items are in the list.

Punctuating Items in a List

Use commas to separate items in a list of three or more items.

Note that commas are used to separate *each* item of the list from the others.

Exercise 2   Punctuating items in a list

Punctuate each of the following sentences correctly. If any sentence is already correctly punctuated, write **OK** in the margin.

Example   The controller met with the sales manager, the tech support manager, and their staffs.

1. Copies of the report went to the president and her secretary.

2. The engineering staff designed the system built the board and wrote the manual within nine months.

3. Each of his first three mystery novels, *Rimshot Greasepit* and *Hindsight,* has an unusual one-word title.

4. They discovered gold silver and platinum coins near the burial site.

5. Another of his shots went over the lake and into the parking lot.

6. The benches have been repainted in red blue green and ocher.

7. She enjoys dancing at the Roxie, the Rosemont Playhouse, and the Westjoy Palace Showroom.

8. The precepts of Marx, Engels and Lenin are followed religiously in Moscow even today.

9. The investment program required a manager an order entry supervisor and an analyst.

10. The first two teams, Loyola and Notre Dame, did well on Thursday.

Coordinate adjectives

Sometimes coordinate adjectives—adjectives that equally describe the same noun and that could be joined by a conjunction like *and*—are written with a comma in place of the conjunction. This removal of the conjunction is usually done to make the sentence more compact and give it a smoother flow.

Coordinate adjectives

A large **and** unfriendly bear entered the camp.
A large, unfriendly bear entered the camp.

When adjectives are not coordinate—that is, when they describe more than just the noun—they are not separated by commas. Compare this example with the last two:

A large grizzly bear entered the camp.

The adjective *large* describes not just *bear* but *grizzly bear*. A helpful test is to try to use *and* between the adjectives. If *and* sounds odd with these words (as in the case of "a large and grizzly bear") or distorts the meaning of the noun-adjective phrase, then a comma should not be used to separate the adjectives.

Exercise 3   Coordinate adjectives

Each of the following sentences contains coordinate adjectives joined by a conjunction. Rewrite each one to replace the conjunction with a comma.

Example   A cold and silent woman entered their apartment.

A cold, silent woman entered
their apartment.

    1. You can rent a newer and tougher truck from Wilbur Rents-It-All.

_____

_____

    2. Her skillfully designed and finely tuned carburetion unit was just in-
stalled last night.

_____

_____

    3. The cold and relentless north wind blew all night.

_____

_____

    4. Barlotti carefully gave instructions to the young and obviously in-
experienced technician.

_____

_____

    5. He sat and watched the clear and placid water for several hours.

_____

_____

Exercise 4   Punctuating coordinate adjectives

Punctuate each of the following sentences correctly.

Example   Jenna's quiet, forceful voice is her best asset.

    1. A calmer more detailed presentation will achieve better results.

2. Three fine journalists have failed to reach the general for an interview.

3. A blue sports sedan is available for your use.

4. The young men listened to the impassioned words of their coach.

5. The Soviets assess the U.N. as a powerless irrelevant institution.

Exercise 5   Punctuating items in a list

Punctuate each sentence of the following paragraph correctly.

The promised democratic elections have been postponed again. An agreement among the council members presidential aides and their staffs prevented local journalists from learning the reasons for this decision. The causes for the new delay have been many. Internal unrest increased last year and threatened to become an issue in any open unrestricted political campaign. The leading opposition candidates, Dr. Mendez Mr. Guttierez Mrs. Perez and others, have not been effective in creating informed active support for their positions. But above all, most urban workers don't seem concerned about the violation of a constitution that is less than six months old.

Compound sentences

Coordinating conjunctions can also join equal independent clauses in a single sentence.

Sam went into business, **and** Douglas joined the army.

Without the conjunction *and,* we would have two separate simple sentences, each containing one independent clause.

Sam went into business. Douglas joined the army.

By joining these clauses with a coordinating conjunction, we can connect them in one sentence and still keep them independent of each other. This kind of coordination helps writing to flow more easily and naturally.

Mark a sentence with two or more independent clauses as if the conjunction were not there.

Sam (went) (into business), and Douglas (joined) the army.

Sentences with only one independent clause are punctuated differently from sentences with two independent clauses. It is important, therefore, to know what each conjunction in a sentence is joining.

A sentence with two subjects and one verb has only one clause. In the same way, a sentence with one subject and two verbs also has only one clause.

Even sentences with two subjects and two verbs have only one clause if both subjects are attached to both verbs.

Two subjects and two verbs—one clause

Carla **and** her mother (planned) the shower **and** (chose) the guests.

This sentence contains only one subject-verb pair. The fact that each side of the pair is compounded does not change the number of clauses it contains.

The two subjects, *Carla* and *mother,* are connected and act like one subject. Likewise, the two verbs, *planned* and *chose,* are connected and act like one verb. Since both subjects do both actions, the sentence contains one independent clause.

The next sentence, on the other hand, has two subjects, two verbs, and two clauses.

Two subjects and two verbs—two clauses

Carla (planned) the shower, **and** her mother (chose) the guests.

This sentence has two subject-verb pairs. Each subject does only one action.

This information can be summarized by the following diagrams.

One clause
1. (subject + subject) + verb
2. subject + (verb + verb)
3. (subject + subject) + (verb + verb)

Two clauses
4. (subject + verb) + (subject + verb)

Exercise 6   One clause or two clauses

Mark each **subject** and **verb** of the following sentences. Then tell whether each sentence has one or two **clauses**.

Example   _2_   It (rained) all weekend, so they (postponed) the trip until

Thursday.

_____ **1.** She played a deaf composer in her first film and a society matron in her next.

_____ **2.** The boys went fishing but caught nothing.

_____ **3.** The gate was damaged in last night's storm, so my father fixed it.

_____ **4.** I will be busy all weekend, but call me on Monday.

_____ **5.** Neither the coach nor the trainer saw the accident.

_____ **6.** The coat is too small for him, but the shirt fits nicely.

_____ **7.** Sue and her father have just left for dinner and a show.

_____ **8.** The explosion destroyed the building, but no one was seriously injured.

_____ **9.** The medals were taken from the box, and the colonel pinned them on the soldier's chest.

_____ **10.** The lamp flickered and went out.

Punctuating compound sentences

Compound sentences can be punctuated in two ways. The first way is with a comma and a coordinating conjunction. The second is with a semicolon.

Comma and conjunction

Two independent (or main) clauses can be joined correctly with a **comma** and a **coordinating conjunction.** The following sentence shows two independent clauses joined by a comma and *or*.

> Jim might have gone to the Coho Club, **or** he might have walked home.

Notice that there is a main clause—with a subject and a verb—on each side of the conjunction. To see this clearly, mark the subject and verb of the above sentence.

Compare that sentence with this one.

> Jim might have gone to the Coho Club **or** walked home.

In this sentence, the conjunction joins two verbs only, so there is no comma used with it.

Note that a comma alone cannot join two independent clauses. A coordinating conjunction must always follow the comma.

Semicolon

As you may recall from Chapter 1, a **semicolon** (;) can also be used to join independent clauses. It is the only punctuation mark that can join independent clauses by itself, in other words, without a coordinating conjunction. Here are a few examples of sentences joined by semicolons.

Separate sentences

> Last year I played intramural football. This year I might try soccer.

Independent clauses joined by semicolon

> Last year I played intramural football; this year I might try soccer.

Do not use a semicolon to join a clause to part of a clause. A semicolon, like a coordinating conjunction, should only be used to join *equal* elements.

You need to be careful when you use the semicolon in your writing. Use it only when the clauses joined are closely allied in meaning, phrased similarly, or follow logically from one another. If you are not sure about using a semicolon, in most cases it is better to use another connector.

Semicolon and conjunctive adverb

A special use of the semicolon combines it with words like *however, moreover,* and *therefore* (called **conjunctive adverbs**) to connect independent clauses. This group is always followed by a comma. The following sentence uses this kind of connector.

> Last year I played intramural football; **however,** this year I might try soccer.

Conjunctive adverbs fall into two groups: those that connect similar ideas and those that connect opposite ideas. They include the following words:

Conjunctive Adverbs

Similarity	**Opposition**
besides	however
consequently	nevertheless
furthermore	
moreover	
therefore	

Exercise 7

Using a comma and a conjunction

Use a **comma** and a **conjunction** to combine each of the following into a compound sentence.

Example

A shawl was draped around her neck. A sash was tied at her waist.

A shawl was draped around her neck, and a sash was tied at her waist.

1. The game was going badly. Raymond left early.

   _____

   _____

2. Congress approved the appropriation bill by a large margin. The president vetoed it.

   _____

   _____

3. The plot was discovered months ago. There have been no arrests.

   _____

   _____

4. You could declare a major this semester. You could wait until your junior year.

_____

_____

5. The film was enjoyed by everyone in the group. It left Shelly strangely annoyed.

_____

_____

6. The architects of environmental policy are sane. They are intelligent. They possess an almost religious depth of purpose.

_____

_____

7. Her purpose was clear. Her language was not.

_____

_____

8. "Breaking with Moscow" is in one sense mistitled. Its author denies having broken with the city of his youth.

_____

_____

9. The colonel emerged from the cocoon of his own view of things. What he saw surprised him.

_____

_____

10. The letter could be printed as it is. It could be heavily edited.

_____

_____

Exercise 8   Using semicolons

Choose three of the following items. Use a **semicolon** to combine the two sentences in each item into a compound sentence. Try to choose the three items for which semicolons make the most sense.

Example   The critics hated every word. The public loved the book anyway.

The critics hated every word; the public

loved the book anyway.

1. We approached the castle at last. A lone dog howled.

2. Each of the committees has submitted its report. Only yours has not been received.

3. The older brother wanted to rise to power. The younger was content with a humble government job.

4. The art of the city was magnificent. The recent restorations should help to justify its reputation.

5. Canadians found themselves with a problem. Relations with France had become dangerously strained.

A. _____

_____

B. _____

_____

C. _____

_____

Exercise 9

Using semicolons with conjunctive adverbs

Rewrite each of the following items using a connector from the list below.

besides	therefore
consequently	however
furthermore	nevertheless
moreover	

Remember that a comma should follow each of the above words.

Example

We arrived at the chancellor's office by 4:30. She had already gone home.

We arrived at the chancellor's office by 4:30; however, she had already gone home.

1. The questions fairly tested our knowledge of the subject. They gave us a chance to show some writing skill.

_____

_____

_____

2. Three of my friends did not study for the exam. They did not pass it.

_____

_____

_____

3. The new government rulings make that investment more expensive that in the past. You should consider other options.

_____

_____

_____

4. The brown coat goes well with these slacks. It is all I can afford right now.

_____

_____

_____

5. Several ministers received threatening letters. Each spoke out against the proposed constitutional changes.

_____

_____

_____

Common errors in writing compound sentences

Three common errors can occur in writing compound sentences.

1. comma splices
2. run-on sentences
3. improperly punctuated coordinating conjunctions

Comma splices

One of the most common punctuation errors is the **comma splice.** It occurs when two independent clauses—groups of words that could be separate sentences by themselves—are joined only by a comma.

Incorrect

Mona is not sick, she just wants to stay home from work.

Each side of the sentence has a subject and verb (_Mona is_ and _she wants_), and there is no conjunction of any kind with the comma. This sentence could be written as two separate sentences.

Correct

Mona is not sick. She just wants to stay home from work.

Comma splices can be corrected by adding the proper punctuation—a period, a semicolon, or, if appropriate, a question mark—or by adding a conjunction after the comma.

Exercise 10 Correcting comma splices

Correct any incorrect punctuation in the following sentences and add coordinating conjunctions where needed. If a sentence is already correct, write **OK** in the margin.

Example The book sold for thousands, ^*but* the movie rights went for a lot more.

1. The senator was nominated for a third term, but he did not run.

2. Valian knew he could not afford to go to college next year, he looked for a full-time job.

3. The bank balance is running low, our paychecks will not be deposited until Monday.

4. New cars are getting more expensive, they are also becoming harder to maintain.

5. I like her way of telling a story, do you?

6. The clothes are missing, the jewelry has not been touched.

7. They wanted to remember the lecture, so they taped it.

8. Juanita enjoys chess, she plays regularly at the Third Avenue Kings and Queens Club.

9. The movie was *Little Caesar,* the character was Rico.

10. The slacks are hard to clean, the legs get mud stained so easily.

Run-on sentences

Another common punctuation error is the **run-on sentence.** It occurs when two independent clauses are printed as one sentence, with no punctuation between them.

Incorrect

I never eat liver the smell makes me sick.

Like comma splices, run-on sentences can be corrected by adding the proper punctuation—a period (or a question mark if the sentence is a question) or a semicolon—or by adding a comma and a conjunction. The above sentence can be corrected in any of these three ways.

Correct

I never eat liver. The smell makes me sick.

I never eat liver; the smell makes me sick.

I never eat liver, for the smell makes me sick.

Run-on sentences are problems of recognition. They occur most often because a writer does not recognize that both clauses are independent. Recognizing independent clauses is the key step in correcting run-on sentences.

Exercise 11 Correcting run-on sentences

Correct any incorrect punctuation in the following sentences and add coordinating conjunctions where needed. If any sentence is already correct, write **OK** in the margin.

Example

These beaches attract thousands in the summer. Everyone wants to cool off.

1. The appointment can wait the letter must be finished.

2. The process is slow and takes a lot of patience.

3. The island was settled quickly the population swelled to several thousand in less than twenty years.

4. Would you read this now I need an answer.

5. Most people stop short of their ability others push themselves well beyond it.

6. The meat is fresh the salad bar is well stocked.

7. The truck was loaded with frozen fish and headed for Chicago supermarkets.

8. Movies bore him so do books and magazines.

9. Noelle wants to write professionally and shows a lot of promise.

10. Marco plans to study art he is already selling his sketches.

Incorrectly punctuated coordinating conjunctions

Sometimes commas are used where they shouldn't be, for instance, with a coordinating conjunction that joins two verbs. At other times a comma is not used with a conjunction when it should be. Here are some examples:

Incorrect—comma not needed

Vanity Fair has been removed from the library, and taken to be rebound.

Incorrect—commas missing

Vanity Fair has been removed from the library and it is being rebound.

The first sentence contains a subject and two verbs. No comma is needed.

Correct

Vanity Fair has been removed from the library and taken to be rebound.

The second sentence contains two independent clauses. A comma must be used with the conjunction *and.*

Correct

Vanity Fair has been removed from the library, and it is being rebound.

Exercise 12 Correcting compound sentences

Correct any incorrect punctuation in the following sentences and add coordinating conjunctions where needed.

If a sentence is already correct, write **OK** on the line. If the sentence is incorrect, use the following abbreviations to tell which error the sentence contains:

CS for comma splice
RO for run-on sentence
CE for comma error (a
    comma must either be
    added or taken out)

Example

_____CS_____ Another delivery was scheduled for tomorrow,⊙

    I
    it should arrive in the afternoon.

_____ 1. Have you solved this problem, I haven't.

_____ 2. She works hard and she is honest.

_____ 3. Diving shops line Seaview Avenue, and most of the side streets.

_____ 4. American farm products are well advertised and attract a large market.

_____ 5. They called a special meeting of the council, the matter was presented in a closed-door session.

_____ 6. The store is closed the streets are dark.

_____ 7. Emilia called at last, and told her sister everything.

_____ 8. He is a cautious driver, the accident couldn't be his fault.

_____ 9. We are just getting dinner ready, so you can eat with us.

_____ **10.** The painting was expensive, it sold for $277,500.

Combining to create compound sentences

Your work in this chapter has two benefits. The most obvious is to help you correct punctuation errors. But the sentence-combining exercises you have done will also help you edit your writing to create a strong final version.

As you have seen in earlier chapters, editing your writing does not mean just correcting its errors. The real goal of editing is to refine rough-draft sentences into strong, clear, pleasing, and readable prose. Sentence combining is a vital part of that process.

When independent clauses are joined, shifts in emphasis occur. Emphasis in writing is created by many elements, including the rhythm of a sentence, its position, its length, and the length of the other sentences in the same paragraph.

Obviously, any two simple sentences that are adjacent to each other *can* be combined. But *should* they be combined?

That is a question for each writer to answer. There is no "correct" solution to any writing problem. The only wrong solution is not to consider sentence-combining possibilities at all, especially those that involve creating or separating compound sentences.

Review Exercise 2 on p. 209 asks you to make these kinds of decisions. Do this exercise carefully, paying attention to the effect of each of your proposed changes. Read the new paragraphs out loud to test the effect of your proposed changes. Don't be afraid to try several possibilities before settling on one of them.

Think of this work as a kind of puzzle. Your goal is to please your ear by writing the most effective combination of short and long sentences possible. It can be enjoyable work, and your writing will improve as a result.

Review exercise 1

Correct all punctuation errors in the following paragraphs.

For centuries flying was a dream but it was a dream that people wanted to come true. The Wright brothers flew the first airplane in 1903, suddenly the idea of flying machines captured the American imagination like never before. Most people thought that airplanes would open up a glorious glamorous future. The human race would certainly benefit from the speed, ease and availability of airplane travel.

That prediction has come true in a short time, and in many ways. Affordable air travel has given people the opportunity to explore distant parts of the world, and the chance to compare their lives with the lives of others. Airplanes and air travel have opened new doors and taught us new lessons.

Review exercise 2

The following sentences contain only one independent clause each. Combine them in ways you consider most effective. Then rewrite your best revision on the lines provided.

Corn was one of the New World's earliest grains. It was grown by Indians before white explorers came to America. Early settlers learned many things from native Americans. One of these things was the cultivation of corn.

That was back in the 1600s. Many improvements have been made in the corn plant since then. Today's ear of corn is sweeter than the early Indian corn. It is also larger and more resistant to severe weather. Corn has been an important part of our diets for a long time. Improvements will guarantee that it continues to be important.

The Midwest states produce a great deal of corn. Consequently, corn can be used to feed cattle as well as people. Beef from corn-fed cattle is tastier than beef from cattle fed any other grain food. Corn is a relatively inexpensive feed for cattle. It also stores well for long periods of time.

Corn has been one of America's greatest gifts to agriculture. It is versatile and hardy. It's nutritious and fun to eat.

_____

_____

_____

_____

_____

_____

_____

_____

_____

_____

_____

_____

Chapter 15 writing assignment

1. In a short paragraph (about half a page), tell why you chose your present major or career. (If it would be helpful, make a list first, as you did in the writing assignments for previous chapters.)
2. Vary the structure and length of your sentences, and make sure that each sentence and all its parts are properly punctuated.
3. Reread what you have written and correct any errors.

16. Subordination

Subordination means combining sentence elements that are *grammatically unequal.* Adjectives and adverbs, for example, are grammatically subordinate to —less important than—the words they describe. Prepositional phrases are always subordinate sentence elements because they always act as adjectives and adverbs.

Dependent clauses

Some sentences, called **complex sentences,** contain clauses that are subordinate to the independent clause. There are three kinds of **subordinate (or dependent) clauses:**

> adjective clauses
> adverb clauses
> noun clauses

Adjective clauses (sometimes called **relative clauses**) act like one-word adjectives by describing nouns and pronouns.

Adverb clauses act like one-word adverbs by describing verbs.

Noun clauses act like one-word nouns. Noun clauses can be subjects; objects of verbs, verbals, or prepositions; complements; and appositives.

Like all clauses, dependent clauses contain a subject and a verb. Unlike independent clauses, however, dependent clauses are introduced by tip-off words that connect the dependent clause to the independent clause it describes.

Let's look at these clauses one at a time.

Adjective clauses

Adjective clauses act like one-word adjectives. They can appear any place in a sentence where a one-word adjective can occur. They can describe any noun or pronoun in a sentence—a subject, an object of a verb, verbal, or preposition, a complement, or an appositive. (Adjective clauses in appositive phrases are especially common.)

Adjective clauses always answer one of the adjective questions:

which?
what kind?
how many (or how much)?
whose?

In addition, each adjective clause starts with a **tip-off word** or a phrase that includes a tip-off word.

Compare the following sentences.

The essay **for my geology class** needs editing.

The essay **that I wrote for my geology class** needs editing.

The main idea of the first sentence is *essay needs editing* (subject + verb + object). You know that *for my geology class* is a prepositional phrase that acts as an adjective describing *essay*.

The main idea of the second sentence is the same as the first, *essay needs editing*. Because *that I wrote for my geology class* describes *essay*, it is an adjective.

The essay **that I wrote for my geology class** needs editing.

Adjective question *which essay?*
Answer *that I wrote for my geology class*

And since *that I wrote for my geology class* contains a subject and a verb, it is a *clause*, not a phrase.

Marking adjective clauses

Adjective clauses are marked with a **long bracket** and an **arrow** that shows which word the adjective clause describes.

The essay **that I wrote for my geology class** needs editing.

Tip-off words for adjective clauses

That is the tip-off word for the adjective clause in the sentence above. Notice that in this case the tip-off word also acts as the object of the verb *wrote*.

Adjective clause

that I wrote for my geology class

Even though *that* is the object of the verb *wrote*, it is positioned at the beginning of the adjective clause. Try writing this clause in normal word order.

Notice also that *that* is a pronoun. Its antecedent (reference word) is *essay*, which is also the word that the whole dependent clause describes.

All tip-off words for adjective clauses are like this one. They are pronouns (and sometimes adjectives) that refer to the same word the clause describes.

The following is a list of tip-off words for adjective clauses.

Tip-off Words for Adjective Clauses

Pronouns	Adjective
who	whose
whom	
which	
that	

Who (subject form) and *whom* (object form) refer only to people. *Which* refers to animals, things, and ideas. It may also refer to groups of people (*the family, which . . . , the class, which . . . , the corporation, which . . .*). *That* may refer to animals, things, ideas, and people (both groups and individuals). But you cannot simply substitute *that* for *which*. Each word serves a different purpose in a sentence, as you will see later in this chapter (p. 219).

"Hidden" tip-off words

Sometimes the tip-off words *that* or *which* are "hidden" in a sentence. Like the *you* missing from but understood in a command, the tip-off word is understood to be in the sentence. Let's look at an example:

> I knew everything he was going to say.

If we supplied the hidden tip-off word, this sentence would read:

> I knew everything that he was going to say.

Whether *that* is included in the sentence or not, we treat the sentence as though it were present. Tip-off words are often omitted in sentences with adjective or noun clauses.

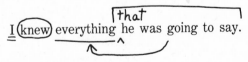

Examples of adjective clauses

Here are some other sentences that contain adjective clauses.

> Jacob Handleman, **who knows your father,** is waiting to see you.

Michelle Arno, **whom you met last winter,** is in town for the board meeting.

I did the readings **that were assigned for today.**

We just met the writer **whose novel we have been discussing.**

Who and *whom*

In the first two examples above, notice the use of *who* and *whom* within the dependent clause.

who knows your father

whom you met last winter

The first clause uses *who* because it is the subject of the verb *knows*.

who (knows) your father

The second clause uses *whom* because it is the object of the verb *met*.

whom you (met) last winter

Notice that the tip-off word appears at the beginning of the clause, no matter how it is used. Try writing *whom you met last winter* in normal word order. You will see clearly that *whom* is an object.

Position of adjective clauses

The normal position of an adjective clause is after the word it describes. Adjective clauses often follow adjective phrases that describe the same word.

The man (in the blue suit) **who is carrying the briefcase** (is) Professor Sen.

Marking sentences completely

Dependent clauses contain verbs that might keep you from finding the main verb of the sentence. So mark them first, before marking the rest of the sentence.

Sentence Marking Order
(Revised)

1. Group dependent clauses (with long brackets), any remaining verbal phrases (with square brackets), and any remaining descriptive phrases (with parentheses).

2. Now mark the verb, subject, and object or complement.
3. Starting at the beginning of the sentence, draw arrows to show what each adjective and adverb word, phrase, or dependent clause describes.

Again, remember that you do not have to mark a phrase within another phrase or dependent clause. Just treat the largest phrase as one word, no matter what other phrases it contains.

Exercise 1   Adjective clauses

In the following sentences, the adjective clauses have been printed in boldface type. Draw an arrow to show which word each clause modifies. Then tell which adjective question the adjective clause answers.

Example

what kind

A messenger **on whom you can rely** will be sent.

_____ 1. Julio saw a painting **that he would like to buy.**

_____ 2. A man **who looks like your father** was in the bank today.

_____ 3. My sociology class, **which I needed in order to graduate,** was just canceled.

_____ 4. They devised a plan **on which everyone could agree.**

_____ 5. She wrote an excellent paper, one **that might be published.**

_____ 6. The afternoon shift, **which I hate,** has just been reassigned.

_____ 7. They gave him anything **that he wanted.**

_____ 8. The couch **that you liked so much** is on sale at Jackson's.

_____ 9. Estes, a doctor **whom I still admire,** revolutionized the practice of medicine in this town.

_____ 10. Courses **that require a lot of reading** aren't very popular in this dorm.

Exercise 2   Adjective clauses

Mark each sentence completely.

Example

Workers who join the strike could be disciplined by the company.

1. Professor Becker, who lectured here last year, will return in July.

2. All donations that we receive are tax-deductible.

3. The finance committee, which approved your loan, just sent this letter.

4. Don't say anything that you might regret later.

5. The boxes that you need will be delivered tomorrow.

6. The wines that they produce are noted for their fragrance.

7. Buckworth has written another book that will make most of its sales in college English classrooms.

8. The Arsten family, which had lived next door to you, is moving again.

9. The page on which he wrote the first draft of the poem is now very valuable.

10. We introduced her to Daley, a policeman who wants to write best sellers.

Exercise 3

Who and *whom* in adjective clauses

A. Write the correct form of **who** and **whom** on the line in each of the following sentences.

Example

We located the person ____who____ has the key.

1. The man _____ made the offer no longer works here.

2. Here is an politician _____ I respect.

3. A resident _____ saw the robbery has been interviewed.

4. Her sister is a researcher with _____ I work.

5. The mayor, for _____ I voted, has recently changed his position on every major issue.

6. Inspector Arnaz, _____ you know, is speaking at noon in the Brown Auditorium.

7. Professor Weiss will always help students _____ ask for his assistance.

8. The report finally went to Annette, for _____ it was originally intended.

9. The hairdresser _____ my sister recommended does very good work.

10. Jenkins, the supply driver _____ received the commendation, was rewarded with an extra week's vacation.

B. Correct any errors in the use of **who** and **whom** in the following sentences. Write **OK** in the margin if a sentence is correct.

Example

Most people ~~who~~ whom we meet at the luncheonette are commuters.

11. Several reporters who you know well are attending the luncheon.

12. The salesperson who helped you yesterday has the day off.

13. An actress whom this agent once represented is now working the New York stage.

14. We didn't know anyone who we could ask.

15. Several young women who entered the competition have since withdrawn under protest.

16. A high official, whom declined to be named, made the announcement this morning.

17. I notified the manufacturer who issued the original warranty.

18. Roberto, who saw the letter, would not comment on its contents.

19. The teachers who you remember are all retired.

20. Each of the tenants who I have spoken to are willing to sign the petition.

Punctuating adjective clauses

Adjective clauses are punctuated like adjective verbal phrases that do not begin a sentence (see Chapter 14). Like such phrases, they can contain both necessary and extra information.

As you recall from Chapter 14, **necessary information** either

1. provides identification or
2. narrows down meaning.

Knowing whether an adjective clause contains necessary or extra information is the key to punctuating it.

Punctuating Adjective Clauses

Separate adjective clauses from the rest of the sentence with commas only if they contain extra information. Do not separate adjective clauses that contain necessary information.

Adjective clauses that contain extra information are sometimes called **nonrestrictive relative clauses** because they do not restrict, or narrow down, the meaning of the words they describe. The following sentences show how these clauses are punctuated.

Extra adjective clauses

Uncle Frank, **for whom my brother works,** hires his relatives whenever possible.

The children still talk about the Bronx Zoo, **which they visited last year.**

Uncle Frank and the Bronx Zoo have already been identified by name. Therefore the adjective clauses contain extra information, which is not essential to the meaning of the sentences.

Necessary adjective clauses (sometimes called **restrictive relative clauses**) are never separated from the rest of the sentence with commas. Here are two examples:

Necessary adjective clause providing identification

This department needs a photocopier **that won't break down.**

Necessary adjective clause narrowing down meaning

People **who have too much money** are welcome at this club.

Note that the tip-off word *which* begins only those clauses containing *extra* information. Clauses beginning with *which* are therefore always separated from the rest of the sentence with commas.

Roughing It, **which** I am reading now, made Kathy laugh out loud.

The tip-off word *that* begins only those clauses containing *necessary* information. Clauses beginning with *that* are never separated from the rest of the sentence with commas.

The book **that** you recommended to me is priceless.

The tip-off words *who, whom,* and *whose,* however, can be used with both extra and necessary clauses.

Exercise 4   Punctuating adjective clauses

Punctuate each of the following sentences correctly. If a sentence is already correct, write **OK** in the margin.

Example   The Stanley Steamers**,**who play in a semipro league**,**have a large

local following.

1. It's hard to find a novel that doesn't contain a lot of violence.

2. Lung cancer which threatens every smoker can now be cured in a great many cases.

3. Grass that roots quickly was planted on the hill.

4. Kentucky bluegrass which roots quickly was planted on the hill.

5. The passengers who followed the steward's instructions were not injured.

6. The band welcomed Ensign Jones who was recently commended for bravery.

7. Venus and Mars which are the two planets closest to Earth can both be seen in the western sky tonight.

8. Our basketball team which won its last five games meets its toughest rival this weekend.

9. Ms. Ramos rehired the supervisors who were laid off last month.

10. Restaurants that offer coupons are doing well.

Adverb clauses

Adverb clauses act like one-word adverbs. They describe verbs, verbals, adjectives, or other adverbs, and always answer one of the adverb questions:

> when?
> where?
> why?
> how?
> under what condition? (or yes or no?)

Marking adverb clauses

Adverb clauses are marked like other dependent clauses—with a **long bracket** and an **arrow** pointing to the word the clause describes.

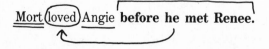

Mort loved Angie **before he met Renee.**

Tip-off words for adverb clauses

All adverb clauses begin with tip-off words. Compare the following sentences.

Rita entered graduate school last fall.

Rita entered graduate school because she wanted a master's degree in business.

The core of each sentence is *Rita entered school,* the independent clause. Each independent clause is followed by an adverb—the first by an adverb phrase and the second by an adverb clause.

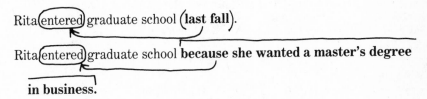

Rita entered graduate school (**last fall**).

Rita entered graduate school **because she wanted a master's degree in business.**

Because she wanted a master's degree in business is an adverb clause. It contains a subject and verb *(she wanted)* and begins with a tip-off word *(because).*

Adverb question   entered *why?*

Answer   *because she wanted a master's degree in business*

Like all adverb clause tip-off words, *because* is a conjunction. It joins the adverb clause to the independent clause and establishes the logic of the relationship between them.

Since this relationship is one of unequals, *because* is a **subordinating conjunction.** You'll recall that "subordinate" means "lesser in rank or order."

Other tip-off words for adverb clauses include the following.

Tip-off Words for Adverb Clauses
(Subordinating Conjunctions)

When?

after	just after
as	just before
as soon as	since (meaning *after)*
before	until
even after	when
even before	whenever
	while

Where?

where	wherever

Why?

because	so (meaning *so that)*
in order that	so that
since (meaning *because)*	

How?

as	as though
as if	

Under what condition? (or yes or no?)

although	if
as long as	though
even if	unless
even though	whether

This list is not complete, but it does contain most of the common tip-off words and phrases. Use it to help you do the exercises in this section.

Examples of adverb clauses

Here are some other sentences that contain adverb clauses.

Under what condition?

The infection can be stopped **if it is treated soon.**

When?

Franklin arrived **just before I did.**

Position of adverb clauses

The normal position of an adverb clause is after the independent clause whose verb it describes. This usually places the adverb clause at the end of the sentence.

They advertised their Christmas specials **as soon as Thanksgiving was over.**

Like other adverbs, adverb clauses can be moved easily to other places in the sentence.

As soon as Thanksgiving was over, they advertised their Christmas specials.

Exercise 5   Adverb clauses

In the following sentences, the adverb clauses have been printed in boldface type. Draw an arrow to show which word each clause modifies. Then tell which adverb question the adverb clause answers.

Example   <u>when</u>   **As soon as she sat down,** the audience

burst into applause.

_____ 1. He always says things like that **when he lectures.**

_____ 2. Sandra will call **after she finishes work.**

_____ 3. **Because the presentation was delayed,** Mr. Pritchard cut short his speech.

_____ 4. The purchase will take place **whether you approve or not.**

_____ 5. **If you release the choke,** the engine will start.

_____ 6. Mary won't speak out **unless she has to.**

_____ 7. We can leave **whenever you wish.**

_____ 8. Reporters were not allowed on the field **until after the plane landed.**

_____ 9. **Since they changed their plans,** they lost their deposit.

_____ 10. Salespeople, **when they speak too fast,** always make me suspicious.

Exercise 6   Adverb clauses

Mark each sentence completely.

Example

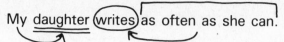My daughter writes as often as she can.

1. The product can be improved if they find more investors.

2. These reservations were made several weeks before the hotel opened.

3. Even though she is seventy-one, Mattie will enter college in the fall.

4. While Juan was in town, he visited his old school again.

5. Although Joe Wisniewski sold his property on Arrow Lake, he comes to see his friends there.

6. They found the cat when they looked near the garbage can.

7. I read several of those books because they were assigned in the humanities seminar.

8. Martin accepted the invitation so that he could meet her parents.

9. The prosecutor waited until the witness arrived.

10. As soon as you find the receipt, return the suitcase to the store.

Punctuating adverb clauses

Most of the time, adverb clauses are punctuated according to their position.

Punctuating Adverb Clauses

1. If the adverb clause is in normal position—that is, after the main clause whose verb it describes—it usually requires no special punctuation.
2. If the adverb clause is not in normal position, it is usually separated from the rest of the sentence with commas.

Adverb clauses that begin a sentence are always separated with commas. The following sentences illustrate the punctuation of adverb clauses.

Adverb clauses out of normal position

After they retired, my parents moved to California.

My parents, **after they retired,** moved to California.

Adverb clause in normal position

My parents moved to California **after they retired.**

Adverb clauses that begin with words like *although* or *even though* are separated from the rest of the sentence with commas, even though they are in their normal position.

Your questions will be answered tomorrow, **although many of them have been discussed before.**

This is because clauses beginning with *although* or *even though* contain information that is relatively unimportant—*extra* information.

Exercise 7   Punctuating adverb clauses

Punctuate each of the following sentences correctly. If a sentence is already correct, write **OK** in the margin.

Example

Until he took Dr. Sherman's class, James had never seen eighteen-century art.

1. We did well on the test although we had little time to study for it.

2. As you read this essay notice how the writer carefully explains each of his reasons.

3. If more capital had been available the manufacturers could have increased production.

4. We had to return early whether we wished to or not.

5. The machinery droned on as we spoke.

6. It can't hurt if you can't feel it.

7. Simonetta speaks as though she is practicing for the U. S. Senate.

8. You should be careful when you are away from home not to carry too much cash at one time.

9. This electronics book was outdated before it was published.

10. Ever since we sold the farm I have missed the smell of black earth.

Combining to create adjective and adverb clauses

Sentence combining can be used to create dependent clauses. For example, the following sentences can be combined so that one is an adjective clause.

> Carlos Ramirez has his own grocery business. He sponsors a Little League team for the neighborhood boys and girls.

Either of these clauses can be made dependent on the other. The question is, which clause should be the dependent clause and which the independent?

The answer depends on which clause the author considers more important. *The most important information should always go in the independent clause.* The two ways of combining these sentences are printed below.

> Carlos Ramirez, who has his own grocery business, sponsors a Little League team for the neighborhood boys and girls.
>
> Carlos Ramirez, who sponsors a Little League team for the neighborhood boys and girls, has his own grocery business.

Though these sentences contain the same information, they emphasize different ideas. Be careful to put the idea you consider most important in the independent clause of the sentence.

Exercise 8   Combining to create adjective and adverb clauses

Combine each of the following groups of sentences into one sentence containing at least one dependent adjective or adverb clause. Make sure that your new sentences are punctuated correctly.

Example

Dana had a very bad dream last week. She has not slept well since.

Dana, who had a very bad dream last week, has not slept well since.

1. The game is not going well. At the same time our team is losing more slowly than usual.

_____

_____

2. Mina cleans up the kitchen. Then she turns on her favorite TV program.

_____

_____

3. The new police promotion list mentions Sgt. Farraro. He used to work with the Sno Kings youth gang.

_____

_____

4. This cosmetic will be popular. It uses a new group of colors. The colors are absolutely nontoxic to the skin.

_____

_____

_____

5. Jerre won the tennis match. He had played very little tennis this year.

_____

_____

Noun clauses

Noun clauses act like nouns in a sentence. They can be anything nouns can be—subjects; objects of verbs, verbals, and prepositions; complements; and appositives. Compare the following sentences.

I know the **answer**.

I know **that the test is tomorrow**.

I know **where the dog hid his dish**.

In each sentence the main subject and verb are *I know*. Each verb is followed by an object that answers the object question *know what?* The first sentence has a one-word object *(answer)*. The next two sentences have clauses as objects: *that the test is tomorrow* and *where the dog hid his dish*. We know that these clauses act as objects because they answer the object question:

> **Object question**   know *what?*
>
> **Answer**   *that the test is tomorrow*

> **Object question**   know *what?*
>
> **Answer**   *where the dog hid his dish*

Each clause contains a subject and a verb (*test is* and *dog hid*), and each begins with a tip-off word (*that* and *where*).

Since these clauses act as objects, we know that they have to be noun clauses. (Don't let the tip-off word *where* fool you. *Where the dog hid his dish* is *not* an adverb clause. A clause that answers the object question is always a noun clause.)

Marking noun clauses

A noun clause is marked with a long bracket. Then an appropriate mark is added to show how the clause is used—an underscore for an object, a double underscore for a subject, and so on.

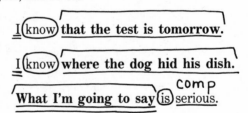

Tip-off words for noun clauses

The most common tip-off word for noun clauses is *that* (used as a conjunction). Other conjunctions used as noun clause tip-off words are printed below.

Tip-off Words for Noun Clauses
Group 1: Conjunctions

how	that
when	(phrases like
where	*certain that* and
why	*afraid that*)
whether	

Pronouns and adjectives can also introduce noun clauses. Unlike conjunctions, these words always have a function within the dependent clause.

Tip-off Words for Noun Clauses
Group 2: Pronouns and Adjectives

who	whoever
whom	whomever
what	whatever
which	whichever

You'll recall that the object form of *who* is *whom*. Choose the correct form of these words based on how they are used in the noun clause. *Who* should be used as a subject or a complement, and *whom* should be used as an object.

Examples of noun clauses

Here are other sentences that contain noun clauses.

Noun clauses as subjects

How we won is still a mystery.
Whichever job you choose is fine with me.

Noun clause as object of verb

We never discovered **why Abraham moved to New York.**

Noun clause as object of preposition

Danny still thinks about **when they met.**

Noun clause as complement

We were **what you wanted us to be.**

Punctuation and position of noun clauses

Noun clauses appear in the same position as a one-word noun. There is no special position rule for noun clauses.

The most common use of noun clauses is in **indirect quotations**—quotations that rephrase a writer's words slightly. The usual tip-off word for indirect quotations is *that.*

Audrey said **that she would be in the office later today.**

Said is the main verb of this sentence. What she said appears in the noun clause, which acts as the object of the verb. (Notice that the speaker's actual words were probably "I will be in the office later today.")

This sentence, by the way, is the equivalent of a three-word sentence. The whole noun clause acts like a one-word object.

1   2   3

Audrey (said) that she would be in the office later today.

Exercise 9   Noun clauses

In the following sentences, the noun clauses have been printed in boldface type. On the lines provided, tell how each noun clause is used.

Example   _object_   I suppose **that you want to borrow my book again.**

                      1. **How much you revise your work** is your decision.

                      2. Then he mentioned **that the exam schedule had been changed.**

                      3. **That you are an honorable man** is well known.

                      4. We can plan the meeting for **whenever you are free.**

                      5. **How Stan gets to the game** is his decision.

                      6. Cynthia told them **whatever they wanted to hear.**

Exercise 10   Noun clauses

Mark each sentence completely.

Example   Jennifer (hoped) that she would get the scholarship.

1. How much your uncle owned is still in question.

2. Alain saw why the ship was rocking so much.

3. After the barbecue, Sheree's father announced that he would retire during the summer.

4. They offered her whatever salary she wanted.

5. Johansen hoped that everything had gone well at the interview.

Noun clauses that weaken sentences

As you have seen in the examples discussed so far, sentences containing noun clauses can be strong and effective sentences.

But many sentences with noun clauses are wordy and weak, and they need to be revised. For instance, many rough-draft sentences place their main idea in a noun clause. Take a look at this sentence.

Weak

What I really mean to say is **that Congress should reconsider its decision.**

Notice how poorly this sentence begins. After eight words we still don't know what the author wants to tell us. The main idea begins with *Congress*.

Now notice the construction of this sentence. *That Congress should reconsider its decision* is a dependent noun clause. Whenever possible, the main idea of a sentence should appear in the main, or the independent, clause.

This sentence could easily be corrected. Simply change the noun clause to an independent clause by eliminating the weak beginning (and the tip-off word).

Stronger

Congress should reconsider its decision.

Sentences like this often occur in rough drafts since the purpose of a rough draft is simply to get ideas down on paper. But such sentences cannot be left unchanged. When you are revising and editing, watch carefully for sentences with weak openings and redraft them when you find them.

Exercise 11   Editing weak sentence openings

Correct any sentence below that contains a weak sentence opening. Write **OK** in the margins of any correct sentences.

Example

I really think that the Civil War was fought for economic reasons.

The Civil War was fought for economic reasons.

1. It seems to me that the Los Angeles Herald Times has an excellent sports staff.

_____

_____

2. The council waited until midnight for the queen's apology.

_____

_____

3. I want to tell you that the Italian Renaissance was more revolutionary than you probably imagine.

_____

_____

4. The author states that the Italian Renaissance was more revolutionary than usually imagined.

_____

_____

5. It is a fact that the history of the Southwest is a history of repeated conquest.

_____

_____

6. It's probably true that campaign promises rarely produce social changes.

_____

_____

Review exercise 1

Mark each sentence in the following paragraph completely. (This passage is taken from James Thurber's "Hell Only Breaks Loose Once," a parody of James M. Cain's suspense novel, *The Postman Only Rings Twice.*)

They kicked me out of college when I was about twenty-seven. I went up to see the Dean and tried to hand him a couple of laughs, but it was no good. He said he couldn't put me back in college, but I could hang around the office and sweep out and wash windows. I figured I'd better be rambling, and I said I had a couple of other offers. He told me to sit down and think it over, so I sat down.

Then she came in the room. She was tall and thin and had a white frowning forehead and soft eyes. She wasn't much to look at, but she was something to think about. As far as she and I were concerned, he wasn't in the room. She leaned over the chair where I was sitting and bit me in the ear.[1]

Review exercise 2

Correct any incorrect punctuation in the following paragraph.

When the wind stopped howling Luke opened his eyes. He could not believe, what had just happened. Heavy furniture was overturned, and a huge bookcase, that once covered a wall, was lying next to him. All of his books which had been so neatly arranged covered the floor. Luke had known how quickly tornadoes can strike. He should have started for the basement, as soon as he heard that warning on the radio. He realized, that he was lucky to be alive. Because he didn't know what else to do he just sat

1. James Thurber, "Hell Only Breaks Loose Once," in *The Middle-Aged Man on the Flying Trapeze* (New York: Universal Library/Grosset & Dunlap, 1935), p. 121.

quietly under the desk for a while. Then he suddenly remembered Eric whose house was under construction. How to call Eric, was the problem.

Review exercise 3

The following paragraphs are composed mainly of simple sentences. Use sentence combining and editing to create coordinate and subordinate clauses and other sentence elements. Remove weak sentence openings.

After you have rewritten the paragraph, reread your version carefully and correct any errors in punctuation.

What many scientists believed for years was this. Primitive human beings learned to stand upright after learning to use tools. But Donald Johanson disproved that theory. He was a scientist. Digging in Ethiopia, he discovered a skeleton of an early prehuman being. It was three million years old.

The creature whose skeleton Johanson found had clearly walked upright. It had walked upright more than a million years before the earliest known tools.

This prehuman creature was given the name "Lucy." Scientists still argue about Lucy. Most discoveries and new ideas cause disagreements among scientists. They divide scientists into supporters and opponents. Nevertheless, Lucy is strong evidence. You can see that it supports Johanson's theory. His theory will stand. It will stand at least until new and different discoveries are made.

_____

_____

_____

_____

_____

_____

_____

_____

_____

_____

_____

_____

_____

_____

_____

Chapter 16 writing assignment

1. Write a short paragraph (about half a page) that defines "maturity." Make some notes that help you plan what you want to say before you actually begin writing the paragraph. This word is not as easy to define as it might first appear.
2. Reread your paragraph carefully and correct any errors. Combine and edit your sentences so that your paragraph flows smoothly.

17. Sentence fragments

Every sentence must contain at least one independent clause. Any sentence that doesn't contain an independent clause is not a real sentence; it's a **fragment** of a sentence. Fragments, whether intentional or not, are usually considered incorrect in formal writing.

Fragments occur when dependent clauses are punctuated as sentences by themselves. Fragments also occur when any part of a sentence that does not contain a subject and verb is punctuated like a complete sentence. Verbal phrases are common fragments. Prepositional phrases and adverb phrases can also be fragments if punctuated by themselves as sentences. *Any* group of words that does not contain an independent clause is a fragment.

Fragments from dependent clauses

Sometimes dependent clauses or phrases that contain dependent clauses are punctuated incorrectly as separate sentences. Dependent clauses contain tip-off words that connect them to something else. They cannot be sentences by themselves.

The following example shows a dependent clause that has been incorrectly punctuated as a sentence.

Fragment from dependent clause

Until we get to a gas station. We will have to drive slowly.

Until we get to a gas station is a dependent clause; its tip-off word is *until*. It cannot be a separate sentence. We can correct this fragment by combining it with the sentence that follows. We replace the period at the end of the fragment with a comma and make the first letter of *We* a small letter.

Sentence with dependent clause

Until we get to a gas station, we will have to drive slowly.

Since the adverb clause begins the sentence, it is set off by a comma.

Exercise 1   Fragments from dependent clauses

Correct any incorrect punctuation in the following, changing capital letters to small letters where needed. If an item is already correct, write **OK** in the margin.

Example

My brother earns extra money by driving a thrift store truck, ~~E~~ven though the job forces him to take all his classes in the morning and evening.

1. I cannot give you a good reason. Why I think Valentia deliberately endangered herself.

2. Several men who work for the county have been using publicly owned construction equipment. Which is supposed to be reserved for highway maintenance.

3. I did not see him. He was not there.

4. You can have. Whatever you want.

5. If the constitution is not approved. Two of the political parties will go underground.

6. The rangers reacted quickly. As soon as they received the call. One of them was on his way to the campsite.

7. The exercise program was to be canceled. Unless more people signed up for it.

8. The tapes that you hold in your hand. Belong to the radio station.

9. The teller was informed. That the checks had just been delivered.

10. She took a job in Chicago. Because her brother lived nearby.

Fragments from verbal phrases

As noted earlier, verbal phrases are common fragments. Here is an example:

Fragment from verbal phrase

My roommate was asked by his sister. **To answer each of the cards.**

Notice that the verbal *to answer* is not a verb and does not have a subject.
   These fragments are corrected like those from dependent clauses—by changing the punctuation between the fragment and the rest of the sentence.

Sentence with verbal phrase

My roommate was asked by his sister **to answer each of the cards.**

Exercise 2   Fragments from verbal phrases

Correct any incorrect punctuation in the following. If a sentence is already correct, write **OK** in the margin.

Example   To be believed completely, He would tell any lie.

1. Finding his first route blocked by house plants. Simon stumbled into the dining room by mistake.

2. A window stood open. To let in the afternoon air.

3. Steadman left to attend graduate school. It was his goal all along.

4. The cattlemen's desire to protect open land. Ultimately resulted, surprisingly, in an even faster closing of the only grazing range in the north country.

5. I heard a morning thrush. Singing to attract a mate.

6. The cultural exchange produced excellent results. Several students agreed to return the following year.

7. The regulation was intended. To reduce paperwork. It seems to be working.

8. A set of armor kept in the museum basement. Once belonged to a Spanish prince.

9. The show first aired in 1967. Only to be removed after a two-week run.

10. They applied a titration technique. To remove all excess xenium required three applications.

Exercise 3   Repunctuating fragments

Rewrite the following paragraph on the lines provided, correcting all fragments.

The boardinghouse had a good reputation. Which meant a lot in those years. It sat on the east end of Forest Avenue. Near the entrance to Arnold Park. It was a big, old house. With a very friendly landlord. I took a room there in 1936. After I first moved north from St. Louis. My job required me to commute to the downtown business district. Mornings I rode the ''L'' train. Which stopped, I recall, two blocks down from the boardinghouse. It took me to the old Goldblatt Building. Where I worked as an accountant. I didn't make much money, but I worked. In the evenings it was back to the boardinghouse. The house was a lot safer than a lot of places. That I could have ended up in. Besides, the jazz clubs weren't so far away. That I couldn't get out when I wanted to. Anyway, I survived.

_____

_____

_____

_____

_____

Fragments from verbal phrases   239

_____

_____

_____

_____

_____

_____

_____

_____

_____

_____

Rewriting fragments

Some fragments are not made simply by incorrect punctuation but by incomplete writing. A group of words that was intended to be a complete sentence lacks a subject, a verb, or both. Longer sentences most often contain this error, as in the example below.

Fragment

The reason that the legislature must come up with a different plan for raising state revenue.

This fragment is not a sentence because it does not contain a verb. It can be corrected by adding a verb and all the additional material needed to complete the thought.

Complete sentence

The _reason_ that the legislature must come up with a different plan

for raising state revenue (is) the lack of public support for Senator

Stewart's bill.

You'll notice, however, that the main verb is now the weak _is_. To create a stronger, more interesting sentence, you may want to think of another main verb and rewrite the sentence a bit.

The <u>lack</u> of public support for Senator Stewart's bill (has forced) the

legislature to come up with a different plan for raising state

revenue.

Remember to use active, informative verbs whenever possible.

Exercise 4 Rewriting fragments

Rewrite each of the following fragments in two different ways.

1. The promotion recently foretold by a fortune gypsy from Hyde Park.

A. _____

_____

_____

B. _____

_____

_____

2. Large baskets containing rolls and bread ready to be delivered by the bakery to the stores.

A. _____

_____

_____

B. _____

_____

_____

3. A discovery of importance shaking up the field of nuclear physics.

A. _____

_____

_____

B. _____

_____

_____

4. The work of a dozen Rembrandts-to-be on display along the warm pavements of Berkeley Street.

A. _____

_____

_____

B. _____

_____

_____

5. A stack of dishes left unwashed in the sink for too long.

A. _____

_____

_____

B. _____

_____

_____

Review exercise

Correct all fragments in the following paragraphs. Combine and revise your sentences as you think necessary. Then write your final version on the lines provided.

Many music videos have interesting directors. And sometimes famous ones. Movie people like John Landis, Tim Hutton, and John Sayles. All have directed videos. So have others. As more Hollywood names get involved in the video business. Music videos get increasingly more expensive. And elaborate. Often look like full-scale Hollywood productions.

On the other hand, there is this point. Because the connection between Hollywood and popular music is so strong. Music stars are becoming movie stars. David Bowie and Sting have already made the switch. Moved from one field of entertainment to another. People see singers involved in elaborate videos. And readily accept them as actors. The acting ability of some music people is amazingly good. And sometimes amazingly bad.

_____

_____

_____

_____

_____

_____

_____

_____

_____

Chapter 17 writing assignment

1. Make a list that compares the singing styles of two popular musicians.
2. Write a short paragraph (about half a page) in which you present and discuss this information.
3. Reread your paragraph carefully and correct any errors. Combine and edit your sentences so that your paragraph flows smoothly.

Section VI

Paragraphs

Though writing good sentences is necessary to all good writing, sentences usually do not stand alone. They are most often parts of paragraphs and longer units of writing, such as essays.

   The next two chapters will discuss the basics of good paragraph writing. The simplest essay is one paragraph in length, and the rules of paragraph structure can apply to longer essays as well.

18. Writing paragraphs

Just as a random collection of words is not a sentence, a random collection of sentences is not a paragraph. A **paragraph** is a group of sentences that are combined to make a point.

There is a kind of "grammar" to a good paragraph, a structure that ties the sentences together in a certain relationship and gives meaning to the whole. Every paragraph that is complete in itself—in other words, every one-paragraph essay—must contain three main parts:

> a main idea
> support for the main idea
> a closing that feels like an ending

Let's look at these parts one at a time.

The main idea

A **main idea** for a paragraph or essay is any thought that

1. can be proved and
2. is worth discussing.

The following are valid main ideas:

Main ideas

Each of my high school science teachers influenced my career choice.

My friend Barry's behavior is an example of good sportsmanship.

This newspaper article is well written.

Exrox makes better office equipment than Ipindoc.

All of these main ideas are provable, and some can be proved in more than one way. In addition, it is not difficult to imagine someone wanting to discuss them or learn about them.

Each of these main ideas has two important elements. Each states a **subject,** or **topic,** to be discussed, and each offers an **opinion** about that subject.

Subject	each of my high school teachers
Opinion	influenced my career choice
Subject	my friend Barry's behavior
Opinion	is an example of good sportsmanship
Subject	this newspaper article
Opinion	is well written
Subject 1	Exrox
Opinion	makes better office equipment
Subject 2	than Ipindoc

Notice that the subject of the main idea is often, but not always, the grammatical subject of the main idea sentence.

A sentence that states only a subject, or topic, cannot be a main idea. Without an opinion, there is nothing to prove. The following sentences are not main ideas. They either lack an opinion or state an opinion not worth discussing or proving.

NOT main ideas

My brother is six feet tall.

Arizona became a state in 1912.

If you cut all your classes, you will probably get bad grades.

Every main idea contains a subject and an opinion worth discussing. A main idea without these elements makes a poor foundation for an essay.

Personal and impersonal writing

Some main ideas, and some essays, are about people and events in our own lives. They are derived from the writer's personal experiences. The writer is prominently featured in this kind of writing. Family, school, work, recreation, romance—all can become main ideas in personal paragraphs and essays.

Two of the sample main ideas in the examples given on pages 246–247 introduce personal essays.

Personal main ideas

Each of my high school science teachers influenced my career choice.

My friend Barry's behavior is an example of good sportsmanship.

Other main ideas do not deal directly with the writer and his or her life. They are about people, things, and ideas that the writer is thinking about, but there are few, if any, references to the writer as a person in the essay.

The following main ideas, also from the examples on pages 246–247, could introduce impersonal essays.

Impersonal main ideas

The newspaper article is well written.

Exrox makes better office equipment than Ipindoc.

The writer of these essays would not have to mention himself or herself at all.

Most of the paragraph assignments in this book have focused on personal main ideas since such paragraphs are easier to write at first. As you progress in college and in the business world, however, you will find that the ability to write impersonal essays becomes more and more important. The rules of good paragraph and essay writing are the same for both personal and impersonal work.

Exercise 1   Subject and opinion in main ideas

Each of the following is a good main idea for an essay. Indicate which portion of the sentence states the **subject** and which states the **opinion**.

Example   Student elections should be delayed until after the trial.

Subject _student elections_

Opinion _should be delayed until after the trial_

1. Early marriage can create many problems.

   Subject _____

   Opinion _____

2. Many former members of this fraternity hold highly respected professional positions.

   Subject _____

   Opinion _____

3. The incumbent mayor will probably win re-election in June.

Subject _____

Opinion _____

4. The money from the cable television company influenced his vote.

Subject _____

Opinion _____

5. The prices for these apartments are too high.

Subject _____

Opinion _____

6. Although they are different in many ways, Mr. Jonas and Ms. Henderson have similar teaching styles.

Subject _____

Opinion _____

7. Although Mr. Jonas and Ms. Henderson have similar teaching styles, they are different in many ways.

Subject _____

Opinion _____

8. Twenty million dollars was hard to raise in the latest effort.

Subject _____

Opinion _____

9. Other opinions should have been sought.

Subject _____

Opinion _____

10. My skiing trips have all been unique and memorable experiences.

Subject _____

Opinion _____

Exercise 2   Identifying main ideas

Five of the following sentences could be main ideas for paragraphs and five could not. Write **YES** next to those that could be main ideas, and **NO** next to those that could not.

Example   ____YES____   Getting good grades can help you get a good job.

_____   **1.** The recent weather is likely to break several records.

_____   **2.** The temperature on September 12 was 107 degrees.

_____   **3.** This house is an excellent buy.

_____   **4.** I will need a car to drive to Florida during spring break.

_____   **5.** Jay Abbott spent most of his life behind bars.

_____   **6.** Your best investment advice will probably not come from your banker.

_____   **7.** Franklin Roosevelt did not create the "Democratic coalition" by himself.

_____   **8.** This cafe has been awarded two stars by the Collegiate Diners' Association.

_____ **9.** The play presented a very realistic view of alcoholism.

_____ **10.** Life had been especially kind to Joan Walstonberg.

Exercise 3   Writing main ideas

Write five main ideas for paragraphs.

1. _____

_____

2. _____

_____

3. _____

_____

4. _____

_____

5. _____

_____

Supporting the main idea

The main idea is the foundation on which a paragraph is built. It states what the writer believes to be true. Once the writer has stated a main idea, he or she must prove that the main idea is correct.

This is done with **supporting ideas.** Supporting ideas are the writer's evidence that the main idea is correct. Without supporting ideas, there is no paragraph; there is only a statement of the writer's opinion.

Supporting evidence can be of many types, including any or all of the following:

       physical descriptions
       stories
       examples
       comparisons

discussion or analysis of a cause and effect relationship
discussion or analysis of a process
definitions
division of a large group into smaller ones
statistical evidence
quotations from authorities
logical and reasonable arguments

Examples of these kinds of supporting evidence will be pointed out in the rest of this chapter. Many of the writing assignments you have been doing have already required you to present supporting details similar to those on this list.

The following paragraphs show the relationship between main ideas and supporting ideas. In the first example, the supporting ideas are descriptions of Annette Dula's state of mind. This description helps convince us that her first statement is true, that she cannot escape her emotional ties to America.

Main idea

    I am not patriotic, but I am a product of America. I believe in freedom of speech, even if it is only token. I take education for granted though we may

Supporting ideas

not receive it equally. I believe in the working of democracy even though it never seems to work. I am forced to accept that I am an American and that here in America lie my cultural roots—whether I like it or not.[1]

In the next example, George Orwell uses both storytelling and description to convince us that his point is true, that as he walked with a man about to be hanged, he saw for the first time that life is important for its own sake.

Main idea

    It is curious, but till that moment I had never realized what it means to destroy a healthy, conscious man. When I saw the prisoner step aside to avoid the puddle, I saw the mystery, the unspeakable wrongness, of cutting a life short when it is in full tide. This man was not dying, he was alive just as we are alive. All the organs of his body were working—bowels digesting food, skin renewing itself, nails growing, tissues forming—all toiling away in sol-

Supporting ideas

emn foolery. His nails would still be growing when he stood on the drop, when he was falling through the air with a tenth-of-a-second to live. His eyes saw the yellow gravel and the grey walls, and his brain still remembered, foresaw, reasoned—reasoned even about puddles. He and we were a party of men walking together, seeing, hearing, feeling, understanding the same world; and in two minutes, with a sudden snap, one of us would be gone—one mind less, one world less.[2]

Exercise 4   Writing supporting ideas

Write a few connected sentences of support for the following main ideas as though they were your own. Then tell what kind of support you are providing. (Use the list on pages 251–252 to guide you.)

1. Annette Dula, "No Home in Africa," *New York Times*, 27 July 1975.
2. George Orwell, "A Hanging," in *Shooting an Elephant and Other Essays* (New York: Harcourt Brace Jovanovich, 1956).

1. The view from the bridge is peaceful.

_____

_____

_____

_____

_____

_____

2. Many employees find themselves in situations that test their honesty.

_____

_____

_____

_____

_____

3. Most of the films released today fall into two groups.

_____

_____

_____

_____

_____

4. It's not as difficult as you might think to learn to dance well.

_____

_____

_____

_____

_____

_____

5. Mrs. Hendrix, my piano teacher, is often too picky.

_____

_____

_____

_____

_____

_____

The closing

Every paragraph and essay that is complete in itself has an effective closing, something that makes the reader feel that the writer is finished.

Effective closings include any of the following:

1. a summary or restatement of the main idea
2. a conclusion that can be drawn, now that the main idea has been proved
3. the repetition of a key phrase from the beginning of the work
4. a particularly effective supporting detail that feels like an ending

The most common closing for paragraphs is actually the last one listed above—the supporting detail that feels like an ending.

Let's look at the closings of the two paragraphs quoted earlier in this chapter. The closing of Annette Dula's paragraph is a restatement of the main idea.

Main idea   I am not patriotic, but I am a product of America. I believe in freedom of speech even if it is only token. I take education for granted though we may not

Supporting ideas   receive it equally. I believe in the working of democracy even though it never seems to work. I am forced to accept that I am an American and that here in

Closing   America lie my cultural roots—whether I like it or not.

George Orwell's closing states a conclusion based on the main idea, followed by a final—and very effective—detail from the story of a prisoner and his guards on the way to the gallows.

Main idea   It is curious, but till that moment I had never realized what it means to destroy a healthy, conscious man. When I saw the prisoner step aside to avoid

Supporting ideas

the puddle, I saw the mystery, the unspeakable wrongness, of cutting a life short when it is in full tide. This man was not dying, he was alive just as we are alive. All the organs of his body were working—bowels digesting food, skin renewing itself, nails growing, tissues forming—all toiling away in solemn foolery. His nails would still be growing when he stood on the drop, when he was falling through the air with a tenth-of-a-second to live. His eyes saw the yellow gravel and the grey walls, and his brain still remembered, foresaw, reasoned—reasoned even about puddles. He and we were a party of men walking together, seeing, hearing, feeling, understanding the same world;

Closing

and in two minutes, with a sudden snap, one of us would be gone—one mind less, one world less.[2]

The paragraph patterns

These main parts of a paragraph can be arranged in a certain number of ways. These arrangements are called **paragraph patterns.**

The most common are the **basic pattern** and the **suspended pattern.** Each starts in the same way—with a statement of the subject of the essay. Each places its body of support in the middle of the paragraph. They differ only in the placement of the main idea.

The basic paragraph pattern

The basic pattern places the main idea where most people would expect to find it—in the introduction of the paragraph, right before the supporting ideas.

The Basic Paragraph Pattern

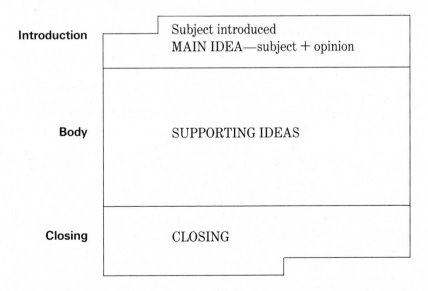

Introduction — Subject introduced
MAIN IDEA—subject + opinion

Body — SUPPORTING IDEAS

Closing — CLOSING

The basic pattern is illustrated in the paragraph that follows.

Introduction	A popular item for tourist shoppers in New York City is a poster originally designed as a cover for *The New Yorker* magazine by the artist Saul Stein-
Main idea	berg. It depicts the world, or at least the West, as seen from the blinkered per- spective of a Manhattanite. Most of the foreground is taken up by Ninth and
	Tenth Avenues, bordered by the Hudson River. New Jersey gets a good deal of
Body (descriptive details)	space; but beyond that, the Middle West is vaguely defined, with obscure places such as Nebraska given uncertain location. The hump of California is depicted with more confidence, bounded on the other side by the Pacific
Closing (final descriptive detail)	Ocean, dotted with some nameless islands against a distant backdrop of China and Japan.[3]

The suspended paragraph pattern

    The suspended pattern places the main idea at the end of the paragraph. There the main idea also serves as a conclusion, since it sums up the ideas that come before.

The Suspended Paragraph Pattern

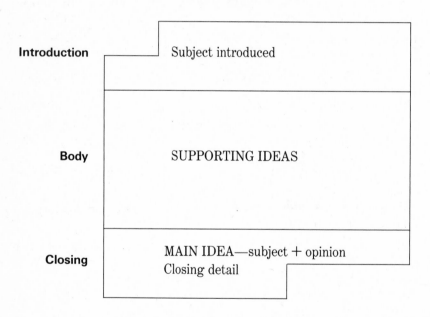

Introduction	Subject introduced
Body	SUPPORTING IDEAS
Closing	MAIN IDEA—subject + opinion Closing detail

    The following paragraph uses the suspended pattern and places the main idea at the end.

Introduction (subject stated)	For half a lifetime, Cyrus Vance had access to the innermost secrets of the American intelligence-gathering machine, which, for $15 billion a year, has concluded that Soviet military power presented a clear and growing threat to the United States. In 1982 Vance took a $3 cab ride across midtown Manhat- tan. His driver was a recent Soviet émigré. Like most Soviet males, he had served a two-year draft period in the armed forces. They talked about the

3. Andrew Cockburn, *The Threat: Inside the Soviet Military Machine* (New York: Random House, 1983), p. 3.

Body (supports main idea with a story) driver's experiences in a tank unit during that time. It was Vance's first opportunity to hear the description of the Soviet threat from the inside, and it was very different from what the secret intelligence briefings had been telling him all along. Vance was surprised to hear that the living conditions of the men were deplorable and that the training for the crews was bad at best. It

Closing (= main idea) sounded like a very different Soviet army from the one depicted by the intelligence briefers over the years.[4]

Review exercise

Mark the **parts** of each of the following paragraphs (introduction, main idea, supporting ideas, closing) by adding horizontal brackets to the text and labeling each part in the margin.

A. Pattern: _____

The rough draft [of a script] is your first attempt to assemble all the elements on which you have been working, to bring order out of chaos. Now your characters must move into action; now they must speak through your dialog. Open the floodgates of your imagination. Write this draft without revisions or polishing and don't plague yourself about its literary quality. If something does not seem quite right, despite your painstaking planning, leave it and plow right along. Bring your work to the climax you have chosen for it.[5]

B. Pattern: _____

Houses are like sentinels in the plain—old keepers of the weather watch. There, in a very little while, wood takes on the appearance of great age. All colors wear soon away in the wind and

---

4. Ibid., pp. 21–22.
5. Constance Nash and Virginia Oakey, *The Television Writer's Handbook* (New York: Barnes & Noble Books, 1978), p. 59.

Review exercise   257

rain, and then the wood is burned gray and the grain appears and the nails turn red with rust. The windowpanes are black and opaque; you imagine there is nothing within, and indeed there are many ghosts, bones given up to the land. They stand here and there against the sky, and you approach them for a longer time than you expect. They belong in the distance; it is their domain.[6]

C. Pattern: _____

The view from the windshield is this: There's that three-to-six-story-high screen, on which titanic monsters or car crashes of megaton explosiveness suddenly appear. Hundreds of vehicles are lined up like pigs before a trough, grunting their approval—horns honking, tape decks blaring, an odd rocket arching toward the screen. If you look past the speaker hung from your window, you gaze on the Texas moon riding high above this most remarkable celebration; you note hibachi campfires, smoke rising from barbequed ribs, lawn chairs planted in the beds of pickup trucks, hammocks strung between speaker poles, patrons splayed out on blankets atop cars, and a Western Rocky Horror punk fest of sixteen-year-olds crowded around the concession stand. You smell pot sweeping through the night, sweet as sagebrush. And all around you Texans are mating. That's summertime at the drive-in movies in, say, Dallas.[7]

---

6. N. Scott Momaday, *The Way to Rainy Mountain* (Albuquerque: University of New Mexico Press, 1969), p. 10.
7. Toby Thompson, "The Twilight of the Drive-In," *American Film*, July/August 1983.

Chapter 18 writing assignment

1. Write a main idea for a paragraph describing the special place you consider your hideaway. Remember that the main idea must contain an opinion about this place. (Often the opinion in a description tells how the place makes the writer feel or explains the visual or emotional impression it makes.)
2. Then jot down a few physical details that support this main idea.
3. Choose an order in which to present these details.
4. Turn these notes into a short descriptive paragraph (about half a page).
5. Check to see that your paragraph really is a paragraph—a group of sentences that, taken together, prove something. Then revise it at least once to make the sentences clearer and to correct any errors.
6. Your instructor may ask that you turn in all copies of your work.

19. The writing process

An efficient way to write is to use the **writing process.** This method divides writing into three stages of activity:

1. thinking and planning
2. writing the rough draft
3. preparing the final copy—revising, editing, and so forth

The first stage is the most important one. If you spend enough time and effort on the thinking and planning stage, you can greatly reduce the time you spend on the second and third stages.

Planning your writing

In the last chapter, you were asked to plan a piece of descriptive writing in a certain way. First you were asked to write a main idea. Then you were asked to make a short list of details that supported your opinion and to choose an order for the items in that list. Finally, you wrote a rough draft.

This kind of planning is important in writing. It's almost impossible to write a rough draft without knowing

1. what you are trying to prove and
2. how you are going to prove it.

To decide on these two essentials, some writers make notes that lead to an outline. Others do something called "clustering." They put the subject of the essay in the center of a blank page and then fill the page with ideas that seem related to the subject. This technique helps writers find a group of ideas that can be structured as an essay. Sometimes a writer decides on a main idea first and then gathers the evidence or arguments that support it. Sometimes a writer gathers the facts first and then decides what they prove. Any of these methods can work well.

Writers have even been known to plan out their ideas by writing rough draft after rough draft, until they find one that makes sense. This method, though, is obviously the slowest and should be avoided whenever possible. For one thing, it is an inefficient use of your time. For another, it tempts you to turn in an unsuccessful draft simply because so much work has already gone into it.

Writing a summary page

Some planning—done on paper, not just in your head—should go into every paragraph you write. At the very least, your notes should include a **summary page,** a piece of scratch paper listing

1. your main idea and
2. your supporting details or arguments, in the order you wish to use them.

The summary page should be logical. The main idea should contain something that can be proved, and the supporting details should truly support the main idea. These details should be mentioned in the most effective order—one that sustains the reader's interest and allows one idea to lead logically to the next.

The more logical this summary is, the better your rough draft will be and the less rewriting you will have to do. Any notes you make to help produce this summary will save you time later on.

For example, suppose you are writing a paragraph about how kind some person is. You might decide to prove that opinion with a few brief stories. But which ones should you use?

You could select the first three stories that come into your head. This will produce a fast summary page but probably not the best one.

On the other hand, you might make a list of ten stories that could prove your point. Then, by selecting the best three, you will produce a very strong essay. (Imagine how much time you'd waste if the three best stories occurred to you only after the rough draft was mostly written.)

Do whatever works for you. Just keep in mind that your goal is to produce high quality work with a minimum of wasted effort.

Exercise 1   Planning your writing

Make whatever notes it takes to produce a summary page for a paragraph on *each* of the following subjects. Be sure that your main idea is listed clearly. Remember that your main idea should include something to prove or discuss. Use a separate sheet of paper for each summary page.

1. playing amateur sports

2. how to study

3. the three major causes of racial disharmony

4. the condition of the inside of my car

Writing the rough draft

Writing the rough draft is the simplest part of the writing process. If you have planned your paragraph carefully, the rough draft will almost write itself. That's the test, in fact, of good planning. A rough draft that becomes a struggle is probably not well planned.

Two general rules apply to rough draft writing:

1. Try to write the rough draft in one sitting and without interruption.
2. Do not edit your rough draft sentences as long as they contain some version of the idea you need.

Apply these rules to the rough drafts you will write in the following exercise.

Exercise 2

Writing the rough draft

Choose the two most successful summaries from Exercise 1 and, using the lines below, turn them into rough drafts.

From summary number _____

_____

_____

_____

_____

_____

_____

_____

_____

_____

From summary number _____

_____

_____

_____

_____

_____

_____

_____

_____

_____

_____

Writing the final version

These steps will help you remake your rough draft into the final version of your paragraph or essay:

1. revising to improve the logical structure of your work
2. editing to improve the clarity and correctness of your sentences
3. creating a clean, attractive, readable final copy

Each of these steps will be discussed below.

Revising to improve structure

Revising to improve structure means rereading and correcting your rough draft to make sure that all parts fit together smoothly and logically. In particular, it means answering the following questions:

1. What is the main idea?
2. What is the subject stated in the main idea?

3. What is the opinion stated in the main idea?
4. Are the supporting details presented in the best order?
5. Do ALL supporting details help prove the main idea?

If you have trouble answering any of these questions, fix the paragraph or essay before going on to the next step.

Exercise 3 Revising to improve structure

Answer the following questions for each of the rough drafts you produced in Exercise 2. Then, on a separate sheet of paper, rewrite each rough draft as necessary to correct any errors in structure.

Rough draft 1:

1. What is the main idea?

_____

_____

2. What is the subject stated in the main idea?

_____

_____

3. What is the opinion stated in the main idea?

_____

_____

4. Are the supporting details presented in the best order? (Tell why you think so or don't think so.)

_____

_____

_____

_____

5. Do ALL supporting details help prove the main idea? (Tell why you think so or don't think so.)

_____

_____

_____

_____

Rough draft 2:

1. What is the main idea?

_____

_____

2. What is the subject stated in the main idea?

_____

_____

3. What is the opinion stated in the main idea?

_____

_____

4. Are the supporting details presented in the best order? (Tell why you think so or don't think so.)

_____

_____

_____

5. Do ALL supporting details help prove the main idea? (Tell why you think so or don't think so.)

_____

_____

_____

_____

Editing sentences

If the structure of your paragraph or essay is sound, you can begin editing your sentences.

All rough drafts need sentence editing. In fact, writing a rough draft means that you have put off editing sentences until the end.

When you edit sentences, you alter their wording so that

1. sentences flow smoothly from one to the other. (This refers both to the flow of ideas and the sentences' rhythm and sound.)
2. individual sentences are

> clear
> concise
> correct
> graceful and pleasing to read.

Not all these goals are met easily. Some writers, including the writer of this book, take years to improve their editing skills.

For the time being, you are asked to edit in order to make your sentences **clear, concise,** and **correct.**

Clarity

Clear writing is writing that is easily understood. Unclear writing results from two main causes—misused words and awkward sentence structure.

The following sentences contain errors of clarity.

Misused words

Reality could be believed from watching that film.

Corrected

The film reflected reality.

The film was believable.

In the first example, both *reality* and *believed* are misused. Reality is not something that can be believed or disbelieved. The writer meant to say that the film seemed real to him or her; the corrected examples do say that simply and concisely.

Awkward construction

If you would read this draft I would appreciate it and add your comments for me.

Corrected

If you would read this draft and add your comments, I would appreciate it.

The first sentence suggests that the writer *(I)* will add the comments. Obviously, the second version is what the writer really meant.

Exercise 4   Editing for clarity

Each of the following sentences is unclear. Rewrite each one so that the meaning is clear.

Example   Antonio will follow to us very soon.

<u>Antonio will follow us very soon.</u>

1. He let himself in and made himself at home petting the cat and to read the newspaper.

  _____

  _____

2. Yelling started up again but ended in friendly laughing as they all sat around looking at each in a very caring way for each other.

  _____

  _____

3. About twelve o'clock on the sliding door we heard a knock.

  _____

  _____

4. Last Friday on the way to school I nearly fell asleep on the road.

  _____

  _____

5. I was starting to get afraid so I called with great anticipation for any news.

  _____

  _____

6. Later I saw her talking to Susan which put a bias opinion in my heart.

  _____

  _____

7. At eight o'clock she picked me up, being only fifteen minutes late.

_____

_____

8. She is generous to give, love, hope, and care very much.

_____

_____

9. I have an employee that sounds like she is frustrated.

_____

_____

10. Everything that is obvious about her supports the image of the cosmopolitan girl on the go.

_____

_____

Conciseness

Concise writing states an idea with a minimum of unnecessary words. This does not mean that every sentence should be short. But no sentence should be wordy or repetitious. Let's look at some examples:

Not concise

It's really easy to see that the writer's goal in writing this short story is to write about his relationship with his father when he was a child and growing up at home.

Corrected

This short story deals with the writer's early relationship with his father.

Notice how the important words are rearranged and the "deadwood" (the unnecessary words) eliminated.

Sentence combining, which you practiced in Chapters 15 and 16, is a useful tool in achieving conciseness. Notice how the following two sentences can be combined.

Uncombined

The children walked across the field. It was covered with snow.

Combined

The children walked across the field covered with snow.

Notice that the second sentence in the first example *(It was covered with snow.)* is built around a very weak subject and verb *(It was)*. Verbs should be strong and, wherever possible, active rather than passive. (You may want to review the discussion of active and passive verbs on page 51 at this point.)

Often the best editing comes from recognizing weak or passive verbs. You can often correct this weakness by finding another word in the sentence that can become the verb.

Weak verb

Their boots made a crunching sound on the gravel as they walked.

Made is the weak verb in this sentence (even though it might be strong in another context, in another sentence). But the sentence contains another word with verb possibilities, *crunching*.

Stronger verb

Their boots crunched the gravel as they walked.

Correcting errors

Naturally, your writing should be grammatically correct. In college and in the business world, writing should contain no errors at all. When what you write is important, you won't receive partial credit for "mostly correct" writing.

Your work in this course is preparing you to correct most common grammatical errors, and you should apply what you have learned to your own writing. Mark sentences if that helps you see how they are constructed. Do whatever helps you to correct the errors your rough draft contains. (Everyone's rough drafts, including those of professional writers, contain errors.)

It is best to search for errors after you have done all your other editing—when your essay is in its final shape in all other respects. You can look upon this search as a kind of final polishing of your paragraph or essay.

Exercise 5   Editing sentences

Edit the following sentences to make them more concise and correct (try to find strong, active replacements for all weak, passive verbs). Do a few versions of each sentence on a separate sheet of paper before you write your final version on the lines below.

Example   The logs were placed in a pretty careful way, stacked in a corner

of the garage against the wall by my brother and me.

My brother and I stacked the logs carefully

in a corner of the garage.

1. We were no more than twenty yards away when I began to think to myself that these faces were not the faces of friendly people.

   _____

   _____

   _____

2. Halfway down the slope I got beside him and was telling him to do the thing we call "snowplowing" and not to lean back.

   _____

   _____

   _____

3. As the second half of the concert was played and the heat increased, the playing was stopped by the band, and another intermission was announced by the band leader.

   _____

   _____

   _____

4. The story began in the ice-cold north in January of 1967 somewhere in the Rocky Mountains of Colorado.

   _____

   _____

   _____

5. It has been a long time since I was told the reasons behind the dean's action when a new course was canceled by the dean.

   _____

6. The beds had just been made by us, and the counselor complimented us in a booming voice.

_____

_____

_____

7. Most everything went well until my sister and I ran over a bump in the road, and our bikes hit it hard.

_____

_____

_____

8. Joe was arrested by narcotics agents who had been specially trained to do undercover work.

_____

_____

_____

9. Since it was coming to an end, I was feeling worse about getting back home from my vacation.

_____

_____

_____

10. The branches of the tree were rustling in the high wind, and she looked at them.

_____

_____

_____

Now that your paragraph or essay is clear, concise, and correct, you have only one more step to take. If you want to make sure that others will respond favorably to your work, you will need to present a clean, neat, and legible final copy. When you are working on the final copy, these are good rules to follow:

1. *Use correct margins and line spacing.* For typed and handwritten college essays, a one-inch margin on all sides is most common. All typed essays should be double spaced. Handwritten essays can be double or single spaced, though handwriting that is difficult to read should always be double spaced.
2. *Make sure all typing and handwriting is free of incidental errors ("typos" and similar mistakes).*
3. *Write a brief, interesting title and center it (without quotation marks or underlining) a few lines above the first paragraph.* Five words or less is a good length for a title of a nonhumorous, nonscientific essay. The title should specifically indicate the subject of your essay. "My Description Essay" would be a poor title for an essay that describes the study you built in your basement. "My Basement Hideaway" would be much stronger and much more specific.
4. *Use only one side of the paper.*
5. *Pay attention to the details that will enhance the readability of your final copy.* You don't want your reader to struggle to read your work or to be discouraged from reading it at all because of its messy appearance. Make your final copy legible and attractive. Write or print neatly. Or use a clean typewriter, a dark ribbon, and good paper (some chemically treated typing papers are difficult to read). Don't let your paper become wrinkled and dog-eared.

Exercise 6 The final copy

Edit and prepare a final copy of one of the rough drafts you revised for Exercise 3. Turn in all your pages, not just the final version.

Review exercise

Edit the following essay so that it is clear, concise, and correct (do not forget about correcting punctuation where needed). You will probably need to do a few versions before you arrive at your final version. Then make a final copy of the essay.

Man's Worst Friend

I don't like dogs. They always seem to me to be more trouble than they're ever worth. One story always comes to my mind, it happens whenever someone talks to me about how wonderful they think dogs are.

Five years ago I flew back to pennsylvania for the summer to visit some relatives. My uncle Ed had an old pug, these dogs are born with bad breathing problems. At the time of this incident the weather was hot and humid making life for all of us very hard. Unfortunately there was a story in the paper about a similar dog who had died the day before from heat exhaustion, making uncle Ed nervous about his own pet. Uncle Ed told us not to take the dog out it was too hot. Because Uncle Ed has such a bad temper, so you would think that my cousin Ted and me would obey his commands, but we wouldn't be real-life kids then.

Ted and I decided Butch needed a little fresh air. It was hot in the house. The pug was named Butch. The leash was carefully snapped onto the collar by us and off the three of us went. We walked all around the neighborhood all over the place until we were tired. A shady tree looked good to us so we sat down there, underneath the tree. Ted reached over to give Butch a little friendly pat on the head and Butch bit Ted and Ted dropped the leash and Butch went roaring away he wasn't chasing a thing he was just running out of meanness.

Ted and I went chasing after Butch, yelling until we couldn't yell anymore. We were sweating all over the place too. Because it must have been close to a hundred degrees. Butch disappeared over a hill. Before then we could see his fat little legs flying. I've never see a fat dog move so quick before. Now we could just hear him bark. Then not a sound was heard. We just stopped and looked at each other, we guessed what had happened.

We went over the hill and there was Butch all four legs spread out from his body lying in a heap. Not moving a muscle. He was dead. We had to go back and tell uncle Ed he was dead. Uncle Ed was furious. Yelled at us calling us careless boys for hours. It seemed unfair. It wasn't our fault.

I think that dog got us into trouble out of meanness. He ran hisself to death because he knew that would be the worst thing he could do to us. Dogs may be smart they are also plenty mean. At least Butch was. I think all dogs are.

Chapter 19 writing assignment

1. Write a main idea for an essay that tells why you would like to have a certain job.
2. Jot down some details that support this main idea. Your supporting details can include notes about something that actually happened to you, various pieces of information that other people have told you, or notes that describe what you think the job would be like.
3. Choose an order in which to present these details.
4. Turn these notes into a one-page essay. Think of a title for your essay.
5. Revise the essay until you come up with a version that is clear, concise, and correct.
6. Turn in a neat final copy of your essay.

Section VII

Other punctuation and spelling skills

When you studied phrases and clauses earlier in this book, you learned how to punctuate them. The next two chapters will tell you more about how to punctuate the various parts of a sentence and will help you review all you have learned about punctuation so far.

The final chapter will show you ways to avoid spelling errors.

20. Other punctuation skills

You'll recall that words and phrases providing extra information are separated by commas from the rest of the sentence. There are also many words and phrases that seem to **interrupt** the clause they're in, and they, too, are usually set off by commas.

Commas with interrupters

The list below contains many of the common interrupters, although it is not a complete list.

Some Common Interrupters

1

besides	therefore	by the way
consequently	as a result	of course
furthermore	yes	for example
however	no	on the one hand
moreover	well	on the other hand
nevertheless	oh	
meanwhile		

names and titles of people spoken to

	2	
I believe		I think
I suppose		it seems to me
	3	
not		according to
such as		but

Let's look at each group more closely.

Group 1   Most of these words and phrases are familiar, and others like them are in common use. Use this list as a reference until you can correctly punctuate any sentence that contains one of them.

The following sentence contains an interrupter from this group.

> The church in the center of the city, **on the other hand,** is more
> than two hundred years old.

The phrase *on the other hand* seems to break the flow of the clause.

Also contained in this group are names of people spoken to. Here is an example:

> **Mr. McCormack,** would you restate your question?

In this sentence, *Mr. McCormack* is the name of a person spoken to. The name of a person spoken to is set off by commas whether it comes at the beginning, at the end, or in the middle of the sentence.

> This is a better book, **Lenore.**
>
> Are you sure, **Steve,** that you don't want a sandwich?

Group 2   The interrupters in this group are clauses. Each contains a subject and a verb.

Because these interrupters are complete clauses, they do not function as interrupters when they are placed at the beginning of a sentence. Compare the following sentences.

> The water, **I believe,** should be tested.
>
> **I believe** the water should be tested.

When clauses like *I believe* begin a sentence, they are the subject and verb of the main clause. The hidden tip-off word *that* introduces the noun clause, which is used as an object (*I believe that the water should be tested.*)

Group 3   The phrases in this group occur frequently in college and business writing. Let's look at two examples:

> History, **according to some writers,** is merely the record of the lives
> of great men.

We spoke to Dr. Granger, **not Dr. Inez,** about the illness.

Notice that *according to* and *not,* like other words in this group, do not stand alone as interrupters (as the words in Group 1 do, for instance). They are followed by other words, and the entire phrase becomes an interrupter. Words in this group function as tip-off words for such interrupter phrases.

Marking interrupters

Interrupters can be marked with a long bracket and the letter **I,** as shown below.

The assignment, ⌐of course,⌐ must be turned in on time.

Punctuating interrupters

Interrupters almost always require special punctuation. The following sentence contains the interrupter *for example.*

One of the actors, **for example,** was educated in England.

Notice that *for example* is separated from the rest of the sentence with commas. This is the interrupter pattern, which you have seen in earlier chapters. Interrupters can appear in three positions—at the beginning, in the middle, or at the end of a sentence—and are always separated from the rest of the sentence by a comma or commas.

> **Mayor,** what do you think is the major problem facing Cleveland today?
>
> Irving's design, **on the other hand,** is much simpler.
>
> I like furry animals, **such as chows and angora cats.**

Note, however, that such words and phrases from Group 1 as *consequently, furthermore, meanwhile,* and *by the way* are rarely used at the end of a sentence.

Exercise 1   Interrupters

Mark and punctuate all interrupters in the following sentences.

Example

⌐Consequently,⌐ the news will be followed by a special sports presentation.

1. Furthermore Ms. Simmons will not be present this evening.

2. The navy it seems to me offers greater opportunities to women in those professions.

3. According to Dr. Homan the test results are correct.

4. On the one hand his grades are very good.

5. Chemical oven cleaners do a very good job however.

6. The cause of his anger moreover has yet to be discovered.

7. The *Saturday Evening Post* for example went out of business.

8. Well they discovered gold and copper in the ore that they tested.

9. The black belt can be worn with the tan pants I think.

10. New York not New Jersey is my uncle's childhood home.

Quotations

Quotations are references to another speaker's or writer's exact words. Quotations often contain a *he said* statement (or some version of it, such as *she was saying, I explained, we will comment, they have proposed,* and so on). This statement introduces the quotation by naming its speaker or writer.

There are two kinds of quotations—**direct quotations,** where the speaker's or writer's words are given exactly, and **indirect quotations,** where the writer's or speaker's words are rephrased by someone else.

Punctuating indirect quotations

You may recall examples of indirect quotations from Chapter 16. Indirect quotations are usually sentences with noun clauses as objects, like the following:

> The manager said **that she was tired.** (Speaker's exact words: *I am tired.*)

The speaker's exact words have been changed (this is what makes the quotation *indirect*). Notice that the noun clause containing the speaker's words acts as the object of the verb. For this reason, indirect quotations like the one above receive no special punctuation.

A variation of this pattern places the *he said* statement (or some version of it) in the middle of the quotation. There it acts like an interrupter.

Compare the following:

A version of *he said* at the beginning

A company representative announced that no more workers would
be laid off this year.

A version of *he said* as an interrupter

No more workers, **a company representative announced,** would be
laid off this year.

(The exact words of this speaker were probably *no more workers will be laid off
this year.*)

Exercise 2

Indirect quotations

Rewrite each of the following into an indirect quotation. Use the interrupter pattern where indicated.

Example

Speaker: Professor Thorsen

Statement: *Class will be dismissed early.*

*Professor Thorsen said that class
would be dismissed early.*

1. Speaker: Sidney

   Statement: *The strike will soon be over.*

   _____

   _____

2. Speaker: An industry spokesperson

   Statement: *A new product will be released before June 15.*

   (Interrupter pattern)

   _____

   _____

3. Speaker: Dr. Velikovsky

Statement: *Your editing skills improve with practice.*

_____

_____

4. Speaker: The ship's captain

Statement: *The damage to the ship was extensive, but no one*

was injured.

(Interrupter pattern)

_____

_____

5. Speaker: My sister

Statement: *Will you be ready by eight o'clock?*

_____

_____

Punctuating direct quotations

In direct quotations, the exact words of the quoted speaker (or writer) are placed within **quotation marks (" ").**

If a version of the *he said* statement introduces or follows the quotation, it is usually separated from the quotation by a comma. Consider these examples:

> Marilyn said, "This test is unusual."
>
> "This student is the best writer I've ever taught," Terry Bijon informed his colleagues.

In both examples, the exact words of the speakers are given, and so they are enclosed in quotation marks. Because each quotation is a complete sentence, it begins with a capital letter.

Note that when a period or a comma follows a direct quotation, it is always placed *within* the quotation marks. Periods and commas are placed within quotation marks even when only one or two words are quoted.

> They called the help they were given "very generous."
>
> She termed his action "preposterous," even though it was predictable.

Punctuating Direct Quotations

1. Place **quotation marks** around the speaker's exact words.
2. Use **commas** to punctuate the *he said* statement, if any, as an interrupter.
3. **Capitalize** the first letter of the speaker's words, no matter where the first letter appears.
4. Use a **question mark** instead of a comma or a period to show a question by the speaker or the writer. Use an **exclamation point** in the same way to indicate an exclamation.

Study the following unpunctuated examples. In all three sentences, the speaker's exact words are *the test will be postponed.*

> The test will be postponed said Dr. Hellman.
> The test said Dr. Hellman will be postponed.
> Dr. Hellman said the test will be postponed.

Now let's apply the punctuation rules one at a time.

1. Place **quotation marks** around the speaker's exact words.

> "The test will be postponed" said Dr. Hellman.
>
> "The test" said Dr. Hellman "will be postponed."
>
> Dr. Hellman said "the test will be postponed."

Notice once again that the periods at the end of the sentences are placed *before* the quotation marks.

2. Use **commas** to punctuate the *he said* statement, if any, as an interrupter.

> "The test will be postponed," said Dr. Hellman.
>
> "The test," said Dr. Hellman, "will be postponed."
>
> Dr. Hellman said, "the test will be postponed."

Here again, the commas are placed *before* the quotation marks.

3. **Capitalize** the first letter of the speaker's words, no matter where the first letter appears.

> "The test will be postponed," said Dr. Hellman.
>
> "The test," said Dr. Hellman, "will be postponed."
>
> Dr. Hellman said, "The test will be postponed."

In the third sentence, the speaker's sentence begins in the middle of the sentence that contains it. Note the capital letter.

The final version of these sentences looks like this.

> "The test will be postponed," said Dr. Hellman.
>
> "The test," said Dr. Hellman, "will be postponed."
>
> Dr. Hellman said, "The test will be postponed."

Now let's look at a new set of sentences that show how to use question marks with quotations.

4. Use a **question mark** instead of a comma or a period to show a question by the speaker or the writer. Use an exclamation point in the same way to indicate an exclamation.

> "Has the test been postponed?" asked Dr. Hellman.
>
> "Has the test," asked Dr. Hellman, "been postponed?"
>
> Dr. Hellman asked, "Has the test been postponed?"

The question marks come where you would expect, *before* the quotation marks. This is because the speaker asks the question.

If the writer of the sentence, and not the speaker, asks the question, then the question mark comes *after* the quotation mark.

> Did Dr. Hellman say, "The test has been postponed"**?**

This rule about question marks applies to exclamation points as well.

Speaker's exclamation

> "Stop that man!" shouted the lady.
>
> The lady shouted, "Stop that man!"

Writer's exclamation

> Don't keep saying, "I'm sorry"!

Never use double punctuation, such as a period and a question mark or a comma and a question mark together. Use only the more important punctuation mark.

Exercise 3   Direct quotations

Each of the following sentences contains a direct quotation. Punctuate these sentences correctly.

Example   "Marcie likes this club," answered Barbara.

1. The manager responded yes I will

2. In the afternoon said Emil Marciano we only need two waiters

3. Where did you find the coat asked Janet

4. Did Walter just say I'm ready

5. The singer asked would you like to hear a new song or an old one

6. The ticket seller replied we only have balcony seats available

7. Labor Day Bill complained is the earliest that I can get away

8. This medicine the pharmacist assured us is as good as any of these others

9. The driver got out of her car and yelled watch where you're going

10. Would you please help me with my groceries

Long quotations and changing speakers

Punctuate quotations that include more than one sentence just like the quotations we have been discussing so far, but keep in mind that a new sentence does NOT require a new set of quotation marks.

Use new quotation marks only to show a new speaker's words. Compare the following examples. The first shows one speaker saying three sentences. The first sentence of the long quotation is introduced by a *he said* statement. (The speaker's exact words are printed in boldface type.)

One speaker

Professor Weintraub said, **"The war continued for several years more. Neither side wanted to admit defeat. Both sides, however, had suffered greatly."**

Now let's see what happens if these comments are made by two speakers. (The first speaker's words are printed in boldface type. The second speaker's words are printed in italics.)

Two speakers

Professor Weintraub said, **"The war continued for several years more."** *"Neither side wanted to admit defeat,"* added Ms. Marshall. *"Both sides, however, had suffered greatly."*

The two sets of quotation marks between *more* and *Neither* show that one quotation has ended and a new one is beginning.

Often, but not always, a new paragraph is also used to show that a new speaker is talking.

Two speakers

Professor Weintraub said, **"The war continued for several years more."**

"Neither side wanted to admit defeat," added Ms. Marshall. *"Both sides, however, had suffered greatly."*

Exercise 4   Direct quotations

Correct any punctuation errors in the following paragraphs. (NOTE: The only errors in this exercise involve the punctuation of quotations.)

"Step aside said Rosie Carter as she pushed her way past me. She gave me such a jolt, completely unexpected, that I was pushed sideways into the tiles of the science building hall. I stopped to watch this human torpedo complete her course and enter one of the classrooms. "Who is this woman I asked." "Doesn't she know how to behave?" I was angry, but my anger soon passed. I walked to the door of Room 205 and noticed Rosie sitting in the front row. The room was full, but the chairs around Rosie were empty. What, I asked myself, "Makes a person act like that"? Later, as I walked the dirt path that led to my dormitory, I decided to find out.

Colon, dash, and hyphen

The **colon (:),** the **dash (—),** and the **hyphen (-)** are punctuation marks with special uses.

Using the Colon, Dash, and Hyphen

Use a **colon** or **dash** to attach a list or an explanation to the end of a sentence.

Use **dashes** to add a list or an explanation in the middle of a sentence.

Use a **hyphen** to form some compound words or to divide a word at the end of a line.

Let's look at these punctuation marks one at a time.

The colon

The colon has several uses. You are probably already familiar with some of them, such as in indicating time.

My 8:15 class usually starts at 8:25.

The colon is also used to add a list or an explanation to the end of an otherwise complete sentence. Study the following sentences.

Colon with a list

I am taking four classes this semester: microbiology, computer science, intermediate statistics, and surfing.

Colon with an explanation

I have very little sympathy for Ray: his decisions have damaged a number of promising careers.

The words that follow the colon are not part of the main clause of the sentence. The colon is required to attach these words to the rest of the sentence.

A colon should not be used to attach words to a sentence if those words are already part of the sentence. The following sentence, for example, is incorrectly punctuated.

Incorrect

This semester I am taking: microbiology, computer science, intermediate statistics, and surfing.

Correct

This semester I am taking⅄ microbiology, computer science, intermediate statistics, and surfing.

The colon is also used after the salutation in business.

Dear Sir:

Dear Ms. Bialy:

The dash

A dash can be used much like a colon—to attach a list or an explanation to the end of a sentence.

Dash with a list

I am taking four classes this semester—microbiology, computer science, intermediate statistics, and surfing.

Dash with an explanation

I have very little sympathy for Ray—his decisions have damaged a number of promising careers.

Dashes can also be used to insert a list or an explanation into the middle of a sentence.

Dashes in the middle of a sentence

I am taking four classes this semester—microbiology, computer science, intermediate statistics, and surfing—and I like all of them but one.

Both the colon and the dash should be used with great care. Writing that contains too many colons or dashes (especially dashes) will appear awkward and overpunctuated.

Exercise 5   Colons and dashes

A. Punctuate each of the following sentences correctly using colons or dashes.

Example

My roommate needs help in two classes: European History and Humanities.

1. The sisters wanted to leave the party was breaking and the hostess was getting tired.

2. Our favorite instructors Dr. Sarandon, Mrs. Endicott, and Mr. Lee are all out sick this week.

3. Each of the panelists had the same question for us why don't we study harder?

4. Stuart told two good stories the one about the ice cream and the one about Frank's red truck.

5. Two brands are under consideration IBM and Xerox.

6. The next two months January and February will be the most difficult.

7. The palace opened its doors early the crowds were becoming too large.

8. The school gave a special citation to two remarkable students Jessie Cates and Bill Martinez.

B. Correct any punctuation errors in the following sentences. If a sentence is already correct, write **OK** in the margin.

Example

The government helps students to attend college by offering͵ loans and grants.

9. The fire marshal announced that: Wembly Street would be closed all afternoon.

10. Three radio stations: WCAZ, WXZF, and WBB, are offering a free vacation.

11. We had hoped to see—Tyrone and Christopher.

12. Janet contributes to all the local charities, including: the Boy Scouts and the Junior Chamber of Commerce.

13. Everyone at the apartment—even the dog was glad to see us, for we were bringing both hamburgers and ice cream.

14. Three engineers were hired today—Jackson, Carlton, and Lee.

15. We met the Flying Freeman Brothers, a circus act.

The hyphen

The **hyphen (-)** is used to form some compound words and to divide a word at the end of a line. (Notice the length of the hyphen. It is less than half as long as a dash.)

Forming compound words

Many English words are made by putting two or more smaller words together. Sometimes the new word (called a **compound word**) is written with a hyphen joining the smaller words. Compound words spelled with a hyphen include

mother-in-law	self-improvement
half-finished	twenty-one, twenty-two, etc.

Some compound words are written without hyphens. These include

freeway	bookmark
spellbound	seatbelt
bedroom	clubhouse

If you are not sure whether a compound word is spelled with a hyphen, consult a dictionary.

Sometimes hyphens are used with a prefix such as *ex-* or *un-*: *ex-wife*, *un-American*. Again, it is best to consult your dictionary if you are unsure whether to use a hyphen with a prefix.

Dividing words at the end of the line

Sometimes only part of a word will fit at the end of a line, and the rest must be carried over to the next line. When a word is divided in this way, a hyphen is used at the end of the first part of the word.

For example, in the sentence below, the word *understood* is carried over from the first line to the second.

> The instructor asked if we **under-
> stood** the assignment.

Notice that the hyphen is placed at the end of the first line, not the beginning of the second.

When words are divided, certain principles must be followed.

1. Divide a word only between syllables. (If you do not know where to break a word into syllables, consult a dictionary.)

base- ment	NOT	bas- ement

2. Do not divide a one-syllable word.

thought	NOT	thou- ght

3. Do not separate a single letter from the rest of the word.

afraid	NOT	a- fraid
mighty	NOT	might- y

4. Avoid separating a two-letter syllable from the end of the word.

pleas- antly	NOT	pleasant- ly

5. Always divide a hyphenated compound word at the hyphen.

self- control	NOT	self-con- trol

Exercise 6   Hyphens

Use a hyphen to divide the following words correctly. Write your divided word on the two lines provided. If any word should not be divided, write the whole word on the first line. (If necessary, use a dictionary to make sure your answers are correct.)

Example   sailboat   _sail–_
                                 boat

1. sweepstakes   _____
                  _____

2. moreover   _____
                  _____

3. paper   _____
                  _____

4. professor   _____
                  _____

5. indeed   _____
                  _____

6. anonymously   ————————

————————

7. through   ————————

————————

8. pattern   ————————

————————

9. punctuation   ————————

————————

10. twenty-seven   ————————

————————

11. fairness   ————————

————————

12. intelligent   ————————

————————

13. green   ————————

————————

14. regular   ————————

————————

15. furtively   ————————

————————

Apostrophes

The **apostrophe (')** is used to make possessive adjectives and contractions.

Apostrophes in possessive adjectives

As you recall from Chapter 12, all nouns and most pronouns form possessive adjectives by using the apostrophe. The following rule will help you to spell these words correctly:

Using Apostrophes in Possessive Adjectives

To form possessive adjectives,

1. write the name of the owner or owners.
2. add an apostrophe to the end of the word that names the owner.
3. add an *s* after the apostrophe if the word that names the owner is either
    a. singular, or
    b. plural not ending in *s*.

This rule is easy to apply and always produces the correct answer. The chief problem in spelling possessive adjectives is the temptation to add the apostrophe inside the name of the owner, not after it.

Be sure to write the word that names the owner or owners first. Then add the apostrophe and, if necessary, the *s*.

Here are some examples of possessive adjectives.

Jerline owns that book. It is _____ book.

1. Write the name of the owner or owners in the sentence.

It is __*Jerline*__ book.

2. Add an apostrophe to the end of the word.

It is __*Jerline'*__ book.

3. Add an *s* after the apostrophe if the word is either
    a. singular, or
    b. plural not ending in *s*.

It is __*Jerline's*__ book.

Since this word is singular, it does need an added *s*. *Jerline's* is the correct possessive adjective form of *Jerline*.

Jerline owns a book. It is **Jerline's** book.

Here is another example:

This school accepts only boys. It is a _____ school.

1. Write the name of the owner or owners in the sentence.

It is a ___boys___ school.

The boys don't own the school, but we all understand the sense in which it "belongs" to them.

2. Add an apostrophe to the end of the word.

It is a ___boys'___ school.

The name of the owner, as always, is printed *before* the apostrophe.

3. Add an *s* after the apostrophe if the word is either
   a. singular, or
   b. plural not ending in *s*.

It is a ___boys'___ school.

Boys is plural, and it already ends in *s*. Another *s* is not needed. *Boys'* is the correct possessive adjective form of *boys*.

This school accepts only boys. It is a **boys'** school.

Let's do one more example.

All of the children own this toy. It is the _____ toy.

The name of the owners is *children*.

It is the ___children___ toy.

An apostrophe is placed after this word.

It is the ___children'___ toy.

An *s* is added because the word is a plural that doesn't end in *s*.

It is the ___children's___ toy.

The correct possessive form of *children* is *children's*.

All of the children own this toy. It is the **children's** toy.

Apostrophe and *s* in possessives

Notice that all the possessives you have seen so far, except personal pronouns and *who*, have ended in *s*. This is true of all possessives except the personal pronouns and *who*. Singular words automatically receive an added *s*, and plurals get one if they need one.

	Singular		Possessive
	Jerline		Jerline's

	Plural		Possessive
	boys		boys'
	children		children's

Possessive forms of most pronouns

As you have learned in Chapter 12, most pronouns form possessives in the same way as nouns.

Pronoun	Possessive
someone	someone's
another	another's
others	others'

Possessive forms of personal pronouns and *who*

The personal pronouns and *who* form possessives in the following way:

Pronoun	Possessive
I	my, mine
you	your, yours
he	his
she	her, hers
it	its
we	our, ours
they	their, theirs
who	whose

The second form of the possessive *(mine, yours, hers, ours,* and *theirs)* is used when a pronoun, not an adjective, is required.

Compare these examples:

You have **my** key.

This key is **mine.**

Exercise 7   Possessive adjectives

Tell whether each of the following is singular or plural by writing **S** or **P** on the line to the left. Then write the correct **possessive form** of the word on the line to the right.

Example   __S__   book _book's_____

1. _____   woman _____

2. _____ women _____

3. _____ games _____

4. _____ Cleveland _____

5. _____ desk _____

6. _____ speedboats _____

7. _____ goose _____

8. _____ mice _____

9. _____ sweepstakes _____

10. _____ accountant _____

11. _____ brother _____

12. _____ businessmen _____

13. _____ porches _____

14. _____ box _____

15. _____ fish _____

Exercise 8   Possessive adjectives in sentences

Complete each of the following with the correct **possessive adjective form** of the word in parentheses.

Example

The ___*Ladies'*___ Aid Society will hold its first fall meeting on
    (Ladies)
September 10.

1. Sharon wants to spend a week at her _____
                                                    (friend)

   apartment.

2. The _____ recoil is not too great.
         (rifle)

3. I followed the _____ orbit across the night sky.
                   (satellite)

4. It took him _____ work to solve that equation.
               (four hours)

5. _____ cat has escaped.
   (Jesse)
6. A _____ sting can be painful.
   (sea urchin)
7. The _____ wife just called.
   (boss)
8. The whole family will go to _____ graduation.
   (Carlos)
9. She checked the _____ temperature first.
   (water)
10. Researchers studied the _____ properties carefully.
    (compound)
11. You are entitled to _____ vacation.
    (two weeks)
12. The _____ popularity has risen rapidly.
    (band)
13. They contributed to the _____ pension fund.
    (players)
14. _____ suits are located in the rear.
    (Men)
15. _____ grades have improved greatly.
    (Willis)

Apostrophes in contractions

Contractions are words and phrases that are shortened because letters are removed. When contractions are created, an apostrophe is used to show where the missing letters would have appeared.

The process is fairly straightforward.

$$\text{do not} \longrightarrow \text{donot} \longrightarrow \text{don't}$$

Common contractions include the following:

Common Contractions

Contractions with *Is* and *Has*

he is	=	he's
she is	=	she's
it is	=	it's
who is	=	who's
there is	=	there's
he has	=	he's
she has	=	she's
it has	=	it's
who has	=	who's
there has	=	there's

Contractions with *Are*

we are   =   we're
you are   =   you're
they are   =   they're

Contraction with *Am*

I am   =   I'm

Contractions with *Would*

I would   =   I'd
you would   =   you'd
he would   =   he'd
she would   =   she'd
it would   =   it'd (a very awkward phase and
                              therefore to be avoided)
we would   =   we'd
you would   =   you'd
they would   =   they'd
who would   =   who'd
there would =   there'd

Contractions with *Not*

does not   =   doesn't
do not   =   don't
is not   =   isn't
are not   =   aren't
was not   =   wasn't
were not   =   weren't
has not   =   hasn't
have not   =   haven't
had not   =   hadn't
cannot   =   can't
could not   =   couldn't
would not   =   wouldn't
will not   =   won't

Notice the last contraction especially since it is not spelled as you might expect.

will not = **won't**

Exercise 9   Contractions

Correct any misspelled contractions in the following sentences. If the sentence is already correct, write **OK** in the margin.

Example

Isn't
~~Is͟n͟t~~ this your first theater class?

1. We didn't find further explanation necessary.

2. Theres more in the refrigerator.

3. The strike was'nt planned properly.

4. Michaels certain we're landing in a few minutes.

5. Shes' never liked another mystery film.

6. Theyre never going to understand his reasons if he won't explain them.

7. Future explorations willn't be funded for some time.

8. These are'nt stone arrowheads.

9. The're natural rock formations.

10. He wondered if he'ld ever make the first string.

Review exercise

Correct all punctuation errors in the following paragraph, including errors with apostrophes.

Two of my friends Aaron, and Patty were discussing their astronomy assignment when Aaron mentioned that some people think, planets like Venus Mars and Jupiter, can influence your life. ''They worry about Venus for instance'' he said. ''because they think it affects their love life.'' According to these people he added, the planets Mars and Jupiter determine how aggressive you are and how much luck you have. ''But thats nonsense, exclaimed Patty. ''Wh'od believe such stuff. I certainly can't''. Aaron agreed that its' silly to assume that planets control every aspect of your life; your career, your family relationships, and your health. But those who hold such beliefs, although they have no scientific basis wont change them easily.

Chapter 20 writing assignment

1. Using the writing process that was discussed in Chapter 19, write a one-page essay analyzing why a fictional character (from a book, film, etc.) acted as he or she did.
2. Your instructor may ask that you turn in your summary page and drafts along with your final copy.

21. Punctuation review

This chapter will review the punctuation principles you have learned so far, give you a few ways to break these rules successfully, and offer paragraphs on which to practice.

Punctuation rules

What follows is a list of all the major punctuation rules you have studied in this text, beginning with those involving the punctuation of clauses.

Punctuating independent clauses

Between every two independent (or main) clauses there must be punctuation, either to separate them into two sentences or to join them in one sentence. The first rule tells us how to join or separate independent clauses.

Punctuation Rule 1
Independent Clauses

To separate or join independent (main) clauses, use the following:

1. period, question mark, or exclamation point—to separate independent clauses

2. semicolon—to join independent clauses
3. comma + coordinating conjunction—to join independent clauses

The following sentences illustrate this rule.

Separated with period

Several cars turned onto the expressway. Jim's car was one of them.

Joined with semicolon

Several cars turned onto the expressway; Jim's car was one of them.

Joined with comma and conjunction

Several cars turned onto the expressway, **and** Jim's car was one of them.

Notice that there is an independent clause on each side of the punctuation.

Punctuating introductory clauses and phrases

You have now dealt with many introductory clauses and phrases. Here is a general rule to help you punctuate them.

Punctuation Rule 2
Introductory Clauses and Phrases

All dependent adjective and adverb clauses, verbal phrases, and appositives that begin a sentence must be separated from the rest of the sentence with a comma.

The following sentences show how this rule works.

Introductory clause

Because he was married before he turned twenty, William Shakespeare faced the dual problems of family and career at an early age.

Introductory verbal phrase

Married before he turned twenty, William Shakespeare faced the dual problems of family and career at an early age.

Introductory appositive

A married man before he turned twenty, William Shakespeare faced the dual problems of family and career at an early age.

Punctuating "extra" clauses and phrases

This rule deals with adjective and adverb clauses and phrases that contain extra information. You learned this rule in Chapter 16, but let's restate it here.

Punctuation Rule 3
Extra Adjective and Adverb Clauses and Phrases

Adjective and adverb clauses, verbal phrases, and appositives that contain extra information must be separated from the rest of the sentence with commas.

Necessary and extra adjective verbal phrases were discussed at length in Chapter 14 (pages 170–171), and adjective clauses were considered in Chapter 16 (pages 212–219). You may recall that extra adjective clauses or verbal phrases can be removed from a sentence without changing its meaning. They provide information that may be interesting and helpful but is not essential to the meaning of the sentence.

Extra adjective clause

Stanley, **who was working in a factory at the time,** wrote several short novels during the early 1970s.

Extra verbal phrase

Stanley, **working in a factory at the time,** wrote several short novels during the early 1970s.

As you may remember from Chapter 14 (pages 178–179), appositives can also be identified as extra or necessary. Extra appositives are not essential to the meaning of the sentence.

Extra appositive

Stanley, **a factory worker at the time,** wrote several short novels during the early 1970s.

Extra adverb clauses are usually introduced by tip-off words like *although* (see Chapter 16, page 225).

Extra adverb clause

Stanley wrote several short novels during the early 1970s, **although he was working in a factory at the time.**

Punctuating interrupters and lists

The next three rules deal with interrupters, lists, and coordinate adjectives.

Punctuation Rule 4
Interrupters

Separate interrupter words, phrases, and clauses from the rest of the sentence with commas. These interrupters include the following:

1

besides	therefore	by the way
consequently	as a result	of course
furthermore	yes	for example
however	no	on the one hand
moreover	well	on the other hand
nevertheless	oh	
meanwhile		

names and titles of people spoken to

2

I believe	I think
I suppose	it seems to me

3

not	according to
such as	but

Keep in mind that interrupters can occur in three positions. The following sentences illustrate these patterns.

Interrupter at beginning

According to reporters, several citizens have mysteriously disappeared from the capital.

Interrupter in middle

Several citizens, **according to reporters,** have mysteriously disappeared from the capital.

Interrupter at end

Several citizens have mysteriously disappeared from the capital, **according to reporters.**

Interrupters in Group 2 are not punctuated as interrupters when they appear at the beginning of the sentence.

"I believe" as an interrupter

Several citizens, **I believe,** have mysteriously disappeared from the capital.

"I believe" at the beginning of a sentence

I believe several citizens have mysteriously disappeared from the capital.

Punctuation Rule 5
Lists

Separate with a comma each item in a list of three or more. Do not separate items in a list of two.

This rule is easily applied, as the following examples show.

List of two items

An earthquake rocked the mountains of **Peru and Chile.**

List of three items

An earthquake rocked the mountains of **Peru, Chile, and Bolivia.**

Note the comma used with *and* in the last example above.

A variation of the list rule involves adjectives that could be joined by *and* but aren't. As you learned in Chapter 15 (page 193), these are called **coordinate adjectives.**

Punctuation Rule 6
Coordinate Adjectives

Use a comma to join adjectives that could be joined by the coordinating conjunction *and*.

Compare the following sentences.

Office politics is a **serious and dangerous** game.
Office politics is a **serious, dangerous** game.

Note that both of the sentences above are correct.

Punctuating direct quotations

You practiced punctuating direct quotations in the last chapter. The rule below sums up the necessary steps.

Punctuation Rule 7
Direct Quotations

1. Place **quotation marks** around the speaker's exact words.
2. Use **commas** to punctuate the *he said* statement, if any, as an interrupter.
3. **Capitalize** the first letter of the speaker's words, no matter where the first letter appears.
4. Use a **question mark** instead of a comma or a period to show a question by the speaker or the writer. Use an **exclamation point** in the same way to indicate an exclamation.
5. Use one set of quotation marks for the words of one speaker, unless those words are interrupted by the writer's comments. Use new quotation marks to show a change of speakers.

This punctuation rule is discussed at length in Chapter 20, on pages 281–283. The following sentence merely illustrates the final effects of applying these steps.

> The sales manager said, "We should take advantage of each of these opportunities."

Notice that the comma and the period appear *before* the quotation marks.

Using the colon, dash, and hyphen

This rule applies to three important, but less common, punctuation marks.

Punctuation Rule 8
Colon, Dash, and Hyphen

Use a **colon** or **dash** to attach a list or an explanation to the end of a sentence.

Use **dashes** to add a list or an explanation in the middle of a sentence.

Use a **hyphen** to form some compound words or to divide a word at the end of a line.

The following sentences show how these marks are used.

Colon before a list or explanation

I took this job for two reasons: advancement and money.

Dash before a list or explanation

I took this job for two reasons—advancement and money.

Dashes with an interrupting list

Two reasons—advancement and money—made me take this job.

Hyphen to form compound words

She is a **well-meaning** but rather **self-centered** person.

Hyphen to divide a word

I took this job because I needed the **challenge** of new responsibilities.

Using commas with conjunctions

You have studied three kinds of conjunctions—coordinating conjunctions and conjunctive adverbs in Chapter 15 and subordinating conjunctions in Chapter 16. When we use all these conjunctions, we often have to use commas as well.

Let's look at these three kinds of conjunctions and see what kind of punctuation should be used with them.

Commas with coordinating conjunctions

Coordinating conjunctions are conjunctions that join equals. They include *and, or, but, nor, yet, for,* and *so.*

The following information summarizes the use of commas with coordinating conjunctions:

1. Conjunction joining a list of two items in an independent clause—NO COMMAS
2. Conjunction joining a list of three or more items in an independent clause— USE COMMAS
3. Conjunctions joining independent clauses—USE COMMAS

The most difficult situations to punctuate correctly involve conjunctions joining two verbs. Sentences where a conjunction joins two verbs in one independent clause are often confused with sentences where a conjunction joins two independent clauses.

Conjunction joining two verbs in one independent clause

Several men **returned** to the cabin and **searched** again for the old iron box.

Conjunction joining two independent clauses

Several **men returned** to the cabin, and **they searched** again for the old iron box.

Commas with subordinating conjunctions

Subordinating conjunctions make a clause (or a phrase) dependent on another clause. Clauses beginning with a subordinating conjunction (for example, *when, while, since, although*) can be noun or adverb clauses and are punctuated according to the rules for such clauses. See Rule 3 in this chapter, as well as the information on when to use commas in Chapter 16.

Commas with conjunctive adverbs

The interrupter rule (Rule 4) shows how to punctuate conjunctive adverbs—words like *however, nevertheless,* and *yet.* When used in combination with a semicolon, these words can join independent clauses. In such cases, the conjunctive adverb is always followed by a comma.

Cobwebs hung from the ceiling; **however,** the tiled floor was spotless.

Notice that both the interrupter rule and the independent clauses rule (Rule 1) are followed. The semicolon joins the two clauses. The interrupter, appearing at the beginning of the second main clause, is punctuated with a comma according to the interrupter pattern.

Breaking punctuation rules

Like all rules, punctuation rules can, and sometimes should, be broken. Of course, we need to know them in order to break them properly; therefore, we still need to learn them.

We should not break punctuation rules on a whim but only when another, more important principle is considered.

The following principles are a guide to how and when you can break the rules you have learned.

1. Do not overpunctuate short sentences.
2. Add commas wherever they are needed to make an unclear sentence clear.
3. It is not necessary to separate simple interrupters that do not "feel" like interrupters.

Take these principles into account when you punctuate. A complete discussion of each principle follows.

Overpunctuating short sentences

To prevent short sentences from appearing overpunctuated, you can leave out commas that normally appear

1. after introductory clauses and phrases.
2. with a conjunction between independent clauses.

The following sentences illustrate these points:

> To win she always fights hard.
> We left and she entered.

These short sentences are clear as they are. Commas after *To win* and *We left* are not necessary, even though the rules call for them.

Adding commas for clarity

Some sentences contain combinations of words that could be read in two ways. To keep readers from misreading a sentence, commas can be used to group phrases properly.

Consider this example:

> In short, sentences must be easily read to be considered well written.

If the comma after *short* were removed, the beginning of the sentence would read

> In short sentences . . .

The comma after *short* prevents anyone from misunderstanding the sentence.

Simple interrupters

Sometimes a simple interrupter, like *however* or *nevertheless*, just doesn't seem to interrupt the sentence. You may leave out the commas in such a sentence.

> She is nevertheless a good student.

Placing commas before and after *nevertheless* would create awkward pauses where none are needed.

Test sentences like this both ways before you decide on no punctuation. Remember that commas are needed with interrupters *most* of the time.

Review exercise 1

Many punctuation marks are missing from the following essay. Add all necessary punctuation. You may need to change the capitalization of some words.

As the summer draws to a close thousands of people all over

the country begin to worry about a major expense how to pay for their season tickets to professional basketball games Season tickets are often a mixed blessing for the people who own them.

On the positive side these tickets do carry a certain prestige. In towns that have a good basketball team and even in towns where a team's talent is questionable season tickets are hard to come by. There may be a long waiting list for season tickets which makes them seem that much more valuable there is always a great demand for tickets during the play-offs and people prize their season tickets especially highly then.

Fans pay a high price for their tickets however. The tickets often cost a great deal of money. The seats are often cramped and far away from the action on the court the fans in the stand occasionally have fantasies about watching the games on television in the comfort of their own living rooms. A friend of mine admitted sometimes during a game I find myself thinking about bowls of popcorn cushioned sofas and bathrooms down the hall.

Nevertheless two things convince most fans to keep their season tickets. First the thrill of watching a game in an arena filled with a lot of noisy excited people is difficult to match true fans will willingly give up money and comfort to be a part of the game as it happens. Second owning season tickets gives fans the chance to really appreciate exceptional athletes like Larry Bird Magic Johnson and Patrick Ewing it's a pleasure to be able to watch every move a gifted player makes. Season tickets provide fans with opportunities that add much to basketball's enjoyment.

Review exercise 2

Correct any incorrect punctuation in the following essay. You may need to change the capitalization of some words.

Whenever I start to feel weighted down by problems I go to the beach the beach is one of the most relaxing places I know.

I'm a city boy a guy used to concrete, and tiny patches of blue sky. I have the chance to feel close to nature at the beach, it's as if the beach touches some kind of primitive core. That we all have. The water is powerful, and deep. The waves keep up a soothing, constant rhythm, as they break against the sand. The summer sun is really hot and makes me think about what living, without modern conveniences, would be like. Sometimes I close my eyes, and pretend I'm a tough gritty prospector in the Nevada desert. Or an explorer in Africa. The sand dunes make the most, comfortable bed in the world. The gulls, overhead, call out to each other. A huge sky completes the picture; when I see that sky I really know: I'm not in the city anymore.

I always get a lot of exercise, at the beach. If it's summer—I like to swim a lot. I especially like the water to be a little cold on hot dry days. At any time of year though, I walk a lot at the beach. It's fun to stroll along look for shells and breathe in the salty air. The beach, I usually go to, is a long one which gives me a good opportunity to stretch my legs.

When I get back to my apartment I feel refreshed ready to jump back into city life. I know I'm, completely, relaxed when I get

home, I always sleep like a log that first night back from the
beach.

Chapter 21 writing assignment

1. Using the writing process discussed in Chapter 19, write a one-page essay on
   one of the following subjects:
   a. the qualities you would look for when choosing a doctor.
   b. the qualities you would look for when choosing a baby sitter.
2. Your instructor may ask that you turn in your summary page and drafts
   along with your final copy.

22. Spelling skills

This chapter will help you to improve your spelling by showing you how to spell many of the words that can cause difficulty.

These words fall into three groups:

1. verbs and nouns with added endings
2. words that sound alike
3. commonly misspelled words ("spelling demons")

Adding endings to verbs and nouns

The most common added endings are *-ing, -ed, -d, -s,* and *-es.*

Adding *-ing*

The *-ing* form is a verbal that can act as a noun, adjective, or adverb; it is also the key word in *-ing* verb phrases (see Chapters 5 and 6). To spell *-ing* forms, follow this rule:

Spelling *-ing* Words

Most *-ing* words are spelled by adding *-ing* to the present tense verb.

Verb	*-ing* word
play	playing
read	reading
sing	singing

For some verbs, however, the last letter is dropped, while for others it is doubled, before *-ing* is added. The following explains these exceptions.

Exception 1
Silent *e*

Drop a final silent *e* before adding *-ing*.

Verb	*-ing* word
love	loving
write	writing
invite	inviting

BUT

see	seeing

(Note that the *e* in *seeing* is not silent.)

Exception 2
Accented Syllables

In most cases, if the last syllable is accented (stressed), double a single consonant preceded by a single vowel before adding *-ing*.

(The **vowels** are *a, e, i, o, u,* and sometimes *y*. The **consonants** are all the remaining letters.)

Verb	*-ing* word
prefer (pre-FER)	preferring
control (con-TROL)	controlling

BUT

Verb	*-ing* word
corner (COR-ner)	cornering
travel (TRA-vel)	traveling

In one-syllable words a single consonant preceded by a single vowel is usually doubled when *-ing* is added.

Verb	*-ing* word
hit	hitting
run	running

BUT

cheer	cheering
swear	swearing

The consonants *w* and *y* are never doubled, however.

Verb	**-*ing* word**
grow	growing
say	saying

Knowing these rules can help you identify the -*ing* forms of similar words, as in these examples:

Verb	**-*ing* word**
bare	baring
bar	barring

Exercise 1   Adding -*ing*

Write the correct -*ing* form of the following verbs.

Example   foretell   *foretelling*

1. reply   _____

2. remove   _____

3. grin   _____

4. tear   _____

5. bore   _____

6. forget   _____

7. proceed   _____

8. tan   _____

9. repel   _____

10. offer   _____

11. characterize   _____

12. program   _____

13. incite   _____

14. rain _____

15. concur _____

Adding *-ed* and *-d*

The endings *-ed* and *-d* are added to regular verbs to create the past tense and past participle. These forms are spelled as follows.

Spelling *-ed* Verbs

Most regular past tense and past participle forms are spelled by adding *-ed* to the present tense verb.

Present tense	Past tense	Past participle
add	added	added
allow	allowed	allowed
ask	asked	asked

As usual, there are exceptions to this rule.

Exception 1
Verbs Ending in *e*

If the last letter is an *e,* simply add *-d.*

Present tense	Past tense	Past participle
close	closed	closed
die	died	died
free	freed	freed

Exception 2
Verbs Ending in *y*

For verbs that end in *-y* preceded by one or more consonants, change the *-y* to *-i* before adding *-ed.*

Present tense	Past tense	Past participle
apply	applied	applied
study	studied	studied
	BUT	
play	played	played

Finally, verbs that double the final consonant when *-ing* is added also double the final consonant when *-ed* is added.

Exception 3
Accented Syllables

If the last syllable is accented (stressed), double a single consonant preceded by a single vowel before adding *-ed.*

Present tense	Past tense	Past participle
prefer (pre-FER)	preferred	preferred
control (con-TROL)	controlled	controlled
	BUT	
corner (COR-ner)	cornered	cornered
travel (TRA-vel)	traveled	traveled

Since the syllable in one-syllable words is always stressed, this exception always applies to one-syllable words—just as in the case of *-ing.*

Present tense	Past tense	Past participle
plan	planned	planned
	BUT	
clean	cleaned	cleaned

As in the case of *-ing,* consonants like *w* and *y* are never doubled.

Present tense	Past tense	Past participle
endow	endowed	endowed
slow	slowed	slowed
play	played	played

Exercise 2   Adding *-ed* and *-d*

Write the correct *-ed* form of the following verbs.

Example   ally   _allied_

    1. patrol   _____

    2. reply   _____

    3. introduce   _____

    4. finish   _____

    5. scan   _____

    6. imagine   _____

    7. walk   _____

    8. like   _____

    9. arrive   _____

    10. start   _____

    11. pass   _____

    12. quiet   _____

    13. attend   _____

    14. regret   _____

    15. alter   _____

Adding -*s* and -*es*

    The same rules apply when you add -*s* to verbs or to nouns. The -*s* ending on a verb denotes the present tense form used with subjects like *he, she,* and *it.* The -*s* on a noun denotes a plural form.

Spelling -*s* Words

Spell the *s*-form of most verbs and nouns by adding -*s* to the root word.

Verb	***s*-form**
see	sees
play	plays

Verb	s-form
find	finds
understand	understands
compare	compares
separate	separates

Noun	Plural
actor	actors
idea	ideas
fortune	fortunes
Pontiac	Pontiacs
sidewalk	sidewalks
Wilson	Wilsons

Exception 1
Words That Add -es

Add -es instead of -s to words that end in an *s, x, z, sh,* or *ch.*

	Verb/noun	s-form
S:	dress	dresses
	boss	bosses
X:	fix	fixes
	ax	axes
Z:	fizz	fizzes
	Perez	Perezes
SH:	flash	flashes
	ash	ashes
CH:	lurch	lurches
	church	churches

Exception 2
Words That End in -o

You usually add -es instead of -s to words that end in *o.*

Verb/noun	s-form
go	goes
potato	potatoes

BUT

radio	radios

Exception 3
Words Ending in -y

For words that end in -y preceded by one or more consonants, change the -y to -i and add -es.

Verb/noun	s-form
apply	applies
study	studies
ferry	ferries
ally	allies
library	libraries
story	stories

BUT

play	plays
delay	delays
alley	alleys
key	keys
Henry	Henrys

Exercise 3   Adding -s to verbs and nouns

Write the correct -s form of the following words.

Example   miss   <u>misses</u>

1. crash   _____

2. flex   _____

3. apply   _____

4. penetrate   _____

5. do   _____

6. tarnish   _____

7. pipe   _____

8. project   _____

9. dentist   _____

10. launch   _____

11. university _____

12. enjoy _____

13. solidify _____

14. enroll _____

15. rock _____

Exercise 4 Correcting word endings

Correct any misspelled words in the following paragraph.

Several horses stampped nervously in the dirt near the water trough. Inside the saloon Sutton was dealling a hand of blackjack. Three men looked on from the bar. Another man stood near the swinging doorrs carveing an apple with a short knife. Sunlight from the windows brightenned the room almost beyond endurance. A fly, buzing in the dusty air, was the last sound anyone remem- berred hearing. Suddenly gunshotts tore the room in half.

Sound-alike words

Sometimes one word sounds so much like another word that the two spellings can become confused. We will look at some of the most common sound-alike words.

Possessives and contractions

Although there are many sound-alike words in English, among the most con- fusing are the following possessive adjectives and contractions.

Its/it's

Its is a possessive adjective meaning "belonging to it." *It's* is a contraction of *it is* or *it has*.

The dog raised **its** head.

It's a beautiful day.
It is a beautiful day.

It's been good to see you.
It has been good to see you.

Your/you're

Your is a possessive adjective meaning "belonging to you." *You're* is a contraction of *you are*.

Did you bring **your** books?

You're the best storyteller in the room.
You are the best storyteller in the room.

Whose/who's

Whose is a possessive adjective used in questions and adjective clauses. *Who's* is a contraction for *who is* or *who has*.

Whose car is this?
I know the woman **whose** car this is.

Who's willing to ask the obvious question?
Who is willing to ask the obvious question?

Their/they're/there

Their is a possessive adjective meaning "belonging to them." *They're* is a contraction of *they are*. *There* is an adverb that usually indicates a place.

Their holiday plans sound interesting.

They're working in the garden.
They are working in the garden.

We work **there**.

In each of the above examples, the word with the apostrophe (') is the contraction in the group. Remember that apostrophes are *always* used to hold the place of missing letters in contractions.

Exercise 5   Possessives and contractions

Correct any misused word in the following sentences. If a sentence is already correct, write **OK** in the margin.

Example

                               its

She left the phone off it's hook.

1. Their trying to correct the problem now.

2. Who's explanation do you believe?

3. There sits an honest man.

4. The personal computer has left it's mark on Western culture.

5. They're working on the problem and will have a solution sometime this week.

6. I read the text of you're speech in the campus newspaper.

7. They're is a young man waiting in the outer office for you.

8. Every dog recognizes its owner.

9. I'm looking for one juror whose on my side.

10. Michael and Inez left there books in the car.

11. Who's standing by the door?

12. Its time to start working on the anthropology project.

13. Your the best man for the position.

14. The eggs are all packed in their containers.

15. I know it's a long trip to be taking on such short notice.

Other sound-alike words

There are other groups of common words that sound alike and are often mistaken for each other. The most common are these:

Accept/except

Accept is a verb meaning "to receive" or "to answer affirmatively." *Except* is a preposition meaning "excluding."

She will not **accept** the truth about Aunt Marge.

He scored better than everyone **except** Bennett.

Alone/along

Alone is an adverb meaning "by oneself." *Along* is an adverb or preposition meaning "with someone else."

I went to the film **alone.**

I went **along** with Helene to the film.

An/and

An is an adjective. It is used instead of *a* when the next word starts with a vowel sound. *And* is a conjunction.

An old tree has fallen behind the garage.

Eric **and** Antony are going to Fort Lauderdale together.

By/buy/bye

By is a preposition meaning "next to" or "through the action of." *Buy* is a verb meaning "to purchase." *Bye* is a form of *goodbye,* meaning "farewell."

This essay was written **by** Andrew over the weekend.

We **buy** a season ticket every year.

Mickey stood on his toes and whispered, **"Bye,** Grandma."

Doing/during

Doing is the *-ing* form of the verb **to do.** *During* is a preposition that introduces a span of time.

Are you **doing** well in geology?

The cat sleeps **during** the day.

Find/fine

Find is a verb meaning "to discover." *Fine,* as an adjective or adverb, refers to the quality of something; as a noun, it means "a penalty," such as a judge might give a traffic offender.

Can Felicia **find** the restaurant?

This is a **fine** day.

Judge Halprin made me pay a $25 **fine**.

Hole/whole

Hole is a noun referring to a cavity or opening made in something. *Whole* is a noun or adjective meaning "everything" or "entire."

You have a **hole** in your sock.

The **whole** story is being rewritten.

Idea/ideal

An *idea* is a thought. An *ideal* is a standard of perfection. *Idea* is always a noun. *Ideal* can be a noun or an adjective.

Governor Black has a good **idea** for reforming the state income tax.

In an **ideal** class, students are free to ask questions.

Loose/lose

Loose (pronounced LOOSS) is an adjective meaning "not tight," referring to how something fits. *Lose* (pronounced LOOZE) is a verb meaning "to mislay something."

These shoes are too **loose** for my feet.

I'm afraid the child will **lose** his way.

Loss/lost

Loss and *lost* are both related to the verb "to lose." *Loss* is a noun made from this verb. *Lost* is the past tense of *lose* and also the past participle used in verb phrases or as an adjective.

Noun

Allen's death was a great **loss** to Mary.

Past tense

I **lost** a lot of time worrying about the test.

Past participle and adjective

The money was **lost** at the roulette table.

We searched for the **lost** child in the woods.

Mind/mine

Mind is a noun that refers to a person's brain or ability to think. *Mine* is a pronoun related to *I* and *me*.

He does all his adding in his **mind**.

The house is **mine**.

No/know

No is an adjective or adverb meaning "not any." It is also a negative response to a question. *Know* is a verb meaning "to be aware of" or "to understand."

I have **no** idea when he'll return.

Did you **know** that Bill found a job?

Pass/passed/past

This group is similar to *lose/lost/loss*. *Pass* is a verb that has several meanings. *Passed* is the past participle form of this verb, used mainly in verb phrases.

Past is a preposition used in prepositional phrases. *Past* is also a noun, adjective, or adverb referring to time gone by. *Past* is never used in verb phrases.

Verb

He cannot **pass** the final exam without more work.

Past participle

My brother has **passed** biology at last.

Past as noun

Memories are shadows of the **past**.

Past as preposition

Silena drove **past** the old courthouse.

Sit/set

These two verbs are often confused. *Sitting* is a position you take. *Setting* is something you do to something else. If something rests undisturbed, it *sits*.

Please **sit** next to Marion.

Why don't you **set** that shovel down?

The vase **sits** on the radiator.

Then/than

Then is an adverb that tells "when." *Than* is a preposition used in comparisons.

We had dinner and **then** went to the movies.

These towels are a much better buy **than** the others.

To/too/two

These words are commonly confused. *To* is a preposition, and it often indicates a direction. It is also used to form infinitives. *Too* is an adverb. When it describes a verb, it means "also." When it describes an adjective, it indicates an excessive amount of something. *Two* is a number.

Study these words carefully. They occur frequently in writing.

Frank drives **to** work at nine.

Alicia wanted to go **too**.

We will return in **two** hours.

Were/where

Were is a past tense form of *to be*. *Where* is an adverb or conjunction that indicates a place.

James and Doree **were** both raised in France.

Where is my brown jacket?

Whether/weather

Whether is a conjunction (tip-off word) that usually introduces a dependent clause or phrase. **Weather** is a noun referring to the climate or an atmospheric condition.

She wondered **whether** Randolph would visit soon.

The **weather** will be cool and dry.

Exercise 6 Other sound-alike words

Correct any misused or misspelled word in the following sentences. (All of the errors involve words discussed above.)

Example

Bruno never did fin~~g~~d his los~~s~~t books.

1. We past the store an several gas stations on the way to Walter's.

2. The find was levied against both of the defendants.

3. The credit sign said, "Bye now, pay later."

4. My uncle doesn't like to loose on poker nights.

5. I have no idea weather you past the restaurant or not.

6. Wendy rode alone with her sisters.

7. How did you no the names of the authors?

8. These vendors do not except credit cards.

9. To many people wanted to use the pool then could comfortably swim there.

10. The Great Santini Brothers are an idea circus act.

11. Miss Hays observed every holiday accept this one.

12. Herman never took a vacation in his hole life.

13. Please pass the cards too the dealer.

14. Would you mine if we borrowed these chairs?

15. He set next to the minister and his wife.

Commonly misspelled words

Some words are commonly misspelled—everyone has trouble with at least some of them. Many of these words are listed below.

Commonly misspelled words

accommodate	appearance
acquainted	article
across	athletics
agreement	attendance
all right	believe
already	benefit
analysis	Britain

business	manufacture
changeable	misspelled
choose	monotonous
comparative	mysterious
conceive	necessary
conscience	noticeable
continuous	occasionally
deceive	occurrence
decision	omitted
definite	opportunity
dependent	particularly
description	pastime
develop	perform
dining room	precede
disappearance	prejudice
disappoint	privilege
dormitory	probably
embarrass	procedure
environment	proceed
equipment	pronunciation
exaggerate	proportion
existence	psychology
extremely	quantity
familiar	receive
fascinate	repetition
foreign	resemblance
formerly	schedule
forty	secretary
grammar	seize
grieve	separate
harass	similar
height	sophomore
hindrance	succeed
imaginary	sympathize
immediately	temperament
incidentally	tendency
independent	therefore
intelligent	tragedy
irresistible	truly
judgment (*or* judgement)	undoubtedly
knowledge	until
leisure	usually
library	valuable
maintenance	writing

Exercise 7   Correcting misspelled words

Correct any misspelled words in the following sentences.

Example
We were embarra~~s~~sed by the notic~~e~~able neglect of the environment.

1. Wes took the baseball equippment back to the dormatory on his way to the libary.

2. Dr. Wescott is already aquainted with fourty of the supervisors.

3. The applicant gave his heigth and weight.

4. Brad was a sophmore when the incedent occured.

5. I beleive Brittain will benifit from the bisiness.

6. It's hard to exadgerate the role of prejidice in this dicision.

7. I am dissappointed in his artical on the Atheletics Department.

8. The film wasn't divelopped until we returned to the city.

9. I wanted to see the maintanance aggreement in writting.

10. Dr. Wasson offered an intelligent response to Benchley's analisis.

11. Desiree imediately walked to the dinning room.

12. The independant comparitive study was undoubtedly valuble.

13. A fly droned monotinously.

14. Packages are recieved in a seperate department.

15. He preceded to tell us the correct pronounciation of the word.

Review exercise

Correct any misspelled words in the following paragraph.

Much of the monney was never recoverred, even though it's owners searched countinuosly for nearly twelve years. Eventtually it was declarred lossed, and traces to its hidding place grew cold. Colonel Akroyd past the secret to his aunt in Georgia an quitely disapeared form the neiborhood. Twenty years later no one re-memberred the military man who inhabitted the corner house. The aunt eventully placed his last letter in her safe deposit box and for-got it. The box and it's contents endded up on a closet shelf in Michigan.

Chapter 22 writing assignment

1. Using the writing process discussed in Chapter 19, write a one-page essay on a topic of your own choice.
2. Your instructor may ask that you turn in your summary page and your drafts along with your final copy.

Answer key

Chapter 1   Exercise 1

1. *dependent;* Because these events occur frequently.

2. *dependent;* As we already told you.

3. *independent*

4. *independent*

5. *dependent;* If she finds her wallet soon.

6. *dependent;* Whom you were hoping to replace.

7. *independent*

8. *dependent;* Although Jerry studied last night.

9. *independent*

10. *dependent;* Which my sister recommended.

11. *independent*

12. *dependent;* When the college considered your application.

13. *independent*

Exercise 1 (cont.)

14. *independent*

15. *dependent;* Before the next installment appears in the local paper.

Exercise 3

1. compound	6. compound
2. complex	7. complex
3. complex	8. compound
4. complex	9. complex
5. compound	10. complex

Review exercise 1

1. A clause is a part of a sentence that contains a subject and a verb but may or may not stand alone.
2. An independent clause is a clause that can stand alone as a complete sentence.
3. A dependent clause is a clause that cannot stand alone as a complete sentence; it always contains a word or words that connect it to another part of a sentence.
4. A simple sentence contains only one independent clause.
5. A compound sentence contains two or more independent clauses joined by a conjunction, a comma and a conjunction, or a semicolon.
6. A complex sentence contains both a dependent and an independent clause.
7. A sentence fragment is a group of words that does not contain at least one independent clause but ends with a period; it may be a dependent clause, or it may be a group of words that does not contain a subject and a verb.

Chapter 2

Exercise 1

1. Wanda laughs at all her jokes.

2. The apartments were being redone for new tenants.

3. The *Titanic* disaster in 1912 changed radio from a toy to an important means of communication.

4. "FM" stands for "frequency modulation."

5. Many of Professor Wang's students will succeed because of her help.

6. Last night's fire shocked the entire community.

7. Antonio's restaurant has been serving fresh fish daily.

8. David discovered a new shortcut to the campus.

Exercise 1 (cont.)

9. No doubt the Lasowskis (will be bringing) their baby from the hospital tomorrow.

10. The entire bucket of roofing tar (splashed) into the pool.

Exercise 3

1. *action;* Byron (showed) great courage during his father's illness.

2. *linking;* Kurt (is) with his children every evening after work.

3. *action;* Yesterday I (saw) Amy Perfito on her way to the beach.

4. *action;* Earvin's suitcase (weighed) close to fifty pounds.

5. *action;* The Lakers (played) their best game last night.

6. *action;* Abdul (looked) everywhere in the theater for his watch.

7. *action;* The example (appears) on page 425.

8. *action;* Her magic tricks always (delight) the younger children.

9. *linking;* The locket (was) in the drawer all the time.

10. *linking;* This earthquake (felt) stronger than the last one.

11. *linking;* The young singer (sounded) like his father.

12. *action;* The bad accident (occurred) on this street last week.

13. *linking;* The sheets (smell) fresh.

14. *action;* For days afterward, I (thought) about her decision to leave school.

15. *action;* The bank (opens) for business at ten on Saturday.

Exercise 5

1. We (agreed) with all of her arguments.

2. The best comedian in the show (was) eleven years old.

3. The manager (spoke) highly of the team's talent.

4. Unlike the last president, Dr. Aaron (places) a high priority on research.

5. Commuters from the northern suburbs (waited) three hours for a train into town this morning.

Exercise 5 (cont.)

6. The manual decarbing <u>assistor</u> (needed) replacement badly.

7. Chen's dancing <u>instructor</u> (called) in sick this week.

8. The <u>puppy</u> (spent) last night in a box in the basement.

9. The oldest <u>student</u> in the class (looks) like a bank president.

10. <u>He</u> (is) actually a prominent local sculptor.

11. WYKY's local <u>weatherman</u> (guessed) wrong this morning.

12. The <u>victims</u> (reported) the burglary themselves.

13. <u>Wrecking Crew</u> (won) the race by four lengths.

14. A painful <u>limp</u> (slowed) his walk.

15. The <u>Consequential Insurance Company</u> (issued) the policy last year.

Exercise 7

1. <u>Demonstrators</u> (swarmed) through the European city.

2. The <u>bookstore</u> (sells) many historical <u>novels</u>.

3. In spite of examples, these <u>instructions</u> (seem) <u>unclear</u>. *Comp*

4. <u>It</u> (was sent) yesterday.

5. <u>This</u> (is) the best <u>college</u> in the state. *comp*

6. The <u>Knights of Columbus</u> (give) charitable <u>meals</u> each year at this time.

7. Few <u>governments</u> (are) <u>ready</u> for tax reform. *Comp.*

8. The new camera operator's <u>work</u> (was) <u>excellent</u>. *Comp*

9. The <u>thunderstorm</u> (woke) him up.

10. <u>Carmen</u> (looked) through the window at the street.

Review exercise

The twentieth <u>century</u> (saw) the <u>birth</u> of a new form of storytelling. An ingenious <u>combination</u> of metal, celluloid, glass, and wiring (produced) a technological <u>breakthrough</u>. The <u>result</u> (had) a tremendous <u>effect</u> on the minds of

Review exercise (cont.)

millions. This art <u>form</u>, of course, (is) the motion <u>picture</u>. [Comp] To many people <u>it</u> (is)

the most important art <u>form</u> [Comp] of the century.

Chapter 3

Exercise 1

1. Why (was) your <u>worksheet</u> <u>late</u>? [Comp]
2. (Is) <u>this</u> your first philosophy <u>course</u>? [Comp]
3. <u>Who</u> (can answer) my <u>question</u>?
4. (Did) this <u>actress</u> (star) in several musical productions?
5. When (is) the next <u>train</u> to Boston?
6. (May) <u>Erica</u> (borrow) your <u>car</u>?
7. (Was) <u>corn</u> also <u>available</u> [comp] in Europe?
8. How (was) your <u>supper</u>?
9. How (do) <u>you</u> (spell) her <u>name</u>?
10. (Can) <u>Chris</u> (watch) <u>TV</u> tonight?

Exercise 3

1. Into the room (walked) three <u>players</u> from the soccer team.

   Three players from the soccer team walked into the room.

2. A blank <u>page</u> (is) the writer's worst <u>enemy</u>. [Comp]

   [This sentence is in normal word order.]

3. To Mr. Hogan (went) the last <u>transceiver</u>.

   The last transceiver went to Mr. Hogan.

4. A fine <u>student</u> <u>he</u> (became)! [Comp]

   He became a fine student.

5. On the shelf (sat) the <u>stack</u> of newspapers.

   The stack of newspapers sat on the shelf.

Exercise 5

1. (Is) this the way to Beauville? *comp*

2. Here (is) a recent map of this region.

3. Who (lives) in the house now?

4. (Read) the article on the back page. *you*

5. What (was) she (doing) near the safe?

6. One book (disappeared) each week of the last month.

7. There (are) no more copies of the essay.

8. (Was) she the first lawyer on the case? *comp*

9. (Stop) at the first apartment on the left. *you*

10. There (were) ants in the kitchen this morning.

Review exercise

(Do) you (need) a copy of one of your files? Here (is) the simplest method. (Press) *you*
the "Fl" key. A list of files on the current disk (will appear) on the computer
screen. Then (move) the cursor with the arrow keys. Once you (have chosen) a *you*
file for copying, (press) the "Enter" key. The computer automatically (copies) *you*
the marked file.

Chapter 4   Exercise 1

1. /the Gatling Gun was invented in the 1800s. /many people thought it *T* *M*
   would change the West.

2. /their new album sold several million copies /this includes sales in Europe *T* *T*
   as well.

3. /the store opened early, /the holiday season must be starting already. *T* *T*

4. /the contract clearly restricts the number of units available to discount *T*
   buyers.

Exercise 1 (cont.)

5. $\overset{S}{\cancel{s}}$urely the technical manual contains several solutions to the problem. $\overset{C}{\cancel{c}}$hoose one of them.

6. $\overset{L}{\cancel{l}}$ater we told Mrs. Gallagher about the snails in the garden. $\overset{S}{s}$he showed us a book on the subject.

7. $\overset{S}{\cancel{s}}$ummer arrived yesterday. $\overset{F}{\cancel{f}}$ew noticed it since the temperature stayed in the fifties.

8. $\overset{T}{\cancel{t}}$he bears discovered the garbage pile in the night. $\overset{T}{t}$his morning the entire area was a mess.

9. $\overset{B}{\cancel{b}}$ooks that have Dr. Hemming's signature on the title page are now worth over $1000 each.

10. $\overset{I}{\cancel{i}}$n the box on the stairs is a small yellow envelope. $\overset{G}{g}$et it for me please if you have the time.

Review exercise

Ellie Sena loves gardening. $\overset{L}{l}$ast year she started her garden early. $\overset{S}{s}$he wanted to grow some peas before the hot weather set in. $\overset{T}{t}$he very next day rain started to fall. $\overset{I}{i}$t continued for a full week until all the gardens in the area looked like huge puddles. $\overset{A}{a}$ll her seeds washed away. Ellie's neighbor Joe Kawecki had put in some squash seeds but they rotted from all the wetness. $\overset{T}{\cancel{t}}$hen the sun finally came out. $\overset{B}{b}$oth Ellie and Joe prepared to start afresh. $\overset{T}{t}$hey now knew the uncertainty that farmers must endure each year.

Chapter 5   Exercise 1

1. The Barkleys (will go) to the Catskills this summer.

2. On weekdays I (eat) a small breakfast.

3. Wilma (had done) the best job possible.

Exercise 1 (cont.)

4. Tonight's dinner (was prepared) by my daughter.

5. Kiley's girlfriend (should bring) extra plates.

6. The game (has lasted) over two hours.

7. We (must read) those novels for our last literature class.

8. Mr. Wilkes (is leaving) for Colorado.

9. The books (should have arrived) by now.

10. Tremaine, a transfer student, (will be joining) us in March.

11. The actors (have been practicing) since May.

12. The girls in the hall (could have been listening.)

13. The poem (might have been recited) more feelingly.

14. Sonya (might have coped) with her transportation problem differently.

15. The box (had) to be sent by courier mail.

Exercise 3

1. The clock (had rung) several times already.

2. We (should have ordered) pizza.

3. Marcy's new job (could be) a wonderful opportunity.

4. The pie (should have been left) in the oven longer.

5. The dog (had become) irritated by all the fire alarms.

6. The computer system (has been installed) by a consultant from Lanfil

    Technologies.

7. She (will have flown) more than ten thousand miles by Tuesday.

8. Shea (has been trying) hard to win the councilman's seat.

9. The boss (will be coming) any minute.

10. Marv Murphy (has been) a broadcaster in this area for more than fifteen

    years.

11. Jim (may have gone) to the Coho Club.

Exercise 3 (cont.)

12. She (practiced) the flute for years before performing in public.

13. The buses (were running) on a special schedule during the snowstorm.

14. The sauce (might taste) peppery.

15. The world (has been made) safe for democracy.

Review exercise

   In my student days, I (had) always (preferred) serious drama, but my friends (were) usually much more (drawn) to musicals. I (would) sometimes (go) along with them to these shows. With all their stage activity, musicals (had) doubtlessly (struck) us as cheerful and exciting entertainment. Their glitter, too, (must have) strongly (appealed) to us, for it (was) such a contrast to the drabness of our small, industrial town. (Could) any of us, though, really (appreciate) the music? I (do) not (recall). Still, it (was) fun to whistle all those tunes afterward. Even now, I (smile) when the radio (plays) a tune that I (had) once (heard) live on a stage.

Chapter 6   Exercise 1

1. bid	bade	bidden
2. teach	taught	taught
3. arrange	arranged	arranged
4. mean	meant	meant
5. delay	delayed	delayed
6. carry	carried	carried
7. die	died	died
8. learn	learned	learned
9. bring	brought	brought
10. hit	hit	hit
11. drive	drove	driven
12. know	knew	known
13. prevail	prevailed	prevailed
14. give	gave	given
15. rise	rose	risen
16. get	got	gotten
17. refer	referred	referred
18. wear	wore	worn
19. run	ran	run
20. grow	grew	grown

Exercise 3

1. *consider, considered, considered;* consider
2. *consider, considered, considered;* is considered
3. *stand, stood, stood;* stood
4. *stand, stood, stood;* was stood
5. *give, gave, given;* will give
6. *give, gave, given;* will be given
7. *use, used, used;* used
8. *suppose, supposed, supposed;* suppose
9. *find, found, found;* found
10. *discover, discovered, discovered;* will discover
11. *turn, turned, turned;* turned
12. *need, needed, needed;* will be needed
13. *enjoy, enjoyed, enjoyed;* enjoyed
14. *has, had, had;* has
15. *awaken, awakened, awakened;* was awakened

Exercise 5

1. *past perfect passive;* had been ranked
2. *present perfect;* has held
3. *past perfect passive;* had been signed
4. *future perfect passive;* will have been mailed
5. *past;* called
6. *past perfect;* had announced
7. *past;* abandoned
8. *present perfect passive;* has been written
9. *present perfect passive;* has been chosen
10. *past;* opened

Exercise 7

1. *present;* respond
2. *present perfect progressive;* have been traveling
3. *present;* says
4. *present progressive;* is seeing
5. *past perfect progressive;* had been dating

Review exercise

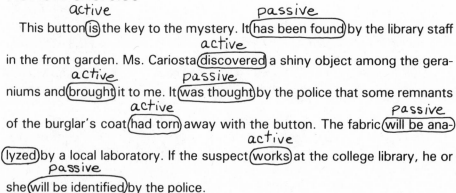

This button <u>is</u> (active) the key to the mystery. It <u>has been found</u> (passive) by the library staff in the front garden. Ms. Cariosta <u>discovered</u> (active) a shiny object among the geraniums and <u>brought</u> (active) it to me. It <u>was thought</u> (passive) by the police that some remnants of the burglar's coat <u>had torn</u> (active) away with the button. The fabric <u>will be analyzed</u> (passive) (active) by a local laboratory. If the suspect <u>works</u> (active) at the college library, he or she <u>will be identified</u> (passive) by the police.

Review exercise (cont.)

The library staff found it in the front garden.
The police thought that some remnants of the burglar's coat had torn away with the button.
A local laboratory will analyze the fabric.
The police will identify the suspect.

Chapter 7

Exercise 1

1. I work
2. you reply
3. he asks
4. they remind
5. she forces
6. we smile
7. it passes
8. you arrange
9. they interview
10. it hurts
11. she sees
12. we enroll
13. she married
14. I sympathize
15. he chooses

Exercise 3

1. I am
2. you have
3. he is
4. they are
5. she has
6. we were
7. he was
8. I was
9. I have
10. he has
11. we are
12. it was
13. she is
14. they have
15. you were

Exercise 5

1. I am in town for just this weekend.

2. She is an excellent employee.

3. They have one of the finest examples of Indian beadwork in the Southwest.

4. He was in the market for a BMW.

5. It is time for another evaluation.

6. You are not what the coach expected.

7. She has only a few weeks to finish her report.

8. You were already a candidate for the promotion.

Exercise 5 (cont.)

9. <u>They</u> are never critical of my efforts.

10. <u>He</u> usually has enough quarters for the washing machines.

Exercise 7

1. We ~~is~~ *are* on her list of available applicants.

2. She ~~have~~ *has* a copy in her desk.

3. He ~~be~~ *is* luckier than most.

4. I ~~is~~ *am* nowhere near a solution to this problem.

5. You ~~has~~ *have* a color television in your room.

6. It ~~were~~ *was* hard enough without Byron's help.

OK 7. We (have) several examples of her art in stock.

8. I never ~~were~~ *was* a student in his upper division course.

OK 9. He (has) an answer for everything.

10. They ~~was~~ *were* not pleased.

Exercise 9

1. The <u>horse</u> ~~have~~ *it* *has* escaped through the break in the fence.

2. The <u>singer</u> ~~are~~ *he or she* *is* often asked about concert tickets.

OK 3. Balcony <u>seats</u> *they* have been available for months.

4. <u>Mario</u> ~~be looking~~ *He* *is* for Ben Garetski.

5. The two faculty <u>members</u> ~~has responded~~ *they* *have* to their complaints.

OK 6. The <u>film</u> *it* is being shot in Brooklyn.

7. The <u>shirt</u> ~~are made~~ *it* *is* in Taiwan.

OK 8. The <u>chicken</u> *it* is cooking in the outdoor grill.

9. <u>Jim and Annette</u> ~~is~~ *They* *are* not attending the concert this evening.

10. The <u>restaurants</u> on this block ~~has offered~~ *they* *have* to support the station.

Review exercise

The idea that there ~~exist~~ *exists* a basic building block of nature called the "atom" ~~go~~ *goes* back to the early Greeks. Atoms are the fundamental unit of all chemical elements, but they ~~is~~ *are* not the most elementary particles of matter. All atoms ~~contains~~ *contain* protons and electrons, as well as other particles. Especially interesting ~~be~~ *is* the fact that regardless of what element they ~~comes~~ *come* from they all ~~looks~~ *look* alike.

Chapter 8   Exercise 1

1. Yesterday <u>he</u> played first trombone in the band concert.

2. <u>I</u> know he wanted to go to college last fall.

3. The <u>registrar</u> published the spring catalogue already.

4. <u>She</u> prepared herself well for her new career.

5. <u>Stanley</u> asked every question he could think of.

6. The <u>dean</u> admitted making the error.

7. The big <u>man</u> frowned, and tears filled his eyes.

8. Michael's <u>Buick</u> roared away from the stop sign.

9. <u>They</u> played in the afternoon and studied at night.

10. <u>Mr. Wagner</u> urged his students to compete in the national science contest.

Exercise 3

OK 1. The <u>gentlemen</u> (like) the restaurant, but their <u>wives</u> (don't).

2. The <u>Harrises</u> (invite) *invited* us to go skiing with them soon.

3. <u>He</u> just (remembered) that <u>he</u> (promise) *promised* to submit an article for the school newspaper.

Exercise 3 (cont.)

4. After much discussion, the judges ~~declare~~ *declared* Another Horse's Color the winner.

5. The band ~~receive~~ *received* an invitation to return.

OK 6. Careless campers (cause) forest fires.

7. Last night the president ~~appear~~ *appeared* on television.

8. This man ~~seem~~ *seemed* ready to go back to work.

9. Brenda ~~correct~~ *corrected* the error in the computer yesterday.

10. This time, the local politicians ~~allow~~ *allowed* the company's engineers to draft their own policy.

Exercise 5

1. Several pieces of wood (were ~~place~~) x *placed* on the worktable.

2. The last bell (has) x already ~~sound~~ *sounded*.

3. This game (should be ~~play~~) x *played* by more than three players.

4. That question (was) x never ~~ask~~ *asked*.

5. The infected organs (will be ~~remove~~) x *removed* Wednesday.

6. Three men (were ~~arrest~~) x *arrested* yesterday for the Lucky's Liquor Barn holdup.

OK 7. We (could serve) them fried eggs and ham for breakfast.

8. The arbitrator's ruling (was ~~appeal~~) x *appealed* to the governing board.

9. Despite the blizzard, the mail (was ~~deliver~~) x *delivered* all week.

10. A new benefit program (was ~~announce~~) x *announced* by the board of directors.

11. Each of the senators (has ~~benefit~~) x *benefited* from the passage of the pension bill.

12. The request for noncompressive widgets (will be ~~process~~) x *processed* by the accounting clerks as soon as we receive a purchase order.

13. The mechanic's accident (was) x probably ~~cause~~ *caused* by a worn gasket.

14. Your film (will) not (be ~~develop~~) x *developed* until Wednesday.

OK 15. Professor Nettelbaum (will) probably (cancel) next week's class.

Exercise 7

1. Their act (is performed) with specially ~~treat~~ *treated* clothing.
2. The police (looked) for signs of ~~force~~ *forced* entry.
OK 3. The Meyers (asked) about our special price on recently repaired vehicles.
4. The fluid (flowed) faster through previously ~~heat~~ *heated* pipes.
5. Please (place) all previously ~~check~~ *checked* baggage on the floor in front of you.
6. The varnish, ~~apply~~ *applied* in layers, (produces) a nice surface shine.
7. Angelica (learned) about his ~~alter~~ *altered* plans only yesterday.
8. A ~~confuse~~ *confused* mayor (spoke) to the town council last night.
9. The cleaners (returned) a ~~wrinkle~~ *wrinkled* pair of pants.
10. The open door (revealed) a ~~surprise~~ *surprised* young boy.

Review exercise

Jim Pruitt ~~call~~ *called* Brad Bradford this morning to have him look at his refrigerator. Jim ~~want~~ *wanted* Brad's opinion about whether to repair or replace it. He knew Brad ~~use~~ *used* to work on refrigerators and air conditioners all through high school. The refrigerator just ~~stop~~ *stopped* working sometime during the night. There ~~were~~ *was* an electrical storm at two in the morning, and Jim ~~were concern~~ *was concerned* that there might have been an electrical overload that ~~damage~~ *damaged* the refrigerator.

Jim did not want to buy a new one if he did not need to, since his daughter was ~~suppose~~ *supposed* to go to college in the fall and Jim could not afford the ~~add~~ *added* expense. Brad ~~look~~ *looked* at the refrigerator carefully but could not find any real damage—just a switch that had become ~~burn~~ *burned*. He ~~replace~~ *replaced* it easily and ~~charge~~ *charged* Jim nothing.

Chapter 9

Exercise 1

1. Next week's <u>game</u> (is played)^x at Shaughnessy Stadium.
2. Loud <u>noises</u> from the new mining operation (have been frightening)^{x x} the children.
3. (Has)^x the <u>money</u> (arrived) yet?
4. The <u>chair</u> (was thrown)^x away last winter.
5. <u>Rain</u> (has been falling)^{x x} for several weeks now.
6. Medical <u>supplies</u> (have) already (been flown)^{x   x} into the stricken area.
7. <u>I</u> (have) never (worn)^x that tie.
8. Colonel <u>Stroud</u> (has been)^x busy for several hours.
9. <u>This</u> (will) just (take) a minute.
10. The birthday <u>cake</u> (could have been made)^{x   x} this morning.

Exercise 3

1. *draw, drew, drawn;* The opening of the pier ~~drawed~~ *drew* a large crowd.
2. *spend, spent, spent;* The customers (spent) most of their money at the kissing booth.
3. *lose, lost, lost;* Misha (lost) several of his best poems during the move.
4. *take, took, taken;* Steve (took) an incomplete in the course.
5. *speak, spoke, spoken;* Dr. Ali ~~spoken~~ *spoke* to him about completing his final essay by June 24.
6. *go, went, gone;* The weatherman ~~gone~~ *went* to a meteorological convention.
7. *ring, rang, rung;* The phone (rang) three times before breakfast.
8. *meet, met, met;* Phil ~~meeted~~ *met* every challenge presented to him.
9. *teach, taught, taught;* She ~~teached~~ *taught* herself to enjoy oysters.
10. *drive, drove, driven;* The manager ~~drived~~ *drove* to the warehouse himself.

Exercise 5

1. *spend, spent, spent;* Three hundred and sixty dollars (were ~~spended~~) on ⟨x spent⟩

   the awards banquet.

2. *find, found, found;* None of the villagers (could be found). ⟨x⟩

3. *break, broke, broken;* The statue (was ~~broke~~) in shipping. ⟨x broken⟩

4. *write, wrote, written;* My instructor (has ~~wrote~~) his own textbook. ⟨x written⟩

5. *tear, tore, torn;* Martin's knee (was ~~tore~~) in the auto accident. ⟨x torn⟩

6. *do, did, done;* Who (has) never (did) a research paper before? ⟨x⟩ ⟨done⟩

7. *grow, grew, grown;* My father (has ~~grew~~) roses for the last fifteen years. ⟨x grown⟩

8. *hit, hit, hit;* Alexander (has ~~hitted~~) a single in his last seventeen games. ⟨x hit⟩

9. *know, knew, known;* She (had known) his secret for a few months. ⟨x⟩

10. *cut, cut, cut;* The skin (was ~~cutted~~) in two places. ⟨x cut⟩

Exercise 7

1. (Has) anyone (brought) mayonnaise? ⟨x⟩

2. Alexander soon (made) plans to invade Greece.

3. Buddy never (meant) to talk that loud.

4. He (had ~~builded~~) these three houses. ⟨x built⟩

5. (Had) you (~~heared~~) about John's scholarship? ⟨x⟩ ⟨heard⟩

6. He (~~spended~~) his last dollar on that beer. ⟨Spent⟩

7. The boys in the back (had told) her not to bother them. ⟨x⟩

8. The sisters (~~founded~~) another reason to avoid going to Aunt Mattie's. ⟨found⟩

9. Will (could ~~sent~~) the letter for you. ⟨Send⟩

10. The groceries (were ~~brung~~) into the house by the neighbor's son. ⟨x brought⟩

Review exercise

Paragraph A

When we arrived at the other end of the valley, we ~~seen~~ that the British sol- ⟨saw⟩
diers ~~was~~ already camped across the river. Captain Wainwright had ~~receive~~ ⟨were⟩ ⟨received⟩

Review exercise (cont.)

orders from General Latrobe not to surrender the valley, so he ~~sended~~ *sent* me and

Will Jennings to scout their position. He also ~~telled~~ *told* us to find out how many

of them there ~~was~~ *were*. Night had just ~~fell~~ *fallen*, and we left immediately. Neither Will

nor I had ~~ate~~ *eaten* any supper.

Paragraph B

We ~~gone~~ *went* by foot to the river's edge and had no trouble until we tried to

cross. We thought that there might be several small boats by the river's

edge, but the Redcoats had ~~sank~~ *sunk* them. If we wanted to cross, it would have

to be by swimming. I turned to Will and I ~~seen~~ *saw* a strange look in his eyes. Then

I remembered. Will had ~~growed~~ *grown* up in the back country and never ~~learn~~ *learned* to

swim. I looked at the water. It had ~~rose~~ *risen* almost to its yearly high, thanks to the

melting spring snow from the mountains. I looked again at Will. He ~~say~~ *said* he

wanted to try, and without looking at me, he ~~bended~~ *bent* down to remove his

boots. I prayed briefly and set to work on mine.

Chapter 10   Exercise 1

1. an ideal solution to the problem
2. between two of my best friends
3. this meal
4. the first sensible suggestion
5. those beautiful stuffed chairs
6. a colorful maze
7. answering her classified ad
8. their new dress design

Exercise 1 (cont.)

9. our English essays

10. its long, bushy tail

Exercise 3

1. writer	writers
2. saying	sayings
3. kiss	kisses
4. box	boxes
5. Benedict	Benedicts
6. applesauce	applesauces
7. video	videos
8. story	stories
9. push	pushes
10. marble	marbles
11. alley	alleys
12. tomato	tomatoes
13. boat	boats
14. dress	dresses
15. essay	essays
16. city	cities
17. rodeo	rodeos
18. driver	drivers
19. fairy	fairies
20. Germany	Germanys

Exercise 5

1. many ~~cousin~~ cousins
2. five new ~~pen~~ pens
3. a few used ~~carburetor~~ carburetors
4. several neighborhood ~~friend~~ friends
5. a large stone library
6. several unused ~~classroom~~ classrooms
7. those wicker baskets
8. several printing ~~press~~ presses
9. one of a few ~~letter~~ letters
10. Barry's last twelve ~~game~~ games

Exercise 7

1. earrings
2. guys
3. desks
4. teen-agers
5. motor

6. motors
7. flowers
8. box
9. friends
10. glasses

Exercise 9

1. The bright lights (shine) across the highway. *they*
2. Chao Li's best friends (are looking) for an apartment. *they*
3. The science writers' convention (has been scheduled) for June in Atlanta. *it*
4. The new delegates (want) to hold the meeting here. *they*
5. Essays (were assigned) yesterday. *they*
6. His car (was parked) in a garage around the corner. *it*
7. The last notes (echo) in the theater. *they*
8. Their story (sounds) interesting. *it*
9. The college (needs) a new law library. *it*
10. The neighborhood's newest stores (have) sales going on right now. *they*

Exercise 11

1. Several ~~goose~~ *geese* have started using the pond at my father's farm.
2. He keeps goats and ~~sheeps~~ *Sheep* most of the year and raises a few cash ~~crop~~ *crops*.
3. The ~~woman~~ *women* in this company are all eligible for promotion.
4. I spoke to the ~~childs~~ *Children* yesterday about their behavior.
5. The office was visited by several ~~salesmans~~ *Salesmen*.
6. Barry bought three new ~~fishes~~ *fish* for his home aquarium—all ~~guppy~~ *guppies*.
7. Janet received several 93s on her physiology exams.
8. Rita received three ~~87~~ *87s* on her recent quizzes.
9. The members of the commission decided the issue for ~~themselfs~~ *themselves*.
10. She broke two of her ~~tooth~~ *teeth* in the fall.

Review exercise

Some evenings both of Jenny's ~~parent~~ *parents* had to work. One such ~~evenings~~ *evening*,
when her favorite baby ~~sitters~~ *sitter* was putting her to bed, Jenny asked her,
"Why does Santa live at the North Pole?" It was just two ~~week~~ *weeks* before

Christmas. The baby sitter was afraid to tell Jenny the truth, for Jenny could
then spoil this ~~Christmases~~ *Christmas* for her two little ~~brother~~ *brothers*. Finally, the ~~women~~ *woman*
smiled at the little girl, showing a gold ~~teeth~~ *tooth*, and told her how Santa's several
~~allergy~~ *allergies* forced him to move north with his many ~~elf~~ *elves*.

The next morning Jenny shared this ~~stories~~ *story* with both her ~~parent~~ *parents*. They
were amused and asked ~~themself~~ *themselves* what they would have told this sharp little
girl in answer to such a ~~questions~~ *question*.

Chapter 11   Exercise 1

1. This ⟨was⟩ next *comp* to the swing.

2. One ⟨does⟩ not ⟨say⟩ such things.

3. She ⟨lifted⟩ herself onto the window ledge.

4. They ⟨know⟩ everyone here.

5. None of the children ⟨has brought⟩ a ball.

6. The dog ⟨buried⟩ it in the yard.

7. I ⟨wrote⟩ that article for the newspaper.

8. Paolo ⟨found⟩ these under the kitchen sink.

9. Two of his cousins ⟨have graduated⟩ already.

10. We ⟨examined⟩ each carefully.

Exercise 3

OK 1. Who plays tennis here?

2. The foreman knows both my brother and ~~I~~ *me*.

Exercise 3 (cont.)

3. Only ~~her~~ she, Dr. Werley's daughter, had both the motive and the opportunity for murder.

4. It was ~~him~~ he on the phone again.

OK 5. Another winter storm will hit us tonight.

6. ~~Whom~~ Who can help you the most?

7. Only you and ~~us~~ we can tell the difference.

OK 8. Whom did you hear on the phone?

9. The least guilty person is ~~him~~ he.

10. I have a candy bar to divide between you and ~~I~~ me.

Review exercise

Roweena has been working with small computers and computer systems for years. For her ~~it~~ this interest started as a hobby. In her junior year at Joliet State College, she entered the local science fair. All of ~~them~~ the entrants showed interesting projects. Roweena's project about computer codes won first prize, and she received a fellowship for graduate school. This fellowship meant a lot, both to her mother and ~~she~~ her. ~~Their~~ The students' adviser, Ms. Christiansen, was proud of ~~them~~ the participants all. But most of all ~~he~~ she was proud of Roweena. [Students' responses may vary.]

Chapter 12   Exercise 1

1. The key chain (saved) my life.
          comp
2. She (is) a model student.
3. The old boxes (were inhabited) by mice.
4. These librarians (take) their work seriously.
                                    comp
5. The largest set (was) not available.
6. The broken statues (can be fixed).
7. His inventory (includes) several new microprocessor chips.

Exercise 1 (cont.)

8. Our minivans (are) an excellent bargain. *[Comp]*

9. The Croton daily newspaper (declared) bankruptcy yesterday.

10. Several recent videos (have featured) famous film actors.

Exercise 3

1. *yes;* to Joseph

2. *no*

3. *yes;* with Marilyn and me

4. *yes;* for the coming symposium

5. *yes;* in chains

6. *yes;* above the village walls

7. *yes;* behind her back

8. *no*

9. *no*

10. *yes;* despite their anxiety

Exercise 5

1. The foreman is a good friend (of you and ~~I~~). *[me]*

2. Sister Alicia gave the letter (to Mrs. Radola and ~~she~~). *[her]*

3. (To ~~who~~) did you give copies (of the contract)? *[whom]*

4. Each (of us) wanted to go on the trip.

5. (For ~~who~~) was this gift purchased? *[whom]*

6. The briefcase was brought (to her)(by the manager and ~~he~~). *[him]*

7. Several new albums were previewed (at the reception).

8. You bought your books (from ~~who~~)? *[whom]*

9. The cabinet's decision was overturned (by the president and him).

10. (By ~~who~~) was the note (to her sister and ~~she~~) written? *[whom] [her]*

Exercise 7

1. The focus (of this discussion) has shifted.
2. She suggested the film (at the NuArt).
3. Several (of these envelopes) have been opened.
4. We played the team (from Argentina).
5. The manager (of the store) (on the corner) suggested several (of these).
6. Ari has received two (of the tickets).
7. The game (of the week) is being televised.
8. The men (in the front office) have spent millions (of dollars).
9. Her friend (in Alabama) wrote another (of her long letters).
10. We need a new committee chairman.

Review exercise

The evening (of the ninth day) (of April) fell, and the rain began. Loud explosions (of thunder) frightened Pablo. Everything (inside the house) rattled slightly. A dog (near the stable) (behind the house) yelped again and again. When he heard the terror (in that dog's bark), Pablo felt more afraid. *comp*

Suddenly the sound (of the thunder) stopped. Pablo slowly opened the curtain (of a window) (in the library). The faint lights (of the stars) twinkled overhead, and the air (outside the window) smelled fresh and cool. *comp* *comp* The lawn (around the house) was a deep, wet combination (of grass and dandelions). *comp* Pablo could just see the dark shape (of the eastern slope) (of the mountains). The sight (of those mountains) was a welcome relief. *comp*

Chapter 13   Exercise 1

1. *when;* Herman seldom opens his junk mail.
2. *where;* The coach threw down his bat.
3. *how;* She easily answered all his questions.

Exercise 1 (cont.)

4. *where;* The dog raced downstairs.

5. *when;* I never expected this promotion.

6. *when;* Yesterday one of the English faculty retired.

7. *how;* Professor Brandt speaks well.

8. *how;* Cautiously, the children entered the dark house.

9. *when;* Now Evelyn likes him.

10. *yes or no;* They have not filled the prescription.

Exercise 3

1. The mail is usually delivered at my house in the morning.

2. These papers fell from your desk.

3. Without any warning, our new teacher canceled all her classes for the rest of the week.

4. Henriette shared her news in a confidential whisper.

5. For his bravery, Melbar received a medal at the banquet.

6. Harold admitted the theft with a sly grin.

7. At the children's party, Ms. Pelotti gave *to* our daughter a very costly present.

8. With great determination, Leon walked toward the door.

9. The darkness keeps the secret well in this tunnel.

10. Did you go to the bookstore by the new route?

Review exercise

Yesterday I stayed inside the house and gave *to* it a good cleaning. *By* This morning all of the rooms sparkled but I felt *comp* very irritable. I needed a change (from my daily routine). I walked out of my front door and immediately felt better. I was in a really energetic mood, so I roamed around my neighborhood for

Review exercise (cont.)

hours. The noise of the traffic and the crush of the crowds seemed oddly ex-
comp
hilarating today.

I went down an unfamiliar street and stumbled into Kaminsky's Produce
to
Shop. Mrs. Kaminsky sold me a huge bunch of carrots with feathery green

tops and three pounds of seedless grapes. I got equally good bargains at the

hardware store and the bakery on the same street. I walked back to the

comp
house with bags under each arm. My legs were tired, but I was humming a

during
little tune. Maybe I will explore new territory tomorrow morning.

Chapter 14   Exercise 1

1. *sing*	singing	to sing	sung
2. *arrange*	arranging	to arrange	arranged
3. *see*	seeing	to see	seen
4. *run*	running	to run	run
5. *plan*	planning	to plan	planned
6. *try*	trying	to try	tried
7. *pass*	passing	to pass	passed
8. *buy*	buying	to buy	bought
9. *teach*	teaching	to teach	taught
10. *find*	finding	to find	found
11. *edit*	editing	to edit	edited
12. *calculate*	calculating	to calculate	calculated
13. *dance*	dancing	to dance	danced
14. *organize*	organizing	to organize	organized
15. *become*	becoming	to become	become

Exercise 3

1. She refused to give up her place in line.

2. Meta has no desire to get married.

3. He found a dollar stuck to the floor of the cafeteria.

4. Jim discovered the dog rummaging through the garbage can.

   comp
5. Opening the presents was my favorite part of Christmas.

6. The outside of the house really needs to be painted.

7. A coil in the heating unit was replaced yesterday.

Exercise 3 (cont.)

8. Ben prefers to eat rare meat.

9. The need to work overwhelmed Barry.

10. Written at the last minute, the story had to be revised.

Exercise 5

1. Hoping to meet women, Kurtis stayed in the library every evening.

OK 2. I have two pairs of jeans. The pair thrown into the corner needs to be washed.

OK 3. Discovering new skills has changed Marissa's life.

OK 4. The soloist playing in tonight's concert has never performed the Brahms sonata before.

5. Zeta Melbourne, giving a one-woman show next week, regularly performs in this auditorium.

6. Arnie VanDerKellen, watching the fireworks, was as delighted as his children with the display.

OK 7. Melba served lunch to some ladies canning tomatoes in the basement.

OK 8. The prince spoke the words written for him by the archbishop.

9. The old family dog, resting by the fire, looks as tired as Grandpa, sleeping in a chair beside him.

OK 10. Several of the governors invited to the reception have publicly refused to attend.

Exercise 7

1. The Shadow Warriors, (a local street gang,) have recently joined with another gang, (the Snow Kings,) in a neighborhood cleanup drive.

2. Michael's brother, (a medical technician,) has promised to pay his tuition this semester.

Exercise 7 (cont.)

3. His brother (the medical technician) has promised to pay Michael's tuition this semester.

4. One of the advertisements was placed by my uncle (the writer).

5. Only one thing, (poverty,) prevented him from being rich.

6. (A detective by nature,) Terry Hruska immediately reconsidered the events of last night.

7. Our great ambition, (to win the game,) made us practice daily.

8. We recently bought one of the better accounting programs, (ProRate.)

9. His friend (Ben) wrote it.

10. Georgina is saving money, (a few dollars each day.)

Exercise 9

OK 1. He placed the order with his uncle **Bill**.

2. The cause of the conflict, **a disagreement over land reform,** was soon forgotten.

3. The gun, **a battered .38,** was recovered from the lake.

4. He said the social welfare system punishes its beneficiaries, **the poor**.

5. The city council plans to rewrite a bylaw, **the one against loitering**.

6. Jamaal is studying the quark, **a subatomic particle**.

7. **A poet of sorts,** he wants to have its name changed to something more pleasing.

8. Consequential Insurance, **our auto insurance company,** waits three months and then pays its claims promptly.

9. She ended the set with her best saloon song, **a slow version of "Torchie."**

OK 10. I finally got the whole story from my friend **the hotshot lawyer**.

Review exercise 1

Sitting on the grass, Louis glanced at the sky. The sun, shining brightly, warmed his face. His gaze returned to a book lying open beside him and to the letter placed within it.

Vacationing in an out-of-the-way spot, he had forgotten school entirely. His two best friends, Marcel and Carolyn, had been a distant memory. Now they had decided to get married, and he had to attend the wedding, a fancy affair probably. Thoroughly disgusted, he reread the letter, written on pale blue paper. The wedding was to be in Dayton, Carolyn's hometown, in September, a month from now.

Gathering up his knapsack, Louis strode toward a speck in the distance, the general store with the island's only telephone. Leaving the island would be hard, but it was time to get back to the world of his friends and the world of work.

Chapter 15

Exercise 1

1. 2 verbs
2. 2 subjects
3. 2 subjects
4. 2 objects of a verb
5. 2 objects of a preposition
6. 2 adverbs
7. 3 appositives
8. 2 verbs
9. 2 complements
10. 3 complements

Exercise 3

1. You can rent a newer, tougher truck from Wilbur Rents-It-All.
2. Her skillfully designed, finely tuned carburetion unit was just installed last night.
3. The cold, relentless north wind blew all night.
4. Barlotti carefully gave instructions to the young, obviously inexperienced technician.
5. He sat and watched the clear, placid water for several hours.

Exercise 5

The promised democratic elections have been postponed again. An agreement among the council members, presidential aides, and their staffs pre-

Exercise 5 (cont.)

vented local journalists from learning the reasons for this decision. The causes for the new delay have been many. Internal unrest increased last year and threatened to become an issue in any open, unrestricted political campaign. The leading opposition candidates, Dr. Mendes, Mr. Guttierez, Mrs. Perez, and others, have not been effective in creating informed, active support for their positions. But above all, most urban workers don't seem concerned about the violation of a constitution that is less than six months old.

Exercise 7

1. The game was going badly, and Raymond left early.
2. Congress approved the appropriation bill by a large margin, but the president vetoed it.
3. The plot was discovered months ago, but there have been no arrests.
4. You could declare a major this semester, or you could wait until your junior year.
5. The film was enjoyed by everyone in the group, but it left Shelly strangely annoyed.
6. The architects of environmental policy are sane and intelligent, and they possess an almost religious depth of purpose.
7. Her purpose was clear, but her language was not.
8. "Breaking with Moscow" is in one sense mistitled, for its author denies having broken with the city of his youth.
9. The colonel emerged from the cocoon of his own view of things, and what he saw surprised him.
10. The letter could be printed as it is, or it could be heavily edited.

Exercise 9

1. The questions fairly tested our knowledge of the subject; moreover, they gave us a chance to show some writing skill.
2. Three of my friends did not study for the exam; consequently, they did not pass it.
3. The new government rulings make that investment more expensive than in the past; therefore, you should consider other options.
4. The brown coat goes well with these slacks; besides, it is all I can afford right now.
5. Several ministers received threatening letters; nevertheless, each spoke out against the proposed constitutional changes.
[Students' responses may vary.]

Exercise 11

1. The appointment can wait. The letter must be finished.
2. *OK*

Exercise 11 (cont.)

3. The island was settled quickly; the population swelled to several thousand in less than twenty years.
4. Would you read this now? I need an answer.
5. Most people stop short of their ability, whereas others push themselves well beyond it.
6. The meat is fresh, and the salad bar is well stocked.
7. *OK*
8. Movies bore him, and so do books and magazines.
9. *OK*
10. Marco plans to study art. He is already selling his sketches.

[Students' responses may vary.]

Review exercise 1

For centuries flying was a dream,but it was a dream that people wanted to come true. The Wright brothers flew the first airplane in 1903. Suddenly the idea of flying machines captured the American imagination like never before. Most people thought that airplanes would open up a glorious,glamorous future. The human race would certainly benefit from the speed, ease,and availability of airplane travel.

That prediction has come true in a short time/and in many ways. Affordable air travel has given people the opportunity to explore distant parts of the world/ and the chance to compare their lives with the lives of others. Airplanes and air travel have opened new doors and taught us new lessons.

Chapter 16   Exercise 1

1. *what kind;* Julio saw a painting **that he would like to buy.**

2. *what kind;* A man **who looks like your father** was in the bank today.

3. *which;* My sociology class, **which I needed in order to graduate,** was just canceled.

4. *what kind;* They devised a plan **on which everyone could agree**.

5. *what kind;* She wrote an excellent paper, one **that might be published**.

6. *which;* The afternoon shift, **which I hate,** has just been reassigned.

Exercise 1 (cont.)

7. *which;* They gave him anything **that he wanted**.

8. *which;* The couch **that you liked so much** is on sale at Jackson's.

9. *what kind;* Estes, a doctor **whom I still admire**, revolutionized the practice of medicine in this town.

10. *what kind;* Courses **that require a lot of reading** aren't very popular in this dorm.

Exercise 3

A.
1. who
2. whom
3. who
4. whom
5. whom
6. whom
7. who
8. whom
9. whom
10. who

B.
11. Several reporters ~~who~~ *whom* you know well are attending the luncheon.

12. *OK*

13. *OK*

14. We didn't know anyone ~~who~~ *whom* we could ask.

15. *OK*

16. A high official, ~~whom~~ *who* declined to be named, made the announcement this morning.

17. *OK*

18. *OK*

19. The teachers ~~who~~ *whom* you remember are all retired.

20. Each of the tenants ~~who~~ *whom* I have spoken to are willing to sign the petition.

Exercise 5

1. *when;* He always says things like that **when he lectures**.

2. *when;* Sandra will call **after she finishes work**.

Exercise 5 (cont.)

3. *why;* **Because the presentation was delayed,** Mr. Pritchard cut short his speech.

4. *under what condition;* The purchase will take place **whether you approve or not**.

5. *under what condition;* **If you release the choke,** the engine will start.

6. *under what condition;* Mary won't speak out **unless she has to**.

7. *when;* We can leave **whenever you wish**.

8. *when;* Reporters were not allowed on the field **until after the plane landed**.

9. *why;* **Since they changed their plans,** they lost their deposit.

10. *when;* Salespeople, **when they speak too fast,** always make me suspicious.

Exercise 7

1. We did well on the test, although we had little time to study for it.

2. As you read this essay, notice how the writer carefully explains each of his reasons.

3. If more capital had been available, the manufacturers could have increased production.

4. *OK*

5. *OK*

6. *OK*

7. *OK*

8. You should be careful, when you are away from home, not to carry too much cash at one time.

9. *OK*

10. Ever since we sold the farm, I have missed the smell of black earth.

Exercise 9

1. subject
2. object
3. subject
4. object
5. subject
6. object

Exercise 11

1. The *Los Angeles Herald Times* has an excellent sports staff.
2. *OK*
3. The Italian Renaissance was more revolutionary than you probably imagine.
4. *OK*
5. The history of the Southwest is a history of repeated conquest.
6. Campaign promises rarely produce social changes.

Chapter 17 Exercise 1

1. I cannot give you a good reason/ ~~W~~(w)hy I think Valentia deliberately endangered herself.

2. Several men who work for the county have been using publicly owned construction equipment, ~~W~~(w)hich is supposed to be reserved for highway maintenance.

3. *OK*

4. You can have/ ~~W~~(w)hatever you want.

5. If the constitution is not approved, ~~T~~(t)wo of the political parties will go underground.

6. The rangers reacted quickly. As soon as they received the call, ~~O~~(o)ne of them was on his way to the campsite.

7. The exercise program was to be canceled, ~~U~~(u)nless more people signed up for it.

8. The tapes that you hold in your hand, ~~B~~(b)elong to the radio station.

9. The teller was informed, ~~T~~(t)hat the checks had just been delivered.

10. She took a job in Chicago, ~~B~~(b)ecause her brother lived nearby.

Exercise 3

The boardinghouse had a good reputation, which meant a lot in those years. It sat on the east end of Forest Avenue near the entrance to Arnold Park. It was a big, old house with a very friendly landlord. I took a room there in 1936 after I first moved north from St. Louis. My job required me to commute to the downtown business district. Mornings I rode the "L" train, which stopped, I recall, two blocks down from the boardinghouse. It took me to the old Goldblatt Building where I worked as an accountant. I didn't make much money, but I worked. In the evenings it was back to the boardinghouse. The house was a lot safer than a lot of places that I could have ended up in. Besides, the jazz clubs weren't so far away that I couldn't get out when I wanted to. Anyway, I survived.

Review exercise

Each student will have an individual response.

Chapter 18

Exercise 1

1. Subject: early marriage
   Opinion: can create many problems
2. Subject: many former members of this fraternity
   Opinion: hold highly respected professional positions
3. Subject: the incumbent mayor
   Opinion: will probably win re-election in June
4. Subject: the money from the cable television company
   Opinion: influenced his vote
5. Subject: the prices for these apartments
   Opinion: are too high
6. Subject: Mr. Jonas and Ms. Henderson
   Opinion: although they are different in many ways, they have similar teaching styles
7. Same as number 6
8. Subject: twenty million dollars
   Opinion: was hard to raise in the latest effort
9. Subject: other opinions
   Opinion: should have been sought
10. Subject: my skiing trips
    Opinion: have all been unique and memorable experiences

Exercise 3

Each student will have an individual response.

Review exercise

A. Pattern: Basic

Introduction & Main idea — The rough draft [of a script] is your first attempt to assemble all the elements on which you have been working, to bring order out of chaos. Now

Review exercise (cont.)

Introduction & main idea (cont.) —

your characters must move into action; now they must speak through your dialog. Open the floodgates of your imagination. Write this draft without revisions or polishing and don't plague yourself about its literary quality. If something does not seem quite right, despite your painstaking planning, leave it

Supporting Ideas Closing —

and plow right along. Bring your work to the climax you have chosen for it.

B. Pattern: Basic

Introduction & main idea —

Houses are like sentinels in the plain—old keepers of the weather watch.

Supporting Ideas —

There, in a very little while, wood takes on the appearance of great age. All colors wear soon away in the wind and rain, and then the wood is burned gray and the grain appears and the nails turn red with rust. The windowpanes are black and opaque; you imagine there is nothing within, and indeed there are many ghosts, bones given up to the land. They stand here and there

Closing —

against the sky, and you approach them for a longer time than you expect. They belong in the distance; it is their domain.

C. Pattern: Suspended

Introduction —

The view from the windshield is this: There's that three-to-six-story-high

Supporting Ideas —

screen, on which titanic monsters or car crashes of megaton explosiveness suddenly appear. Hundreds of vehicles are lined up like pigs before a trough, grunting their approval—horns honking, tape decks blaring, an odd rocket arching toward the screen. If you look past the speaker hung from your window, you gaze on the Texas moon riding high above this most remarkable celebration; you note hibachi campfires, smoke rising from barbequed ribs, lawn chairs planted in the beds of pickup trucks, hammocks strung between speaker poles, patrons splayed out on blankets atop cars, and a Western

Review exercise (cont.)

Supporting Ideas (cont.)

Closing & Main idea

Rocky Horror punk fest of sixteen-year-olds crowded around the concession stand. You smell pot sweeping through the night, sweet as sagebrush. And all around you Texans are mating. That's summertime at the drive-in movies in, say, Dallas.

Chapter 19   Exercises 1, 3, and 5

Each student will have an individual response.

Review exercise

Each student will have an individual response.

Chapter 20   Exercise 1

1. Furthermore, Ms. Simmons will not be present this evening.
2. The navy, it seems to me, offers great opportunities to women in those professions.
3. According to Dr. Homan, the test results are correct.
4. On the one hand, his grades are very good.
5. Chemical oven cleaners do a very good job, however.
6. The cause of his anger, moreover, has yet to be discovered.
7. The *Saturday Evening Post*, for example, went out of business.
8. Well, they discovered gold and copper in the ore that they tested.
9. The black belt can be worn with the tan pants, I think.
10. New York, not New Jersey, is my uncle's childhood home.

Exercise 3

1. The manager responded, "yes, I will."
2. "In the afternoon," said Emil Marciano, "we only need two waiters."
3. "Where did you find the coat?" asked Janet.

Exercise 3 (cont.)

4. Did Walter just say, "I'm ready"?

5. The singer asked, "Would you like to hear a new song or an old one?"

6. The ticket seller replied, "We only have balcony seats available."

7. "Labor Day," Bill complained, "is the earliest that I can get away."

8. "This medicine," the pharmacist assured us, "is as good as any of these others."

9. The driver got out of her car and yelled, "Watch where you're going!"

10. "Would you please help me with my groceries?"

Exercise 5

A. 1. The sisters wanted to leave; the party was breaking and the hostess was getting tired. [dash would also be acceptable]

2. Our favorite instructors—Dr. Sarandon, Mrs. Endicott, and Mr. Lee—are all out sick this week.

3. Each of the panelists had the same question for us: why don't we study harder?

4. Stuart told two good stories—the one about the ice cream and the one about Frank's red truck. [colon would also be acceptable]

5. Two brands are under consideration—IBM and Xerox. [colon would also be acceptable]

6. The next two months—January and February—will be the most difficult.

7. The palace opened its doors early: the crowds were becoming too large. [dash would also be acceptable]

8. The school gave a special citation to two remarkable students—Jessie Cates and Bill Martinez. [colon would also be acceptable]

B. 9. The fire marshal announced that Wembly Street would be closed all afternoon.

Exercise 5 (cont.)

10. Three radio stations, WCAZ, WXZF, and WBB, are offering a free
    vacation.

11. We had hoped to see Tyrone and Christopher.

12. Janet contributes to all the local charities, including the Boy Scouts
    and the Junior Chamber of Commerce.

13. Everyone at the apartment—even the dog was glad to see us, for
    we were bringing both hamburgers and ice cream.

14. *OK*

15. We met the Flying Freeman Brothers, a circus act.

Exercise 7

1. *S*; woman's
2. *P*; women's
3. *P*; games'
4. *S*; Cleveland's
5. *S*; desk's
6. *P*; speedboats'
7. *S*; goose's
8. *P*; mice's
9. *P*; sweepstakes'
10. *S*; accountant's
11. *S*; brother's
12. *P*; businessmen's
13. *P*; porches'
14. *S*; box's
15. *S* and *P*; fish's

Exercise 9

1. *OK*

2. There's more in the refrigerator.

3. The strike ~~was'nt~~ wasn't planned properly.

4. Michael's certain we're landing in a few minutes.

5. She's never liked another mystery film.

6. They're never going to understand his reasons if he won't explain them.

7. Future explorations ~~willn't~~ won't be funded for some time.

8. These ~~are'nt~~ aren't stone arrowheads.

9. ~~The're~~ They're natural rock formations.

10. He wondered if ~~he'ld~~ he'd ever make the first string.

Review exercise

Two of my friends, Aaron, and Patty, were discussing their astronomy assignment, when Aaron mentioned that some people think, planets like Venus, Mars, and Jupiter, can influence your life. "They worry about Venus, for instance," he said, "because they think it affects their love life." "According to these people, he added, the planets Mars and Jupiter determine how aggressive you are and how much luck you have." "But thats nonsense! exclaimed Patty. "Who'd believe such stuff? I certainly can't." Aaron agreed that its silly to assume that planets control every aspect of your life, your career, your family relationships, and your health. But those who hold such beliefs, although they have no scientific basis, wont change them easily.

Chapter 21 Review exercise 1

As the summer draws to a close, thousands of people all over the country begin to worry about a major expense: how to pay for their season tickets to professional basketball games. Season tickets are often a mixed blessing for the people who own them.

On the positive side, these tickets do carry a certain prestige. In towns that have a good basketball team and even in towns where a team's talent is questionable, season tickets are hard to come by. There may be a long waiting list for season tickets, which makes them seem that much more valuable. There is always a great demand for tickets during the play-offs, and people prize their season tickets especially highly then.

Fans pay a high price for their tickets, however. The tickets often cost a great deal of money. The seats are often cramped and far away from the action on the court. The fans in the stand occasionally have fantasies about watching the games on television in the comfort of their own living rooms. A

Review exercise 1 (cont.)

friend of mine admitted,"Sometimes during a game, I find myself thinking about

bowls of popcorn,cushioned sofas,and bathrooms down the hall."

Nevertheless,two things convince most fans to keep their season tickets.

First,the thrill of watching a game in an arena filled with a lot of noisy,excited

people is difficult to match.True fans will willingly give up money and comfort

to be part of the game as it happens. Second,owning season tickets gives

fans the chance to really appreciate exceptional athletes like Larry Bird,Magic

Johnson,and Patrick Ewing.It's a pleasure to be able to watch every move a

gifted player makes. Season tickets provide fans with opportunities that add

much to basketball's enjoyment.

Chapter 22

Exercise 1

1. replying
2. removing
3. grinning
4. tearing
5. boring
6. forgetting
7. proceeding
8. tanning
9. repelling
10. offering
11. characterizing
12. programming
13. inciting
14. raining
15. concurring

Exercise 3

1. crashes
2. flexes
3. applies
4. penetrates
5. does
6. tarnishes
7. pipes
8. projects
9. dentists
10. launches
11. universities
12. enjoys
13. solidifies
14. enrolls
15. rocks

Exercise 5

1. ~~Their~~ They're trying to correct the problem now.
2. ~~Who's~~ Whose explanation do you believe?

OK 3. There sits an honest man.

Exercise 5 (cont.)

4. The personal computer has left ~~it's~~ _its_ mark on Western culture.

OK 5. They're working on the problem and will have a solution sometime this week.

6. I read the text of ~~you're~~ _your_ speech in the campus newspaper.

7. ~~They're~~ _There_ is a young man waiting in the outer office for you.

OK 8. Every dog recognizes its owner.

9. I'm looking for one juror ~~whose~~ _who's_ on my side.

10. Michael and Inez left ~~there~~ _their_ books in the car.

OK 11. Who's standing by the door?

12. ~~Its~~ _It's_ time to start working on the anthropology project.

13. ~~Your~~ _You're_ the best man for the position.

OK 14. The eggs are all packed in their containers.

OK 15. I know it's a long trip to be taking on such short notice.

Exercise 7

1. Wes took the baseball ~~equippment~~ _equipment_ back to the ~~dormatory~~ _dormitory_ on his way to the ~~libary~~ _library_.

2. Dr. Wescott is already ~~aquainted~~ _acquainted_ with ~~fourty~~ _forty_ of the supervisors.

3. The applicant gave his ~~heigth~~ _height_ and weight.

4. Brad was a ~~sophmore~~ _sophomore_ when the ~~incedent occured~~ _incident occurred_.

5. I ~~beleive Brittain~~ _believe Britain_ will ~~benifit~~ _benefit_ from the ~~bisiness~~ _business_.

6. It's hard to ~~exadgerate~~ _exaggerate_ the role of ~~prejidice~~ _prejudice_ in this ~~dicision~~ _decision_.

7. I am ~~dissappointed~~ _disappointed_ in his ~~artical~~ _article_ on the ~~Atheletics~~ _Athletics_ Department.

8. The film wasn't ~~divelopped~~ _developed_ until we returned to the city.

9. I wanted to see the ~~maintanance aggreement~~ _maintenance agreement_ in ~~writting~~ _writing_.

10. Dr. Wasson offered an intelligent response to Benchley's ~~analisis~~ _analysis_.

11. Desiree ~~imediately~~ _immediately_ walked to the ~~dinning~~ _dining_ room.

Exercise 7 (cont.)

12. The ~~independant comparitive~~ study was undoubtedly ~~valuble~~.
independent comparative ... *valuable*

13. A fly droned ~~monotinously~~.
monotonously

14. Packages are ~~recieved~~ in a ~~seperate~~ department.
received ... *separate*

15. He ~~preceded~~ to tell us the correct ~~pronounciation~~ of the word.
proceeded ... *pronunciation*

Review exercise

Much of the ~~monney~~ was never ~~recoverred~~, even though ~~it's~~ owners searched ~~countinuously~~ for nearly twelve years. ~~Eventtually~~ it was ~~declarred~~ ~~lossed~~, and traces to its ~~hidding~~ place grew cold. Colonel Akroyd ~~past~~ the secret to his aunt in Georgia ~~an quitely disapeared form the neiborhood.~~
money ... *recovered* ... *its* ... *Continuously* ... *Eventually* ... *declared* ... *lost* ... *hiding* ... *passed* ... *and quietly disappeared from the neighborhood.*

Twenty years later no one ~~rememberred~~ the military man who ~~inhabitted~~ the corner house. The aunt ~~eventully~~ placed his last letter in her safe deposit box and forgot it. The box and ~~it's~~ contents ~~endded~~ up on a closet shelf in

Michigan.
remembered ... *inhabited* ... *eventually* ... *its* ... *ended*

Index

Verbals and verbal phrases *(continued)*
  as adverbs, 166, 168–169
  as appositives, 176
  complements of, 165
  dangling, 173
  described by adverbs, 220
  as fragments, 236, 238
  infinitives, 90, 163
  -ing words, 163, 312–314
  marking, 167
  as nouns, 166, 169, 176
  past participles, 88, 163
  present participles, 163
  punctuating, 168–171, 301–302
  and verbs, 163, 166

Verbs and verb phrases, 2, 10–13, 37–105
  action, 10–11, 20, 40–41
  adding endings to, 312–319
  of being, 12–13
  as coordinate elements, 187, 188, 306

future tense form of, 52–54
helping, 39–40, 77, 86, 93–94, 95
-ing form of, 48, 163, 312–314
interrupted by adverbs, 43–45
irregular, 49, 93–105, 163
linking, 10, 12–13, 20, 40–41, 127
marking, 11, 41
past participle form of, *see* Past participles
past tense form of, *see* Past tense
perfect tense of, 53, 56–58
present tense form of, *see* Present tense
principal parts of, 48–49, 94–98
progressive tense of, 53, 61–63
in questions, 24–25
regular, *see* Regular verbs
of seeming and sensation, 13
simple tense of, 52–54
tenses of, 52–63
to be, 71, 77, 105, 119
to do, 77
to go, 105
to have, 71, 77
and verbals, 163, 166

voice of, *see* Active voice; Passive voice
weak, 269
see also Subject-verb agreement
Voice, *see* Active voice; Passive voice
Vowels, 313

Were/where, **326**
Whether/weather, **326**
Which, **219**
Who/whom, **125–126**
  in adjective clauses, 130, 214, 219
  choosing forms of, 128, 294
  in noun clauses, 229
  in questions, 25
Whole/hole, **324**
Whose/who's, **321**
Writing process, 260–272

Your/you're, **321**